Dyslexic Dick

True Adventures of My World

By Richard "Dick" W. Kraemer

The book cover graphic illustrations and design were provided by Robert Sabin of Sabin Design Studio P.O. Box 3237 Idyllwild, CA. 92549

ISBN-13: 978-1469986463

ISBN-10: 1469986469

Dedication

In loving memory of my parents, who just wanted the best for their children.

Table of Contents

Foreword

Twenty percent of the American public has a reading and writing disability, of those Americans 70% are Dyslexic.

The following institutions support the above information:

> ➢ The National Institute of Child Health and Human Development
> ➢ National Adult Literacy Survey
> ➢ U.S. Department of Education
> ➢ National Institute of Heath

According to the U.S. Census result for 2011 using the American population figures for 2009, there are more than 43 million people who have Dyslexia in the United States today.

About The Author

Dick Kraemer is a United States Marine Corps Vietnam Era veteran. He joined the Amalgamated Lithographers of America in 1979, where he worked as a printer. In 1989, Dick earned his A.A.S. degree in Business Management at Orange County Community College. He pursued a career in information systems in many Fortune 500 companies, working his way up from computer operator to the position of Director of Production for Automatic Data Processing Inc, in 1998. In 2003, Dick changed his career to become a top selling real estate agent for some of the largest firms in upstate New York. Dick now lives in Warwick New York, with his wife of 34 years and daughter.

Preface

I first discovered that I had dyslexia when I was 44 years old. At the time, I reached the peak of my career as a Director of Production in information technology for the fixed income service bureau, a division of ADP Automatic Data Processing Inc. My mother was dying of cancer and I was helping her put her affairs in order before her agonizing death. She had pulled out a box that she had hidden away for years, and handed me a big folded piece of vanilla crepe paper. I open the paper to reveal my first kindergarten attempt at spelling my full name, and that almost every letter was painted in the reverse image. Shocked at what I had discovered, I looked at her and asked, "I'm Dyslexic?" My mother acknowledged, and told me that she and my father had learned of my dyslexia when I was 13 years old. She continued to explain how my parents decided to keep it a secret from me and everyone else they could. My parents thought I would grow out of it. Blinded with anger of what I learned, knowing that I had certainly not grown out of my dyslexia. My life shot before my eyes, of all the difficulties I had even to this day due to dyslexia. Later that evening at home I had sworn my wife to secrecy, had a few drinks, and decided to bury this family secret forever. After 10 years of concealment of my learning disability, I had done an in depth research on dyslexia. I discovered that 1 out of 5 Americans have a reading and writing disability in which 70% are dyslexic that is about 43 million people. In addition, because of the social effects of growing up as a perceived illiterate through learned behavior, a dyslexic's personality becomes defensive by hiding the disability. Some of the personality traits of a dyslexic are isolation, only 25% are married or in a long-term relationship. They are masters of deception when it comes to concealing their disability.

Because dyslexics feel inadequate personally and socially, there is a very high rate of long-term depression, drug and/or alcohol abuse. During my research I had this Big Ah-Ha moment, these were all the personality traits I had experienced, although I went through life thinking that I suffered from a bad case of stupidity. But, now this problem has a name-Dyslexia. Then for the first time I took a trip down memory lane to my childhood, and began to write. I never wanted to go back there before, because I didn't want to remember those days. When I started writing, I couldn't stop. Once I finished writing I realized that I had lived a pretty crazy childhood, filled with many funny, suspenseful and emotional stories. So strap on your seatbelts and keep your hands inside the window. This is your wild ride of Dyslexic Dick, True Adventures of My World.

Acknowledgement

Because of my dyslexia that I continue to overcome even to this day, this book would never have been published if it were not for my lovely wife June. It was her command of the written English language, editing skills, and encouragement that helped bring this book to life. She helped bring this book into reality as she struggles with her own disabilities with partial blindness and Myotonic Dystrophy, and cares for our darling adult daughter who suffers with the same disease. So if you don't like the book, it's my wife's fault. If you like the book, I'll take all the credit.

Dick Kraemer Jr.

Introduction

This is a true story of a typical American family in the middle of the 1960's in upstate New York, about 35 miles northwest from New York City. A history changing time in our country, we just finished playing nuclear war chicken with Cuba & Russia, our president was bumped off by the mob or the C.I.A, the Beatles had invaded our shores, black people were marching in the streets for their civil rights while getting beaten by police, the United States was involved saving another country from communism in Viet Nam, and still the decade had more in store for us. Yes, I could remember it all because of the wonder of television every night at 6PM, you could see mostly uncensored in those day's news broadcasts of people getting killed, beaten and civil unrest, all in your living room on your black and white TV.

My father was a Medic in the Korean War and was decorated with 2 bronze stars and two purple hearts. In the Korean War, the enemy did not get the rules of war memo from the Geneva Convention - they thought that the red crosses with white background on the Medic uniforms were used for target practice. His name was Dick Kraemer. On his 17th birthday, he joined the army to save the Korean people from communism. His profession was a plumber for a plumbing company in Rockland County New York. Dick was a very likable with quite a sense of humor, a hard working, tough guy and if you didn't like him, he didn't give a fuck.

My mother was a housewife of the 60's, with a Beehive hairdo, a seasonal job as a sales clerk in W.T. Grants, very loving, and had a bad temper. Her name was Jeanie; she loved her kids and her husband, an all American home maker. This woman was a clean freak, and would suck the kids into this cleaning frenzy. I would be cleaning the bathroom every Saturday morning and would have to stand inspection before I could go to my next cleaning assignment.

My Brother Ike and Sister Gina had their own cleaning crosses to bear - if we were lucky, we would be done by lunchtime. Jeanie had other interests too, like pissing off the old man but only before the breaking point. She loved getting involved in Cub Scouts. Mom was our Den Mother for the neighborhood. She also loved making rum fruitcakes and holiday nut wreaths, for the holidays to make a couple of extra bucks for Christmas.

My Brother Ike is two years younger than I and basically farther down the family food chain. Ever since he was born, his mission in life has been to always try to one up me. My younger brother and I would be in a constant battle of sibling rivalry and would drive my parents crazy. The other side of my relationship with Ike was that he was my best friend. Although at the time neither one of us knew it.

My little sister Gina was a pretty little blue-eyed blond girl and was protected from the rest of the litter. Not only was she 3 years younger than I was, and a girl, but also because some psychologist in the early 60's determined that she was mentally disabled. Because she didn't begin to talk as fast as me and my brother, and she would stutter when she did start to talk. Later the labels changed to learning disabled, and in high school before she graduated it was Dyslexia. Later in life, I discovered that I too was diagnosed with Dyslexia. My parents knew it, but decided not to tell me. Because in those days Dyslexia was not such a well-known diagnosis and there was no cure. The teaching techniques for Dyslexic children were just being developed and were not available to my sister or me. So what's a parent to do? A psychologist tells you that your child has short-term memory loss, and will have way below average reading/writing skills or not read/write at all. How does a parent manage the prospect of having illiterates in the family? The way my parents handled Gina was they told her that she was Special. Being a Special kid, in the family or in school does not make for a great childhood. But the psychologist in the early 60's determined that was the right way to handle Gina. Then the psychologist determined I had Dyslexia at 13 years old, and my parents decided they would not tell me.

This leads us to the main character myself, Dick Kraemer Jr. A.K.A. Little Dick. Yah, the old man named me after himself. It was a family tradition to name your first son after yourself, his father my grandfather's name was Dick, actually, Richard Kraemer was the legal name and Dick was a nickname. Everyone that knew them called them Dick, not Rich or Richard, it was an accepted nickname up to the 1950's. However, as the sexual revolution had started to unfold, and Dick had a more accepted meaning, it was, you got it, and I have it, The Penis. Now at ten years old and becoming aware of my own anatomy, and because all of the other boys my age were becoming aware that a penis was more popularly referred to as a dick, I was The Dick of the Neighborhood. The name itself wasn't the only reason I've had more then my share of fights with most of the kids in the hood, but it didn't help. I wasn't a type of kid that was looking for a fight; in fact, I was the type that would avoid a fight at almost any cost. But some times I would pay that cost, and get that good beating I so much deserved and sometimes I'd win and sometimes I'd lose, but one thing you could be sure of was that if you messed with me you were not going away clean. I was the class clown, blond haired, blue eyed, all American kid, and the eldest of two other children. So being the son of Dick, My father Big Dick then I had to be called Little Dick or Dickie, and that's how my friends and family referred to me as A.K.A., The Little Penis. There was no way to get around the name, my mother use to yell at the top of her lungs for me for dinner, the neighbors thought she was a nymphomaniac. I finally bought a watch, so I would be home before dinner, which saved a couple of ass whippings.

Chapter 1- One Classic American Family

My mother and father had lived in a big subdivision of track homes in Stony Point in Rockland County, New York, until the fall of 1967; I was 11 years old and in the fourth grade. My parents had purchased their first two bedroom home with the help from my mother's parents, Nana and Pop-Pop, my grandparents, in 1961.

In those days before leaving Stony Point, I hardly saw my father. He was busy trying to make a living to support our ever-growing family; learning a trade as a plumber, and paying a mortgage. He had three jobs back then he was a plumber five days a week from 8 AM to 6 PM, then he worked at the Nyack drive-in from 8:30 PM to 12 AM, and on the weekends, he drove a school bus for field trips. When looking at this schedule, you could see that we saw him at dinnertime, and in the morning before school. My dad realized that he had been missing out on the father and family time, and sometimes he took Ike or me on those field trips with him.

The bus would be so full kids that the only way for me to go with him was to sit next to him on a metal heater box in the driver cockpit. We went on a ferry once to the Statue of Liberty; I remember seeing the blue green waters of the Hudson River and the pilot whales swimming along side us. Today, for you tourists, you could expect to see gray waters, and the Frog Man from Homeland Security. Another memorable field trip with my dad and me was to Yankee Stadium, I remember walking up within the old Stadium to the upper most nosebleeds, and never getting a glimpse of the ball field until I approached the last level. I walked out of the darkness of the stadium hallway into the covered bleachers. I stopped and looked in total amazement of how the baseball field was so green; the white lines contrasted against the red brown dirt of the infield and out field.

I yelled at the top of my lungs "It's in color!"

The man making his way past me, stopped, looked at me weird, then looked at my dad and said, "Is that your kid?"

Dad said, looking at me, "Yeah."

The man continued past me, and looking back at me, he said, "Ah Ha."

I looked at my dad, and said, "On TV, the field is in black and white."

Then dad looked at me like I was a knucklehead, and shook his head. My dad must have thought that was a brilliant deduction.

We would also get into the drive-in for free, until they found out how many kids my father had. My dad would drive as all to the drive-in early; and he was dressed in his all white uniform. He would work collecting the money at the ticket booth, and directing traffic in the movie lot. We would keep busy before the movie would start by taking train rides on this kid-sized railroad that also was part of the drive-in. This train was only big enough for kids; adults were not allowed to ride with the kids. So, my mother used to let Ike and I ride on the train alone. The train engineer would make sure that all the kids were sitting down, strap them in, then blow his whistle, toot his horn, and then take off. On one occasion, my brother and I were in the last car on the train. Ike had unbuckled his strap, and holding onto the handlebars, he stood up.

I said, "What are you doing, sit down!"

Ike said, "My strap is off!"

I pulled him down and said, "Wait until we stop!" The train is now at full speed, whistle blowing and horn tooting loud.

Ike said, "No, I have to tell the man!", then he stood up.

Ike yelled, "Hey, Mister!"

Suddenly, everything went black we were in the tunnel. Then, to my horror, I realized Ike was gone! I looked back and my brother was lying on the tracks face down. His forehead hit the top of the tunnel and he did a complete flip out of the last train car.

We came out of the tunnel, there was a stampede of adults running on the tracks, the train had slammed on its brakes, and people were screaming. The parents started taking their kids off the train, and they were crying. I looked at where the tunnel began; there was Ike on his hands and knees. My mother had Gina in her arms, and she was standing next to Ike, with her hand on his head and crying. The train engineer was looking him over and helping him to his feet. Just then, my dad was on the scene and took over; he had been an Army medic in the Korean War. My father picked up Ike, took him to the snack bar, put ice on his head, and cleaned up his skinned knees. My father said that he was okay and we all went back to the car. Once in the car, my father slapped me in the back of my head, and said, "Why didn't you look after your little brother?"

I said, "I told him sit down!"

Then Ike said, "No, you didn't!"

Then I looked at my brother, all beaten up, holding an ice bag to his little noggin, and then I looked at my dad. Then my dad closed the door and went back to work.

I felt sorry for my little brother, he didn't look good. I was thinking that maybe he had brain damage, so I asked him his name, where he lived, and how old he was. He got all the answers right.

Then I asked him, "Ike, do you remember me telling you to sit down?"

He said, "No!"

I said to my mother, "Mom, I think Ike has amnesia."

My mother turned around, with a really mad look on her face, and said, "Leave your brother alone, he is hurt." That is when I knew to drop the subject; the case was closed, that this would go down in history that I let my little brother get the snot knocked out of him In the Great Train Accident at the Nyack Drive-In. But, wait, I had thought immediately, remembering something that I learned in school.

If a person loses their memory due to a blow to the head, and diagnosed with amnesia, it is possible for that person to regain their memory with the same like blow to the head.

Then I thought, maybe I learned it from, "The Three Stooges". But, I have the answer. I had found the solution to Ike's problem, but decided not to try my experiment in the back seat of the car. I waited for the opportunity. The drive-in was playing the new Beatles movie, "Help" and dad comes back to the car after the lot had been filled. We all liked the music, except my father he hated the Beatles and thought they were a bunch of idiots.

After getting home that evening, we went to bed. I climbed from the top of the bunk bed, and grabbed the Webster's dictionary from the bookshelf. I quietly walked over to the bottom bunk where my brother was laying. I explained my Amnesia diagnosis to Ike and the cure, and even offered to look it up in the dictionary as evidence. He was not buying it on my prognosis, so I decided to proceed with my experiment. I raised the book above my head, but my brother covered his forehead, and then screamed, "Mom!" Then my father yelled from the living room, "You kids better go to sleep in there, it's late."

Then my brother yelled back, "Dickie is trying to hit me!" I quickly dropped the book, hopped into the top bunk, and pulled the covers over me. The door opened up partly, and only my mother's head pops in with this twisted evil face and she said softly, "Dick, if you touch your brother, I'm going to beat the shit out of you, understand me?" Then there was silence, is as if time stood still for that moment. The door flew open, and then she said in a lower growling voice, "Well, do you?"

I said, in a panic, "Yes, yes, yes," pulling the covers over my face. Then the door slammed shut. I thought that was scarier then any monster I had ever seen on TV.

This would be my last memory of the Nyack Drive In days, I assume that after the Great Train Tragedy, management told my father not to bring his kids to work anymore. I later learned that the drive-in discontinued those train rides, because of liability concerns. I hope it wasn't because I didn't look out for the family crash dummy.

As I stated at the beginning of this chapter, my father was a hard-working and loving family man. He always did his best in anything he tried to do he was not a quitter. My mother was born a devout Catholic, and raised the children as such. She was a very loving soul and she put her kids as her top priority in life. All the years I had known her, I had never heard her gossip or talk ill of anyone. I thought this to be quite extraordinary, almost saint like. If somebody was talking about someone else unfavorably at some point in a conversation, even if she thought it, she never spoke it to anyone else. But, this quality would have a double-edged sword, if she did have a question or a beef with you, she'd be in your face telling you or asking you what exactly was on her mind. She didn't bother wasting her breath, talking behind one's back, when she could go right to the source and settle any open issues. This rule would stand for any living human being on the planet. Maybe because she grew up with five brothers and one other sister, or maybe her mother's upbringing is the reason for mom's unique personality traits, one could only guess.

We had many happy outings with my mom. She would pack Ike, Gina, and myself in the car, and go to the Seven Lakes Drive, New York State parks, where there are a series of state parks, like Lake Welch, Lake Sebago, Bear Mountain, and others. They would have beaches where you could swim, in one of the many lakes, go roller-skating, or ice skating, and even go to the zoo. In the summertime, we would make it to the lakes about two or three times a week.

On one memorable excursion, we went to Lake Welch, one of our favorite places to go. There was swimming in a big lake, a white sandy beach, full service snack bar, you could even rent a rowboat. As like many summer days, it was hot and sunny, we ate our cream cheese and pimento sandwiches, and drank our ice-cold Pepsi cola, as we sat on my father's old Army blanket on the beach. We always had to wait 20 min. after eating before we could go swimming, because my mother told us that we could get cramps and drown. After baking in the sun for what seemed like an eternity, we would run down to the water because the sand was so hot, it would burn our feet.

Once in the water, it was my job as always to look after my little brother and sister. There is no getting around the fact that my basic family position was the big brother, the oldest child of the clan, Mr. Responsible, and their safety rested on my shoulders, and sometimes literally. We would spend hours in the water, most times until my mother would be as red as a lobster and ready to go home. At the time, Gina was about six years old, and needed the greatest amount of my attention. Sometimes, I would carry her in my arms to the deeper part of the water, and we would splash around. She was like a little monkey in the water. I was standing about mid-chest in the water, and on this day I decided to put Gina on my shoulders.

Walking with her on my shoulders in chest high water, I start to lose my balance a little, and I took a couple of steps backwards. Suddenly, I plunged under the water about 2 feet, and Gina is still on my shoulders. My feet firmly placed on the newly found lower lake bottom, I look up to see Gina above the water surface about mid-chest. I can not let her go, for fear that, I would lose her, and she didn't know how to swim. Looking up at her, I could see she was crying, through my last bubbles of breath leaving me to the surface. I have no more oxygen, and start to gag. All of a sudden, I felt Gina leave my shoulders, and then I felt a great thrust upwards.

Gasping for air, when I come to the surface, I see a bunch of people running towards me. Someone huge carried me under his arm, then laid me face down in the sand, and turned my head to one side.

Then I heard a man's voice yell, "Breathe!"
Then I felt a great weight on my back, it was crushing, and water gushed from my mouth.

The man yelled again, "Breathe!" Again, I felt the great crushing weight on my back, then more water came from my mouth, I started to cough. The man turned me over on my back then sat me up. I kept coughing, gasping for air for a few moments, and then started to cry. I looked at this man for the first time, he was a big, heavy, bald guy and he smiled. The man said," It's okay, little feller."

I said as I was crying, "Where's my sister?"
He pointed to his left, and there was Gina in the arms of my mother. They, too, were crying. The man helped me to my feet, and dusted some sand off me. Then he said, "You know, son, you did great job saving your sister, look, she didn't even get her hair wet."

I looked at Gina, and sure enough, her blond hair was bone dry.

I turned to the man, and said, "Thank you, Mister, for saving us", as I wiped away my tears. He said, "Sure, kid." Then he rubbed his hand on my head. The man walked over to my mother, and explained how he found the situation. He said that he was sitting on the beach, and looking at his kids playing, when he noticed a smaller than usual child, in equal chest high water; where there were kids twice Gina's age in the same area. He got up, walked to the waters edge, noticed that Gina was crying, he could see my blond head submerged beneath her. That's when he sprang into action, grabbing us both from the water. My mother thanked the man, and we all walked back to our blanket. Mom was pretty shaken over this near drowning of Gina and I, her hands were shaking as she hugged us both with a towel to dry us off.

When we got home later that day, mom sat down with me in my bedroom alone. She said," Why didn't you get Gina off your shoulders, you could have drowned."

I said, "I was afraid I'd lose her, and she doesn't know how to swim."

She said, "I could have lost you both, from here on, do not take your sister in the deep water." Then she gave me a long hug, and told me that she loved me and was proud of me.

Looking back on these loving, tender moments alone with my mother is what I remember most about her. There was this close child/parent bond she held for all her kids. Also, this was the cementing of my responsibility of being the Big Brother, the protector of all the Kraemer children. How many people could say that they saved someone from drowning, and the victim didn't even get her hair wet?

There was a lot of preparation before going on one of our day excursions. My mother was very organized, first that housework would be completed, and then she would sometimes have to run to the store to get a few things to make lunch, prepare lunch, pack, and plan the evening meal, then jump in the car with Gina. Then she would round up Ike and me, somewhere in the neighborhood, then we'd be off before 10:30 AM. But, if that schedule got messed up by 15 minutes, the outing was off.

One time, my brother and I decided to go to the store without my mother knowing where we were going. We walked almost all the way home, and all of a sudden, coming around the corner was my mother in her 1961 two tone Plymouth Fury. When she saw us, the car sped straight toward us; she then slammed on the brakes with tires screeching to a stop. She growled, "Get in the car!" Then she drove back to the house, parked the car, and turned around to us with very mad face. Then she yelled, "Do You Know What Time It Is?"

I looked puzzled, and I was trying to think of the right answer.

I said, "I don't know, I don't have a watch."

She said, in a very soft voice, "It's 11 o'clock, smart guy."

Then she yelled, "I Been Looking for You for 30 Min.! Where Were You?"

Ike said, "We went to the store to buy some Batman cards and soda."

Then she said to us, in a very soft voice again, "Well, guess what?"

Then there was silence for a moment, and I did not say anything this time, even though I knew the answer.

She said, with a smile on her face, and almost laughing, "We're not going to the beach today, you're going to stay in your room until dinnertime."

Then she yelled, "Now Get In The House!"

The back door of the car flew open, and we ran into the house.

Once in the house, I could hear the car horn sound, one blast after another, over and over again. I thought my mom wanted us, so I looked out the front door, then stepped out on the front stoop. I saw my mother hitting the steering wheel with both her hands rapidly, and looking straight up at the roof of the car. Not sure what to do, I just stood on the front steps looking at her with my mouth open. Then she stopped, and looked at me, as Gina was crying in the front seat, and pointed at me. I thought that meant, "go to your room", and I did.

Ike and I stayed in our bedroom with 90° heat with not so much as a breeze coming through the window, and we were silent until 5:30 PM. We did go to the bathroom a couple of times to get some water, but it was a quick in and out, hoping not to make eye contact with my mother. When we came out for dinner, everything was back to normal.

After that memorable lesson, we were always around the house if we were going on one of our outings, and always told my mother where we were going.

But, more importantly, all of my siblings and I are very well organized and punctual people. In fact, I have been late for an appointment less then 10 times in my entire life, including the above childhood experience. In addition, my siblings including myself are hard working to a fault, in fact most of us are considered workaholics. This quality trait has been ingrained in our upbringing, and the assurance that we will never go hungry. So, we did inherit and learn some good qualities from our parents, as well as the bad.

Living in that little two bedroom house in Stony Point was getting too small for our growing family. Ike, Gina, and I shared the same bedroom which was 9 x 12, and it seemed like we were living in a submarine. So it was decided by my parents that we needed a bigger place to live. When they searched in the surrounding towns in the area, they found nothing they could afford, unless they lived in a crummy neighborhood, and that was out of the question. So they started to look in Orange County, New York, where the homes where more affordable in nice neighborhoods, and most of all, great schools.

They finally found their dream house on Elm Street in Highland Mills, New York, and quickly put their house on the market. After a few short weeks, they had a buyer for their home in Stony Point, but the buyers needed to move in quickly, and they were willing to pay the full asking price. My parents made an offer to the owners of the house in Highland Mills in September 1967. It was accepted, with a stipulation, that they would not be able to move in until June 1968. After great thought, my parents had decided that they liked the house so much, they were willing to wait until next summer, sell their current home in October 1967, and move into an apartment in Central Valley, New York until the house in Highland Mills was vacant.

This would mean that the Kraemer children would start school in the same school district as our new home in Highland Mills.

In addition, there was a newer sense of urgency to move to a bigger home-my mother was pregnant with her fourth child.

Now that the plan for action had been devised, my parents informed their families of the plan. As stated earlier in this chapter, my grandparents, Nana and Pop-Pop, had assisted my parents in buying the Stony Point house. My Nana was not fond of my parents plan to move 36 miles north, where now she lived only 5 min. from her home and job to our home in Stony Point. When we moved to our new home, my grandparents would maybe see the family once or twice a month at best. This plan did not bode well with my grandmother, so she decided to make it very difficult for my parents.

The way my grandparents helped my parents get the house was that they lent them most of the down payment money which would be paid back monthly with a higher than normal interest rate. This down payment would be secured by having my parents and grandparents names on the deed. So for six years, my father was mostly working three jobs, paying the mortgage, the taxes, the down payment loan with higher than market rate interest, and all of the other family expenses-all without complaint as agreed, just a working man trying to do his best for his family.

My grandmother decided to make a power play to discourage my parent's plans. I should note that my grandfather, Pop Pop, was a wonderful man, but very low key, and could not talk my grandmother out of what she was about to do.

My grandmother had informed my parents that since they were getting such a good price for the Stony Point house, that my parents should give half of the equity earned from the proceeds of the sale to my grandparents. My parents were shocked, and then for a second thought my Nana was joking.

My mother looked at her and said," Ma, you're joking, right?"

Then my grandmother, with a stern stoned face said, "No, I'm not kidding." And my grandmother went on to say, "If you refuse to split half the profit from the sale of the house, I will not sign the deed for transfer to your buyers."

This is when a firestorm of yelling, screaming, and insults had ensued and ended with my grandparents storming out of the house.

My parents felt that if they borrowed money and made all the payments with interest, then that was the end of the business transaction with my grandparents. Now they changed the rules, and also wanted half of the proceeds from the house, too. There was no way around it legally, and my grandmother knew it.

My parents decided to follow through with their plans, pay my grandmother, and move to Orange County. If they did not, they would've buckled under my grandmother's control, and that was simply not going to happen.

This would be the breaking point for my father's relationship with my Nana. The relationship between the two had been rocky to begin with. My mother and father both said it was all about greed, and about what my grandmother thought was fair. My grandparents during that time were well to do financially, before the Great Stony Point Heist. Maybe it's because my grandparents grew up during the Depression, and that was the reason for my Nana's action.

But, when you put money against life long relationships with family, and make no attempt to fix it for a lifetime, is it really worth it?

Chapter 2 - Coming to Small Town U.S.A.

In October 1967, we closed on our small home, and moved into a very large apartment above Tomas's Real Estate in Central Valley. Our soon to be new home was less then 2 miles away, and our new school was right across the street from the apartment. Those few winter and spring months took a little getting used to; starting in a new school when the school year had already begun. Making new friends, at first, was easier for my brother than it was for me, but that was always the case. However, we had adjusted pretty well, and the apartment was twice the size of our old house, so we all had our own bedroom.

In the spring of 1968, as we started to prepare for our move to our new home, Martin Luther King Jr. had been assassinated and race riots erupted all over the country. These were scary times in America, seeing cities burning, people getting beaten or killed on the six o'clock news. In Vietnam, the Tet Offensive was well on its way, bombing the country into a parking lot, protesters were marching in the streets, and burning draft cards. Then, the first week in June 1968, Robert F Kennedy was assassinated, because it looked like he might be the next elected president.

Then also in June 1968, we finally moved to our new home on Elm Street in Highland Mills, New York. As we drove into this little hamlet and turned onto our new street, you would swear the you were in a Norman Rockwell painting. The houses on our street were built in the early 1900s, it was a nicely maintained neighborhood, and most houses had flowers on their front lawn. We pulled into the driveway of this big white with dark green trim colonial home, and then went into the house for the first time as a family; there was a moment of euphoria for my parents and all of the children. There had been a long wait for my family to move to our new home.

Ike, Gina, and I ran upstairs to stake our claim of one of three bedrooms even though my parents knew where we were going to sleep. Yes, it was one of those moments that felt like this could be Utopia for my family in this huge five-bedroom house, in this pretty little hamlet in upstate New York.

However, Utopia was a fictional island with people living perfect lives. The Kraemer's are far from perfect, and just wanted to achieve the American dream. We will take it.

As we started to move in and unpack, it was hard not to notice how pregnant my mother was, she was eight months along, and could not even fit behind the steering wheel to drive. So, the kids helped mom with the unpacking, and my uncles and father did all the heavy lifting.

About two weeks later, we finally unpacked and started a new project, getting the nursery ready for the new baby. Because my parents did not know what sex the little monkey was going to be, they decided on neutral color paint for the nursery. My mother decided lavender, under protest from my father, because if the baby was a boy, he thought the color was too" gay". Nevertheless, my dad, Ike and I had painted this big room down stairs, and my father said that if the little creep was a boy, he would repaint the room.

In the first week in July, my mother was over nine months pregnant, and it looked like she was going to explode into a million pieces at any given moment. So my parents decided that they would schedule an induced labor, and give birth to this Mammoth baby. So on July 6, 1968, my father drove mom to the hospital in Goshen, then dropped Ike and Gina off at my grandparents, and dad and I returned home. My father waited for the hospital or mom to call when she started to go into labor. We waited a couple of hours, then finally the phone rang, and dad answered. As my father spoke on the phone, I overheard him say, "Yes, Doctor." Then, as he listened on the phone, he grasped the counter in the kitchen, and looked outside the window up to the sky for a few moments. Then he said, "I'll be right there."

He hung the phone up, and then he turned his back to me, placed his other hand on the counter, and continued to look outside the window up in the sky.

I said, "What did the doctor say? Is the baby coming, or what?"

He turned to me, and said, "They found out that your mother is going to have twins."

My eyes opened wide, and I yelled, "Twins, two, boys or girls?"

He looked at me troubled, and in a low voice, he said, "Girls, but there could be a problem." He said as he looked down at me, with this face of fear, "You don't understand."

I said, "What?"

Then he said, "This is a small hospital, they do not have many experiences of delivering twins, and we could lose your mother, and or the twins."

Then I knew that this could be a tragedy, and the reason for my father's fear.

We got in the car, and drove 9 miles to the hospital in total silence, it seemed like it took forever to get there. We walked into the waiting room, and inquired about my mom. They said they were prepping her for delivery, and asked if my father wanted to see her before she went in. He did go in to see mom, while I waited for about 20 minutes. Then my father came back to the waiting room, and asked the desk clerk where the hospital chapel was. My dad and I walked into the chapel and sat down in the front pew. My father then knelt down, and put one arm around my shoulder, pulling me forward. I knelt beside him.

Then he said, in a soft voice, "Dick, pray for your mother and the babies."

I looked at him as he put his folded hands to his forehead, and tears started to run down his face. I then folded my hands, looked down to the floor, and began to pray. It seemed that at this very moment that time just stopped.

I could not remember if we were there praying for 15 minutes or 1 1/2 hours. However, I do know what happened next. As I started looking up at the altar in a much darkened chapel, the sun began to shine through the big stained glass window, and then grew brighter and brighter. The front of the chapel suddenly filled with sunlight. It was so bright, that it was blinding. Then, the door of the chapel opened. Then a voice called, "Mr. Kraemer."

My father turned, and said, "Yes."

It was the desk clerk, she said, "Mr. Kraemer, they need you in maternity." We went with the desk clerk to the waiting room, and then she paged the doctor.

The doctor came out with his surgical mask over his face, walked up to my father, and removed the mask. The doctor revealed his big smile, and said, "Mr. Kraemer, you have two beautiful healthy baby girls, and mother is fine." The doctor went on to say, "This is the first time we have delivered twins in this hospital."

Looking at my father, you could see the relief in his face. We went in to see my mother, she looked very tired, drugged up, and asked for a cigarette. Then we went to the nursery to see my little sisters; they were about 6 1/2 pounds apiece, and looked like two big prunes. This was a fine day in the Kraemer family. My parents decided that they would call the girls Pat and Pam.

The hospital had later gotten a baby photograph from my mom, and they blew it up as a mural on one of the walls of the maternity ward, it stayed there for over 15 years. My father had thought that they should have paid a royalty after getting the hospital bill. My mother also decided after having this litter, she would go on the Pill.

One summer day shortly after my mother returned from the hospital, she had decided that Ike and I needed haircuts. So, she sent us to Tulli's Barber Shop in our small town. The owner was an old Italian man, was about 4'10" with Coke bottle glasses, and a black beret. If he wasn't cutting hair, you would find him either standing outside his shop smoking a cigarette, or sitting in one of two Barber chairs reading the paper. He was very friendly. My parents would send Ike and me together to Tulli when we needed a haircut. My brother and I had walked up the street to his shop with some money mom had given us. When I met Tulli for the first time, it was somewhat strange to have an adult be as tall as I was.

I said, "Hi, me and my brother need a haircut."

Tulli said, "Ah, you two da Kraemer boys?"

I said, "Yes."

He said, "Gooda, you mama , she ah called, sitta righta down," dusting off the chair with a sheet.I sat down and took off my glasses, as Ike took a seat in one of the waiting chairs. Tulli then threw a clean sheet over me, and fixed it to my neck.

He said, "My name a is Tullio, but everyone a calls me Tulli, what'sa your name?"

I said, "Dick," as he pulled out a scissor and comb from his pocket.

He said, "Well, Dick, are you a Catholic," looking at me in the mirror.

I said, "Yes, sir, I would like just a trim, leave the hair over the ears, just cut the front just below the eyebrows, and cut the back straight, but over the collar. Okay?"

Tulli said, "Ah, okay." Then he turned the barber chair 180 degrees facing the window, and began to cut. As he did, I could only see my blond hair fall on my lap or the floor. Immediately, I realized that there was way too much hair falling as he pushed my head forward. Then he turned on the electric shears, and ran it up the back of my neck and up my head. It was then that I knew this haircut was not what I asked for. Tulli tilted my head straight and stood in front of me. Then, he cut all the hair off my forehead, with one quick snip of his scissors. Finally, he rubbed some hair tonic on my head, and combed what little hair I had left. Then he swung the chair facing the mirror again, as I scrambled to put my glasses back on. Tulli had unbuttoned the sheet from my neck, and brushed some hair off me. I had discovered that I had a dorky 1940's wet head hair do, complete with pompadour.

I looked straight at Tulli, with a pissed off face, and said, "This is NOT the haircut I asked for," as I stood up.

Tulli looked at me, and held his hand up, "No, nota exactly."

I said, holding up my hands, too, "No, not even close."

Then, with a smile, he said, "Yes, very close a, you mama, she called a me and told da me exactly how to cut you hair, Dick."

I threw up my hands and slapped them down to my sides. I realized my mother had called ahead to direct Tulli how to cut my hair over the phone. Ike saw that I was pissed off, and started laughing as he sat in the barber chair. My brother did not care about his hair because he was going to get a crew cut, and there is no way Tulli was going to screw that up. The haircut assaults lasted about 10 minutes for Ike and me.

After Ike's buzz cut, I paid Tulli, and as we walked out of his shop, he said, "Okay, a boys, thank a you, see you a next time."

I turned, and as I walked away, I said, under my breath, "Not in my lifetime."

As we walked back home, I couldn't help but think how stupid I looked. I looked like Ronald Reagan walking along with my sidekick monkey, Bonzo. As soon as I got home, I washed out the hair tonic, and I gave my brother a banana. Then I wore a baseball cap for about a month. I was forced to get a few more haircuts from Tulli, before I could pay for my own haircuts. He was always a friendly old man, and we had many good conversations on the sidewalk as I grew up.

Shortly after the twins were born, it was apparent that my responsibilities as the oldest child of the clan had just multiplied by two. This would entail all aspects of caring for infants, which I had no previous experience with, nor was I prepared for. My brother was also drafted as my junior partner in baby care 101 Training. My sister, Gina, at age 11, was a little too young at that time to be taking care of Pat and Pam, but she was perfect for keeping the babies amused for hours. She would stand there for hours, playing with the little Rug rats. Sometimes, Gina would stand over one baby's crib shaking a rattle, making smiley faces, and tickling the little bugger, then the other baby would start crying, and she would switch her attention to the other side of the room. This daily exercise would go on for hours, and would drive anyone out of their mind, but not my sister. Surely, there would be times where Pat and Pam would both be crying, and she would run from one crib to another like a ping-pong ball, trying to keep the peace, and then she would have a melt down moment, cry, and get some help. Gina became very handy in our Kraemer baby care team. My mother had given all the other kids basic training in baby care from feeding to diaper changing. The first time I changed Pat's diaper, I thought I was going to vomit. The babies were fed baby formula from a can, so their poop would come out in a watery pea green and stank like hell. One of Ike's first experiences changing a diaper was with Pam. When he undid the baby's diaper, he started wiping her down, and she peed a 2-foot water fountain right in Ike's face. He stepped back quickly, put both of his open hands on his face, trying to wipe the urine off.

With his eyes closed, he yelled, "My eyes are burning, I can't see," as he walked backward, tripped on a toy, and fell on his back to the floor. I quickly ran to him, and helped him to his feet, and guided him to the bathroom. My mom, hearing all the commotion, came on the scene, held Ike's head in the sink, and turned on the water as Ike screamed, "I can't see!" I went back and finished changing Pam, as she giggled. After a few minutes, my brother emerged from the bathroom with his face all red from the scrubbing mom gave him, and his eyes were all blood shot.

Ike said, "Mom, maybe I should go to the eye doctor, and see if I'm alright."

Mom said, "You'll be fine, you can't go blind from baby pee."

Ike shied away from changing diapers for a couple of days after his Golden shower/Near Peepee Blindness experience, then he was back with the team, up to his elbows in shitty diapers with the rest of us.

What surprised me was my father, he, too, knew how to change diapers right off the bat. It just surprised me because I never saw him do anything remotely associated with the feminine side of humanity. He did not do any housework, and didn't cook, except some times he would barbecue a few times. What also pretty much shocked me, at first, was the way he coddled the twins. He would bounce them on his knee, and talk baby talk to them. At dinnertime, mom would feed one baby, and dad would feed the other one while we were eating. Before that point in my lifetime memories, nothing came between my father and his food at dinnertime. He would do airplane noises, and then zoomed the spoon into the weasel's mouth. When I first witnessed this phenomenon, I was dumbfounded. I thought, "Was this the same person my father?" On the other hand, I thought that maybe he had been hit on the head at the job. Then, some of the old memories when I was about five years old would come back to me. I do remember my father lying on the floor with Ike, Gina, and me, playing with us. He would have me stand on his hands, while he was flat on his back, and lift me up as though he was bench-pressing me. He also would have wrestling matches with the three of us, and throw us down on an old red couch. In addition, anytime the Mets were on TV, we all sat on the floor and watched the game with dad on those hot summer nights. Yes, all those memories came rushing back to me. This was the father I knew all along; I just had not seen this side of him for quite a while.

My mom, for the most part, had it pretty good with all of us chipping in helping with the twins. All that intensive training of the older kids really paid off, and lightened the load for her. This was not Easy Street; she would still do a lot of work. Even though we helped, my mother did not sit back sipping a piña colada on a chaise lounge in the backyard, taking in the sun. No, that was not my mother's persona; she was always in motion and doing something. She would have many things to do, cooking, cleaning every day, sewing, painting, wall papering help with all the kids homework, and projects, and in her spare time, ceramics. My mother worked as if she was on fire, especially after the twins were born. In addition, mom had become more hyperactive, and had developed a fine hair trigger to her temper after the babies were born. So, a woman that I had known all my life, who had a lot of energy, emotion, and a short temper before, now had magnified those innermost qualities after childbirth. My dad said that it was her hormones acting up, and blew it off at the time. However, it was not until a few years later that we connected the dots. After my mom had the babies, she had two personal objectives, never get pregnant again, and to lose weight. In those days, the magic of medicine had introduced a few new drugs to the market. The birth control pill was the only surefire way that my mother would never get pregnant again. Therefore, she took The Pill, and at the risk of the Pope finding out, but she thought the risk was worth it. Now she was having a weight problem after giving birth to the Mother Load, so she decided to try diet pills. What a miracle drug, a pill that helps you lose weight! What else could a woman ask for? In the late 1960s, many of the doctors were pushing these diet pills, and the clinical studies showed phenomenal results. This diet pill phenomenon swept through almost every American family in the country like wildfire. Anyone that wanted to lose weight could take this magical pill, and shed all the pounds they wanted. What people in any social class did not know was that they were taking Speed or Black

Beauties. When my mother took these pills home from the doctor's office, she would take six different colored pills. There were pink, orange, blue, yellow, and red ones, but the Speed was the black capsules. The Speed, AKA Biphetamine was an Amphetamine/Dexamphetamine combination, and the effects were hyperactivity, insomnia, heightened irritability, and dry mouth. This pill was a personality enhancer for mom, and that was not a good thing. In all defense to both parents, they did not even know my mom was taking a narcotic. Just like hundreds of thousands of unsuspecting straight-laced Americans across the country taking Amphetamines as diet pills. There used to be an old saying that, "Speed Kills," and at first thought, you may think that if you overdose, you could die of a heart attack. This is true that it could kill you that way. However, that was not the reason for the "Speed Kills" statement. It was because of the amount of rage that could be amassed under the influence of Speed, that the user could become homicidal. Although, mom never killed any of the children, that doesn't mean that she was not thinking about it, and I would be the first one to go.

The Highland Mills house in the summer of 1968.

A rare Kraemer family photo on our front porch, after the twins were baptized in the summer of 1968.

Chapter 3 - Welcome to The Neighborhood

In the fall of 1968, after moving to Highland Mills, we now have to take the bus to school in Central Valley. After school on one hot day, all the kids would get in line to board the school bus. On this day, I was almost at the end of the line, and this bus would be getting packed to full capacity. As I boarded the bus, all the front and middle seats were taken. I moved towards the back of the bus looking for a seat, and the kids behind me were pushing from behind. I was carrying a couple of books under my arm and a couple of pencils in my hand. Suddenly, someone from behind pushed me very hard, and I turned around quickly to regain my balance. Then this little kid, about eight years old, started screaming and crying. I turned to look at him, he was holding one hand over his left eye, wailing, and he was pointing at me. Immediately, all the kids on the bus all stood up, started climbing over the seats, the kid's two older brothers, Ray and Jay, made it to the injured boy. The two brothers assumed that I had poked the boy in the eye on purpose. Then the brothers proceeded to throw several punches from two different directions, with an additional 50 kids out of their seats in riot mode. The bus driver had made it to the back of the bus, broke up the brawl, determined the injured boy needed medical attention, and moved all the brothers and myself off the bus. Once off the bus, the driver told me to stay next to the bus, and the bus driver went into the school with the boy and his brothers, to call an ambulance. About 2 minutes later, the bus driver returned by herself, I started to board the bus, and the bus driver stopped me.

She said, "Oh, no, you don't," as she pulled me off the first step of the bus by my shirt.

I said, "How do I get home?"

She said, with a snarl, "Call your parents," as she slammed the door in my face.

The school bus drove off in a big puff of oily smoke. As it did, I caught a glance of Ike sitting on the bus, looking back at me. I walked back into the school, it seemed deserted because it was 20 minutes since school had ended. As I walked through the empty hallway, the only thing that I could hear was the nurse in her office trying to attend to the kid. I walked into the administration office, and asked the fat lady if I could use the phone.

She said, "Are you Dickie Kraemer, the one that stabbed that boy in the eye?"

I said, "It was an accident, I didn't mean to do it."

She said, "I'll call your parents," as she picked up the phone in one hand and then asked for my number.
I could not remember it, so she looked in her black book. She then dialed the number, and said, "Hello, Mrs. Kraemer, (pause), this is Mrs. Dumpy from the Central Valley Elementary School, your son has been involved in stabbing another boy on the bus."
Then the fat lady stopped talking, and I could hear my mother through the phone receiver.
Then Mrs. Dumpy said, "Your son is in the administration office, (pause), okay."
She hung up the phone, and said "Your mother will be here soon, sit over there." As I walked over to the seat, I could see out the office window into the hall, the ambulance crew was taking the boy in a stretcher, with his brothers walking behind him. They could see me in the office, banged on the window, and made death threats as they passed. My mother finally arrived, and asked me what had happened. I explained to her in detail about the accident. Also, how everyone thought I had done it on purpose.

Then, Mrs. Dumpy said, "That's not what the boy's brothers said!"

Mom said, "What did they say?"

Mrs. Dumpy said, "They said your son stabbed the boy in the eye because he wanted his seat."

My mother suddenly grabbed my hand, and walked over to the front desk, with an angry face.

Then, she said in a loud voice, "You think my son stabbed a boy in the eye, so he could get his seat?"
Mrs. Dumpy backed away from the desk, fearing that mom was going to jump over the desk, and said, nervously, "I don't know, I wasn't there… But the children said that…."

Mom stopped her by putting up a hand, and said, "We will get to the bottom of this."
Then mom turned around and walked out of the office, pulling me along by the hand.

Once at home, my mother sat down with me and went over the incident about three times. My mother called Dad's job, and left a message to call home. It was late in the afternoon when my father called, and said he would be right home. Once my father got home, we went over the incident a few more times. My parents had gotten nervous and started talking about being sued and losing the house. My father had to calm Mom down because she started to become hysterical. Then my father started to act like Perry Mason, then told mom and me not to talk to anybody, and if anyone asks about this incident, tell them to talk to him. About an hour later, the phone rang, and my dad answered, it was the father of the injured boy, and he wanted to come to the house for a conversation. My father agreed to the meeting, and hung up the phone. A few moments later, the man arrived in front of the house, and my father met him on the sidewalk. We could not hear their conversation from inside the house. My Dad and the man talked for about 10 minutes. Then the man drove off, and my dad came back into the house. The man told my father that the boy had surgery, he had a small hole in his eye. The doctors said that he should recover to full sight, but they will know more in a few days. The man then said that his sons had told him that I had attacked the small boy. My dad then told the man my version of the accident, and told him that I was not the kind of kid who would stab someone in the eye, so he could get their seat on a school bus. Dad went on to say that, maybe his sons might have elaborated on the incident, during the time of the crisis, and the man should cross-examine his son's story. The man told dad he was certain of his son's story and had threatened to get the police involved. My father calmly said that if his son had done this on purpose, he would bring him to the police station himself. He told the man that he should go back and question his sons about the incident again, before going to the police to save himself from embarrassment. The man promised to talk to his boys, and would call my father later. Later on, after dinner, the phone rang, it was the father of the boy. He had questioned each of his sons in detail, discovered that this was an accident, and he had apologized. My dad asked how his son was doing in the hospital, and also asked, as the boy progressed, if the man would let us know how he was doing. In addition, he asked the man or his wife to call the school in the morning to clarify that this was an accident, and to clear up any misunderstanding of the incident. The man assured my father that he would take care of it.

The next day, my mother went with me and made sure that Mrs. Dumpy and the rest of the school knew that I was not a pencil-wielding maniac willing to stab little boys in the eye to get a seat on a bus. Mom also bought all the Kraemer kids a pencil case, to guard against any accidents in the future.

I would later learn that the victim of the accident had recovered without any permanent eye damage. As for his two brothers, they never bothered with me again, with the exception of a few insults. I had heard from one of my friends that their father was so pissed off, that the brothers had elaborated on this story, from the accident, that they were beaten badly for it.

My parents always came up with great ideas to keep the kids busy, they felt strongly about the old saying, "Idle time is the devil's workshop."

As soon as we moved to our new home, my mom signed us kids up for everything, and it happened suddenly almost overnight. She was a very friendly person, and quickly networked with other parents in the hamlet and she had a huge folder of applications when she returned home one evening. This is how her recruitment speech went at the dinner table that evening:

After dinner we all cleaned off the table and the kids were about to start washing the dishes. She came in with this big folder, and told everyone to sit back down, including my father.

My mom said, with a smile, "I have good news for everyone."

Gina perked up and said, "We're going to get a cat?"

My dad said quickly, "No cats."

Then mom said," You're going to join the Brownies, meetings are Tuesdays after school." She continued, "The meeting is at the school, the late bus will take you home."

Gina said, "Do I get a uniform?"

Mom said, "Yes."

My Dad sat back, and quickly placed his left hand on the table, then started making rolling, tapping noises with his fingers.

Then, my mother said, "Ike, you're going to join the Cub Scouts."

Ike said, "Why?"

My mom went on to say, "Because it's good for you, and Dick was a Cub Scout, the meetings are on Wednesdays at four o'clock in town at the Presbyterian Church."

Ike then said cheerfully, as he looked at my father, "Do I get a uniform?"

Before Dad could speak, my mother said, with a smile, "Yes, of course, honey."

Immediately, my father sat straight up in the chair and put both hands on the table.

Then he said, "How much is this shit going to cost me, Jeanie?"

She looked at my father, with a straight face, and said, "Wait, I'm not finished."

My father then raised his eyebrows, and said in a feminine voice, "Oh, there's more?" Then he sat back in the chair, crossed his legs, then his arms.

My mother then looked at me, and said, "Dick, you're old enough to join the Boy Scouts."

I said, "Mom, I don't want to join the Boy Scouts."

My mother said, with a concerned tone, "Why? You'll meet kids in school there, and make friends."

Since the move to Orange County to this point, I had more enemies and no friends. What concerned me was the prospect of making more enemies or meeting the ones I already had at Boy Scouts.

I said, "No, I don't want to!"

My dad said, "I was a Boy Scout, you'll learn to survive in the wilderness, and first aid."

I said, "I don't want to join the Boy Scouts!"

My mom said, with a smile, "Well, guess what? You already did!"

Looking at her, knowing I had lost the fight, I needed to be a smart ass and create a diversion.

I looked at her, and said, "Will I get a uniform?"

She looked at my father, straight faced, and said, "Yes."

My dad, looking at mom, with his arms still crossed, said, "Is there anything the kids could join that doesn't cost money?"

My mother said, as she stood up with her folder, "Yes, Dick and Ike are going to be Altar Boys at St. Patrick's Church."

Ike and I looked at each other, as if one of us knew about this.

My father said, "Are you sure? Because they have to wear those Penguin outfits, don't they?"

Mother said, "Yes, the cassocks are supplied by the church."

My dad said, "Well, that's a relief. So, how much is this going to cost?"

Mom opened up the folder, got a pen, and then started to add under her breath.

My father started to tap his feet.

Mom looked up, and said, "Dick and Ike, start doing the dishes." Ike and I walked to the sink, started working, and braced ourselves for a tsunami.

My mother said, "I have it, one hundred and twenty-eight dollars and thirty-seven cents."

My father jumped up, as he did, the chair flipped behind him. He yelled, "Are You Fucking Crazy?"

Ike and I turned around to see my mother glaring at my father, as if she was burning holes in his forehead from the other side of the room. Then, mom turned red, leaned forward, and yelled, "New Uniforms Cost Money, Asshole!"

At this point, my brother and I had seen this screen play before, and decided to "Exit, stage right".

My mother blocked us with her arm, and said, "Get back to work."

We went back to the sink, and started to wash dishes again.

Then, dad said with a low growl, "Why do they need new fuck 'n uniforms?"

Mom looked at him, annoyed, and then ripped open the folder. She was tapping her right foot, and calculating under her breath.

My dad picked up the chair, and moved it under the table.

Mom, then said, "Ike could wear Dick's old Cub Scout uniform." I could hear Ike softly sigh because he always got my old clothes.

Then she said, "I saw a used Boy Scout uniform shirt, for Dick, a hat, scarf, but no pants in a thrift shop in Monroe for $15. He could go for a few weeks in his school pants."

Then she sat down, still looking in the folder, and said, "But I couldn't find a used uniform for Gina, so we'll have to buy it new.

My dad said, "How much is that?"

She said, "$44.72."

My father just shook his head, and placed a hand on his baldhead, and said, "You're kidding?"

My mom looked at him, and with those blue eyes, without saying a word, as if to say, "This is the best deal you're going to get and you'd better take it."

Then he said, as he walked out of the room, "Yeah, okay, you're driving me to the poor house."

My mother went in the opposite direction to the nursery to attend to the twins.

My father was not opposed to the kids joining these American organizations, in fact he encouraged it. He was just trying to save a buck. My mom and dad liked the idea of us joining American community institutions not only to teach their kids life skills, and make friends, but also to teach and show their patriotism.

During this time, it was late August 1968, the Democratic Convention in Chicago was on, and antiwar protesters were rioting in the streets, the police and National Guard were trying to restore order. This troubled my parents greatly, to see chaos in the streets of one of the biggest American cities in the country, because they supported the war in Vietnam. My father thought that it was his patriotic duty as an American, and war veteran to take a few days off from work, go out to Chicago, and crack a few long hair skulls, and maybe some Democrats if they happened to get the way of his bat just to help restore order. My mother was against the idea, because we could not afford the time off from his job.

Therefore, my father would have to settle for confrontations with antiwar protesters in the New York area, which there were many.

As Ike and I washed the dishes, after the family recruitment seminar, which I thought went smoothly considering past budget battles my parents had fought through. I had a feeling that something was missing from this picture. The following morning, as my father went to work, mom told me to get some packages out of the trunk of the car. When I opened the trunk, I looked in the bags to discover Gina's Brownie uniform, and my used Boy Scout uniform. Then, later, that same morning, I found my old Cub Scout uniform in Ike's closet. It had been altered, and had new patches of the Highland Mills pack. This was one of those "Ah ha!" moments, realizing that the whole budget negotiation the night before was a sham, and my mother had duped my dad. She had learned from experience that asking for money of any amount for a kid activity was going to meet opposition, because money was tight. Therefore, she decided to ask for the most amount of money first, because she would've preferred to purchase new uniforms for her children. However, if that tactic failed, the plan "B" would go into effect, with or without my dad's approval. Her strategy proved to work in this case, and the bonus was my father's approval. This was one of my earliest lessons in negotiation,-ask for the Moon, have a plan" B", and settle for what you really want. There was nothing I could do about being drafted into the Boy Scouts or The Archdiocese. Knowing that blowing the cover on my mom's scam would not serve me well, I decided to keep quiet about my discovery.

There was a code of loyalty in my family that also existed in a crime family, the code of silence. But in our family, we had two under bosses. The Kraemer kids would serve both bosses. If one kid would learn something about one parent that would disturb the peace if the other parent found out, we were silent.

This would prove to be an effective way to keep the peace, and the kids would benefit, most of the time, for their loyalty. This code of silence would go unspoken and expected, just like the above example. There would be times where a situation would arise that one of my parents felt that they needed to say," Don't tell your mother/or father, just for clarification. Breaking this sacred code would not serve any child well, because the result would erupt into a big fight between my parents. The offending parent would be pissed off at you, and they would get even. The rest of the kids would treat you like a rat that could not be trusted. If you were stupid enough to try extortion or blackmail on my parents, they would encourage you to tell the other parent. Then say something like, "But do you think it's the right thing to do?" This implied to me that the next time my parents had been backing out of the driveway, that they might not see me.

As mentioned earlier, my mother was a devout Catholic and all the Kraemer children were raised as such. My parents were married in the Catholic Church. Ike, Gina, and I were baptized, had first communion, and were confirmed. Pat and Pam, later in life, would also go through the same process. Once a week, after school for many years, my brother, sister, and myself went to catechism (religious training), and would attend church every Sunday. There was a standing rule in my family-all children must have religious training, and go to church every Sunday, no exceptions. There was one exception, if you were so sick you could not get out of bed, if so you stayed in bed all day Sunday. My mother sometimes could not make it to church services, but the Kraemer children always did.

My father was born and raised as a Lutheran, and his family was religious. When he was a boy, he belonged to a choir, and went to church every Sunday. My dad, for the most part, never went to Sunday Catholic church services, unless my mother badgered him so badly that he would go, just to shut her up. He just did not like the way the Catholic services were organized in the following ways:

He would have to follow the mass in several different sections in the book, and always lost his place.

He would have to stand, sit, and kneel several times without verbal prompting from the priest during mass, and if he had lost his place in the book, he would have to mimic what other parishioners were doing. This would mean that he would be one of the last people to kneel, sit, and stand during the service. This would make him feel like an outsider or an amateur Catholic. I do remember that as he got older, he had acquired a smooth transition from a standing position to a half sit-half kneel move that he could recover from without being detected.

My father believed in God wanted his children to believe in God and get religion. Therefore, even though he did not like the Catholic religion, he felt it was best for his children.

The St. Patrick's Church was led, at the time, by a pastor named Father Karate. The father was a strict old-fashioned Catholic, a no-nonsense kind of person. In those days, the training of an Altar Boy was pretty much on the job training. First, you have to be a confirmed Catholic. Second, you would have to know each of the steps of the mass. Third, you have to pay attention. The father would make a few dry runs of the mass with you and an experienced altar boy before mass, and then, its show time. The lead altar boy,(the one with experience) would do all of the bell ringing, assist the priest with the wine, water, sacrament, then assist giving out the wafers A. K. A.(The Body of Christ). During the mass, for the most part, I was moving along side the lead altar boy, sometimes I was on the other side of the altar, and other times I was sitting, standing, or kneeling next to the priest or the altar boy. After the mass, in the little room in the back of the church, Father Karate would give you feed back on how you did during the service. He was not shy, critical at times, fair, and truthful. He was also a perfectionist, in which high standards were expected. Being on the altar, a representative of the Catholic religion in front of a church full of parishioners was an honor, but nerve racking. If you ever saw a Catholic mass, the amount of sitting, kneeling, genuflecting, standing, making signs of the cross, and all of them combined several times, can be confusing. Now, the people in the pews can pretty much follow the mass, if they mess up, they could cover it up without being noticed. But when I am on the altar (God's Stage), and I make a mistake, it's in front of 100 people, Father Karate, and most of all, God, I would feel ashamed of myself. One thing you could pretty much count on was if I made a mistake, Father Karate would catch it and tell me about it.

One time, I was wearing a cassock (altar boy's robe) that was too long for my height. When I was making my way from one side of the altar to the other, I had to stop in front of the altar, and genuflect before making it to the other side. When I genuflected, my foot stepped on the inside of the cassock, and when I quickly stood up, my body thrusted forward, propelled my head into the top step of the altar, with a loud thud. I could hear the crowded church feel the pain, like at a football game, "AAAAAAHHHHHH!" My head hurt at first, and then the embarrassment took over. On my knees, I recovered my glasses from the altar and put them back on. I looked up at the altar to see Father Karate looking at me over it, with both hands raised. Realizing that the mass is in `Freeze Frame', I quickly got to my feet, and made it to the other side of the altar.

The mass resumes, my head still hurting, about 2 minutes later it was time to assist the priest with the wine and water. As I walked up the steps to the altar, I stepped on the inside of my cassock again, thrusting my body forward, hitting my chest full force on the steps.

I could hear the parishioners let out a loud"OOOOOHHHHH!"

I scrambled to my feet, and reached the top step of the altar. Father Karate looked at me concerned, and said, "Son, go sit this one out, I think you may be hurt." I walked down from the altar, and sat down at the lower portion of it, facing everyone in the church. Now this is awkward, the Quarter Back of God has benched me, and everyone knew it. During the rest of the mass, anytime there was a moment that I should have been involved, I would start to get up to help the priest. The Father would then make eye contact with me, hold up his hand, and wave me off, and then point for me to sit down. After mass, I did not want to hang around to hear what a screw-up I was, so I slid out the back door.

Then I quickly made my way through the parking lot, and I heard Father Karate yell, "Dickie Kraemer,"
I thought maybe I would make believe I did not hear him. So, I kept walking.

Then, The Father yelled, even louder, "Dickie Kraemer, come here!"
There was no way to make as if I did not hear him, so I turned around, and walked back to the church.

When I reached the priest, he said, "Let me see your head."

As he looked at my head, he said, "You've got a bump on your noggin; let's put some ice on it."
We walked into the back room of the church, he wrapped ice in a cloth, and gave it to me.

Father Karate, then said, "Put that on your head, and sit down."
The priest then went to the closet, pulled out the cassock I wore, and looked at it.

The Father said, "Ah, this is a priest cassock, it's way too big for you. I'm sorry, Mrs. Morrow must have put it in the wrong closet."

He went on to say, "How are you feeling? I guess you feel embarrassed about falling during mass. Well, let me tell you, I make mistakes, too. We are all human, and God knows that."

I told him that I felt stupid about this, and other mistakes I had made in the past, and he assured me that I would get better as time went on, and I did. He offered to drive me home, but I declined, and said I felt much better

I never told my parents what happened that day. From that day forward, I had discovered that Father Karate was a kind, caring man of the cloth, and not someone that I should fear because he has a Hot Line to the Lord.

My brother actually had picked up faster on being an altar boy than me. When my brother and I we were ready to go on as a team, my family, including my father, had gone to the service. Ike and I did a great job that Sunday, and our parents were very proud of us. My mother, during those days, use to ask us what we wanted to be when we grew up, hoping that one of us would say a priest. We never said it. Sometimes after asking us, she would say, "What about entering the priesthood?" Then we would confirm for her that we would never be priests.

Boy Scouts

The Boy Scout meetings were held on Thursdays at 7 PM, in the basement of St. Patrick's Church, I would walk there after dinner. There had been about 30 kids in our troop, most of them were my age or older, some I had already known from school. I was happy to find out that the new enemies I had made recently were not members of our troop. The meeting began with the Pledge of Allegiance, and then we recited The Scout's Oath. Then, everyone would sit down and the Scoutmaster and Assistant Troop leaders would discuss troop business like fund raising, planned trips, and volunteering for public services. Then they would announce the testing schedule for merit badges or scouts moving to the next rank. They would announce the classes held that night, an award ceremony, and they would pick two scouts to stay after the meeting to clean up and put away the chairs. These meetings were boring until the part of training classes, testing, and snack time. They would teach all sorts of things, like how to read a map, and compass, camping, hiking, and first aid.

One time, during the meeting, a boy fell out of his chair onto the floor, his arms and legs flailing about, foaming at the mouth, and he turned pale. All the scouts converged on this boy to try to help. In about 5 seconds, they had this kid's shirt unbuttoned, pants undone, and a bunch of scouts held his arms and legs. Then, the Scoutmaster made it through the crowd, and pulled the belt off the boy's pants and put it between the kid's teeth.

The Scoutmaster then knelt next to the boy, and said, "Someone, get a blanket."

Then an Assistant Troop Leader said, "Do you think we should call an ambulance?"

The Scoutmaster said, "No, I know this boy's parents, he is having an epileptic seizure."
After a few minutes, the boy's seizure stopped, and he threw up, then started to cry. You could see that the boy felt embarrassed afterward about what happened. I went over to him and told him that he should not feel that way. Then he joked about it a little, and said that he will remember to take his medication next time. Also, later that evening, a boy had asked an Assistant Troop Leader, if he could get credit for his First Aid merit badge for helping out with this incident.

The Troop Leader looked at him, annoyed, and said, "No."
Then the boy, not satisfied with that answer decided to ask the Scoutmaster.

The Scoutmaster looked at the boy, puzzled, "There were about 10 scouts involved in this incident, and no one else is asking for credit. Why should you?"

The boy said, "Because I asked first."

The Scoutmaster then said, in a very loud voice, "Anyone that was involved in John's incident, please come to the front of the room."

The group of boys gathered in front of the room.

The Scoutmaster then said, "Bill, here thinks he should get credit for his first aid merit badge for helping a fellow scout when he was in trouble, does anybody else want that credit, too?"

All the boys shook their heads, no, in silence.

The Scoutmaster, looked down at Bill, and said, "I believe that's your answer."

There is always moments in life where you say, "I don't want to be that guy," this was one of those times.

Chapter 4 - The Paperboy

A couple of months after I moved to Highland Mills, I found out that the neighbor paperboy was about to quit his early morning route. I immediately talked to the boy, and he agreed to train me. I delivered the papers with him for about week and then I was on my own. Now I had my own newspaper delivery business, and was pulling down the big bucks. On any typical day, at 12 years old, and starting at 4:00 AM; wintertime seemed the most memorable, waking to the sound of a Big Ben wind up alarm clock with huge bells on it. The sound of that clock was so loud that your heart would skip a beat as you woke up. Then my morning would begin with my feet hitting the cold, hard, wooden plank flooring, and turning on the light, to which Ike would turn and pull the covers over his warm little head. I would get dressed in long Johns that I had already slept in, two pairs of socks, an old pair of pants, and a sweatshirt. Then I would run down stairs, and look outside the front door to see if the paper delivery driver had left my bundles of papers. I had nicknames for the delivery drivers-they were Knucklehead, Jerk off, And Asshole. Depending on what day it was, I knew where the papers would be left. Knucklehead would leave the papers anywhere but in front of my house-he would leave them anywhere within a 2 house radius, but he would deliver early. Jerk-Off would always be late, but he would set them on the front porch, and Ass Hole would deliver anytime, but would deliver the papers out of my sight from any window in my house-in the gutter, under my father's truck, in the bushes, or in front of the big elm trees in front of my house. These guys would rotate days, and so I never got down their schedule. I would call the newspaper to complain, and they said that they would talk to the driver, but nothing ever changed. I later learned by catching quick glimpses of the drivers, that they all looked the same; in fact, I came to the conclusion that it was one driver. It was Scumbag all along. So on my last day that I gave up my paper route, I decided to get even. Right now, I'm getting a little off track, I'll tell you later how I handled Scumbag.

I looked outside, and thanked God, the papers were sitting on the sidewalk, but the bad news is that they were sitting on 4 inches of new fallen snow. In those days, in upstate New York, it wasn't unusual to see that it occurred 3 or 4 times a week, sometimes more. Also, in those days, the weather forecasting was very bad; in fact, the only time they were right was when the snow was coming down. The TV weatherman would say, "It's snowing outside and we are expecting anywhere from 2 to 10 inches, depending where you are." This guy is broadcasting from the Empire state building in New York City within a 150-mile radius, and if you're a blind man sitting in your apartment, this information was very helpful. Great job being a weatherman in those days, and the percentage of being right was higher.

I put on my green rubber boots in the mudroom, my blue parka with the fake fur animal trim around the hood, a knitted ski mask, and leather gloves-as I walk out the door, the thermometer read -5°. I took my Red Flyer sled from the side of the house and walked down the short driveway to newspapers. I would cut only one string on the bundles of papers, with my official Boy Scout pocketknife, so I could slip the papers out of the bundle and not lose them to the +20 mile-per-hour wind. I would then tie the bundles to the sled with some rope. I would deliver to all the people in the village first in a three-block radius, almost all of them inside the storm door and some in the mail or milk boxes by the door. There were no plastic paper tubes on the road in those days. I would then walk through the heart of the village where there was a couple of stores, shops, and the village hall. It was still dark and no one was open. Once in a while, the bakery truck used to drop off hot, fresh hard rolls and pastry to Frank's Meat Market. Before I would walk past there, I would mostly take a hard roll, and leave a dime in the bag.

I would then go to the next section of the route on the eastern side of the village; it was called Mount Holy Shit I Do This for $16.25 a Week. This part of my route was a newer development of bi-levels that were built on a side of a mountain that started being built in 1961. This part of Holy Shit was a very steep hill of snow/ice packed road with about 12 houses. The only way to walk up this hill was to walk in the outer part of the snow bank, placing me in about 2 or 3 inches of new snow to get enough traction up. As I climbed the hill, I would wrap the sled rope around my wrist, because a few times in the past, I had fallen, let go of the sled, and screamed every curse I knew, at the top of my lungs. The next level of Holy Shit was level street in a "T", but most of the houses were on a steep hill, and the papers were delivered to the door.

I had this one customer on this block that had to be with the mob. He had this brand-new red Cadillac, Greek statues of Venus on the brick pillars at the end of his driveway, and bronze stair hand railings. I heard one of his friends call him Tony Two Lips; this guy looked like he was hit a few times in the face with an ugly mallet, and his lips were huge. His wife was really hot, and very well dressed. They also had two very vicious Doberman pincers that had bitten me a few times. So my approach to this house was guarded, I learned to carry my bicycle lock and chain in my coat pocket, just in case. The people were great tippers, sometimes they would give me five dollars on collection day, and say to keep the change-the bill was a $1.60 a week.

I would make it the end of the block, and there would be another hill about 300 feet, where I would make a right to another semi-level street, go to the end of the block and intersect on another street. There was a bigger hill that was steeper than the first. But the only difference was my direction of the route was down this snow/ice packed mountain road, and I had to turn back on the road I was once on before.

I had planned this route out this way because of three
important reasons. They are:

1) If I were to go all the way down this snow/ice packed
   mountain, there would be no way to stop at the end of
   the road. I would go across a state highway that has
   traffic now, and if a car or truck didn't make me road
   kill, I would run up the snow bank, take flight and go
   through a plate glass window of Potter's Beauty Parlor
   were I would get a major make over.

2) I needed to deliver two additional papers on the very
   corner of that street.

3) I needed to slow down for my first descent from the hill
   I climbed at first.

When getting prepared for my stunt, I lay my
newspapers evenly on the sled, and tie them down. Then I lay
my belly on the sled, wrap the sled around my wrist, wipe off
my glasses, and do the sign of the cross on my forehead. Now
I start down the hill and then I take my left foot and take an
ever so slight kick off. As I'm picking up speed, my glasses
start to fog up, but I can't wipe them off because both hands
have a death grip on the wooden handle stick. Still gaining
more speed, I move the sled to the far left side of the road. As
I approach the 90° right turn on this road, I start dragging my
right foot, and pulling hard on the right side of the handle
stick.
My target is the snow bank on the left side of this intersection,
after I hit the snow bank, there were mixed results depending
on road and snow conditions. They are:

A. A lot of new fallen snow, 12 inches or more, and the
   plow had passed this street, head first and half my
   body in the snow bank. No injury.

B. New fallen snow, 6 inches or less, winter "frozen-snow bank" without the road being plowed-I would bank the turn, fly across the road, go up the opposite side snow bank and land runners down on my customers lawn. Or I would bank the turn, shoot down the street, pulling hard left and dragging my left foot resulting into a series of 360° turns in the middle of the street and/or flipping over. No injury and the preferred way to land.

C. New fallen snow, 6 inches or less, mid-winter "frozen snow bank" with the road being plowed, I would hit the snow bank and shoot over it with a 1 1/2 twist down an embankment; hitting a tree, a swing set, a metal garbage can or a car was not uncommon. Injuries where possible, but the "B" result could be possible also.

D. New fallen snow, with 2 inches or less over top of an iced up road and a "frozen snow bank" without the road being plowed. Injuries where unavoidable, and "B" and "C" results were possible, but of course, so was the road kill or the make over at the beauty parlor was an option, too.

Now that I had delivered those two papers, I was ready for my final descent down Mount Holy Shit. This road, too, led right into the state highway, it's becoming light and there is traffic moving. My target destination is at the bottom of the hill, on the left is the back of Beatties Exxon gas station which faces the state highway, it is the only choice.

When getting ready for my next stunt, I lay my newspapers evenly on the sled, and tie them down. Then I lay my belly on the sled, wrap the sled rope around my wrist, wipe off my glasses, and do the sign of the cross on my forehead. Now, I start down the hill and then I take my left foot and take an ever so slight kick off. As I'm picking up speed, my glasses start to fog up, but I can't wipe them off because both hands have a death grip on the wooden handle stick. Still gaining more speed, I move the sled to the far right of the road. As I approach the back of the gas station for a 60° left turn to the snow bank, I start dragging my left foot and pulling hard on the left side of the handle stick. My target is the snow bank on the left side of the road, after I hit the snow bank, I would land in the back of the vacant lot of this gas station. Most of the time, I would land pretty much unharmed, but sometimes gaining too much speed, I had crashed into 55 gallon oil drums, a wooden fence-head first, a tree, tires or a junk car.

My route was almost complete now that I had the thrill for the day; I walked to the end of the village to deliver to a trailer park hidden down this long tree lined road. Then I would quickly back track through the village where people are starting to clear off their cars and shovel. I would make it back to my house on Elm Street where I'd see my brother shoveling my father's truck out, and I'd ask if there was school. If there was not school that day, I would help dig out dad. If there were, I'd run in the house, change my clothes, eat if there was time, and then run down to the end of the street to catch the bus.

In those days, to close the school for snow, it would have to be still coming down and a lot more then 4 inches. It is important to note here the time frame; I wake up at 4:00 AM, deliver 128 newspapers, go home, get undressed, get dressed again, wash up, brush my teeth, make my bed, and maybe eat if I had time, then catch the bus. The bus stops at the end of my Street at 6:45 AM, and they are not waiting for anyone. If I miss the bus, there will be hell to pay. First, if my father hadn't left for work by that time, he was running late, and dropping me off at school 10 miles out of his way is not going to happen. So that leaves Mom, she would have to get Pat and Pam dressed, then herself, warm up the car, if it would start in sub-zero weather, put them in the car, and drive me to school 9 miles round trip. Oh, yeah, my mom was going to take me to school, because the Lord knows, I needed the education. In fact, she would've carried me on her back to make sure I would get that schooling. But she would have gone into a fit of rage, start cursing, her light blue eyes would bulge out of her eye sockets, she would start stomping her feet, and start throwing things. If she broke anything, she would say, "See what you made me do?", then she would start crying. This would be a very scary and bizarre scene, but would not be a corporal offense; therefore, I would not get a beating for this. But, there is a very real threat of being forced to give up my paper route.

So, being on schedule was imperative, if I want to make the big bucks.

Looking back on those paper route days, my parents encouraged me to do this as a way of teaching me what it takes to earn a dollar. There were no handouts in my house, you earned the money you spent.

If I walked up to my parents, and asked for money, they would say, "What for?"

I would say, "I want to buy the new Beatles 'Let It Be' album." They would say, "No!" Then if it were my mother, she would wait a minute, and say, "Maybe if you're good, you'll get it for Christmas."

In the above case, if I'm asking for money for new Beatles music in February, it's going to be a long wait for Christmas, and I'm not waiting.

But back to the point, no handouts, no allowance, no way, no how!

But, there were some extra chores around the house. In which you could earn some money. But there were very few 'extra chores' that were outside our regular chores to be paid for. The wage scale was very low, about $.75 a day; I would let Ike rake in this boatload of cash.

My brother, Ike, also had two of his own paper routes, too. One was a weekly town newspaper called the Photo News that had about 75 customers. The other was a Newburgh evening paper he delivered to about 45 customers after school. As soon as my brother and me were tall enough to look over the lawn mower handle bars, old enough to hold a snow shovel, or rake, we had a new and ever lasting chore. My dad had his own personal landscaping crew, one of the many joys of fatherhood.

In a later chapter, I will tell you how I settled the score with the newspaper delivery driver, Scumbag.

The Kraemer family in our dining room during Christmas 1968

Chapter 5 - The Holidays

When the holidays rolled around at my home, mom was Mrs. Claus, and dad was Mr. Scrooge. Their characters were well defined approaching the holidays. The fact is that right after Thanksgiving you knew that Christmas was right around the corner, not by the calendar, but by the intense fighting about money. The closer we got to December 25, the more frequent the money bouts became. Before the twins were born, my mom used to work part time as a sales clerk for WT Grants in the fabric department in Rockland County. She would start in September when the kids were in school, and weekends, when she would get a babysitter. Then she would end her part-time employment on Christmas Eve. The primary reason she worked was to purchase Christmas gifts. My mother used all of her free time working during that half of the year, so her children would have a better Christmas then the last. Nevertheless, even though she worked all those months, she would always overspend on gifts and out spend her earnings. When the Christmas Deficit was realized, it was "Deck the Halls with Screams and Shouting." This holiday ritual would go on year after year, mom would overspend and dad would yell about how he was going to pay for it. After the twins were born, my mother could not work her holiday part time job anymore, and the holiday gift giving expenses had escalated. This made for some of the most memorable holidays of happiness, and the most turbulent. The more my father tried to stop mom from overspending on the holidays, the more my mother would spend. My father never did get control of the Holiday Spending Frenzy. Years later, instead of dad yelling about how much was spent on Christmas, he turned to pleas of mercy, which seemed to work better.

After Thanksgiving, we would receive the Sears Christmas Catalog in the mail and this was our dream book.

The moment that catalog arrived, Ike, Gina, and I would mull through it for hours, making up our gift list. The funny thing was that I believe my mother never really looked at these lists and if she did, it was only a glance. Mrs. Claus intuitively knew what her kids wanted for Christmas. She would observe us at a store, overhear our conversations, sometimes during the year we might ask for something, or she would ask us. The Kraemer children only had two chances of receiving a gift-your birthday or Christmas. My parents, under no circumstances, were going to buy you something that you wanted unless it was purchased for and given to you on birthdays or on Christmas. If you wanted something so badly that you had to have it outside those two dates, you had to figure out how to pay for it with your money. We were not poor. We were middle class. The parental principle of no gifts except for birthdays and Christmas was based on two factors. First, the Kraemer children were overindulged at Christmas and on birthdays; both parents will admit to that fact. Second, the principle lesson of self-reliance, the value of the dollar, and that you had to work for what you wanted in life.

The first week of December, mom would break out the Christmas decorations, and made our house look as though Santa lived there. In each window of the house, mom would install one electric candlestick with a blue bulb, in the living room picture window; there would be electric candelabra. In the hallway and doorways, she would drape and string imitation garland laced with fake poinsettia leaves. Then she would place real poinsettia plants in various places in the house. We had an upright piano in the hallway where she set up a Nativity scene on top. My mother had made the Nativity set from ceramic molds, and had hand painted each piece. She had spent about a year working on this Nativity set, and it was one of her finest works. My mother was a ceramic maniac, once she started the hobby she could not stop. The house was filled with ceramic knickknacks and statuettes, all done from scratch and hand painted. During the holiday season, we would put away all the everyday ceramic figurines, and replace them with all the holiday decoration ceramics. Mom's holiday creativity did not stop with ceramics; she also made tree ornaments, nut wreathes, and rum fruitcakes. If anyone on the planet had the spirit of Christmas, it was my mom, Mrs. Claus. It was not the money that was spent, or how well the house had been decorated, but how much time and effort it took her to prepare for that final day, December 25.

My father's involvement at Christmas time was picking up the tab, stringing the lights in front of the house, getting a wreath, and the tree. The stringing of the lights was an easy job, we put one string right above the porch gutters, and had it done before the Sunday Giant football game. The ceremony of getting the tree and wreath had many different variations, and it was always centered on price. In the early days, mom, dad, and all the kids used to go hunt for the perfect tree. That ceremony wore off quickly because mom used to pick out the most expensive tree on the lot. Then there were the times my father would fly solo a couple of days before Christmas, and come home drunk with a tree. This would prove not to be the best approach; because my father would always say that, the tree looked a lot prettier the night before, looking at the ugly shrub the following day. Then there was the take one or both of your sons approach to the tree search safari. My dad's ceremony of finding the perfect Christmas tree with one or both of his sons seemed to take hold for a few years.

I remember one time, dad and I were on our tree excursion about two weeks before Christmas. It was a Saturday, and we took off a little after noon. The first order of business was that we had to have lunch, most times when dad and I had lunch out, we would get hot dogs. Most times, he would find a hot dog cart over on the side of the road, but in December, you would be hard pressed to find one. On this day, we went to Newburgh to a place called Pete's Hot Dogs. This tube steak palace, now world renowned, was just a shack in those days, about five blocks south from Broadway, in the center of Newburgh, just off 9W, on S. Williams St. As dad pulled up in front of the hot dog place, we noticed a vacant lot that was being used to sell Christmas trees, what luck! We walked into Pete's, dad ordered his usual two dogs with mustard and red onion sauce, and I had two with hot dog relish. The place was packed with customers, but we managed to wedge ourselves into some stand up counter space in front of the window. We both ate and drank our Cokes, looking out the window, without saying a word. As my father finished, he noticed two black men standing next to his truck looking in the back of it. In the bed of the truck, he had tools, a crated cast iron tub, and toilet, a lot of copper pipe and tubing.

He said, "Wait here."

Then he quickly walked outside and approached the two men. Dad said, "You see anything you like?"

The two men turned around, startled, and one said, "No, man, we're just looking."

Dad said, "Looks like you're shopping to me, keep walking."

The other man stepped towards my dad, and said, "Hey, fuck you, honky," raising his finger in my father's face. Suddenly, my father slapped the hand from his face, and then he thrusted both hands into the man's chest, causing the man to fall backwards into the snow bank.

Then my father grabbed a three-foot lead pipe from the back of his truck, and held it to his side. As the one man scrambled to his feet, the other started to come closer to dad. As my dad raised the pipe, a fat man dressed all in white, in his 50s, ran out of the hot dog place with a baseball bat.

The fat man yelled, "Didn't I tell you fuckers never to come around here again?"

As the two black men took a couple of steps backwards, the fat man raised the bat, as if he was going to hit one out of the park.

Then one of the black men pointed at dad, and said, "We'll see ya again, Honky."

My dad yelled, "Fuck waiting for tomorrow, come and get it, you Jive Ass Turkey!"

As my father walked towards the two men, they turned and ran down the block. I walked out onto the sidewalk, knowing that it was safe to come out.

The fat man lowered the bat to his side, and said, "Those two are brothers, and one of them just got out of the joint, I called the cops on them before, but they always show up too late."

My dad placed the pipe in the back of the truck, and said, "Yeah, well, thanks a lot, Pete."

As the fat man walked back inside, he said, "Sorry about all of this."

Dad said, "No problem." Then my father looked at me, and said, calmly, "Let's take a look at those trees." Then he pointed to the vacant lot full of trees next door. I looked at him, confused, because a minute before he almost had a street fight, the next minute he is touched by the Christmas spirit, and wants to pick out a tree.

I said, "Yeah, okay."

He said, "Wait over there by the fire," pointing to the 55 gallon drum full of burning wood. Then he jumped into the truck, and backed it up about 100 feet, so he could keep an eye on it. When he got out, he grabbed the iron pipe out of the back of the truck, and walked to the fire.

The man tending to the tree lot said, "Hi, do you want a tree?"

Dad smiled, and said, "No, I want your money, you son of a bitch!"

The man, wide-eyed and startled, took two steps back with his arms raised, and said, "Dick Kraemer, you mother fucker, how are you doing!"

Dad said, "Billy Dolan, Tommy told me you had a Christmas tree stand up here!"

Billy said, "Yeah, I got laid off last month. Is this your son?"

Dad said," Yeah, his name is Dick, too, say hello to Mr. Dolan."

I said, "Hi."

Billy said, "Holy shit, Dick, he looks exactly like you when you were a kid!"

Dad said, with a smile, "Yeah, scary, huh?"

My dad and Billy talked for a while catching up from the last 15 years. It turns out that they were friends since grammar school; both joined the Army around the same time. After about 20 minutes, the conversation turned to business, and we looked over some trees. Billy had given us a discount, so we loaded up the tree and wreath in the back of the truck, and we took an old rope to tie it down. As we drove away, it started to snow. My father wanted to make sure that we didn't get home too quickly after getting the tree, so we would let mom think that we searched for hours looking for the one special Christmas tree. Therefore, dad decided to take the scenic route home, and traveled on route 9W South. When we traveled for about 10 minutes, the snow started to come down harder.

Dad said, "You know what happened back there with those two niggers?"

I said, "Yeah."

He said, "It never happened, you got that?"

I looked at him, and said, "Why? They were going to rip you off."

He let out a sigh, shook his head and said, "Your mother won't see it that way. She'll never understand, and she'll think that I put you in danger."

I said, "But you did the right thing, and you didn't put me in any danger."

Dad said, "Your mother would not see it that way, I don't need a hassle from your old lady, and so it never fuck 'n happened. Got it?"

Then he looked over at me, waiting for my answer.

I said, "Yeah, I got it."

As we got onto route 293 heading towards West Point, dad put on his country Western station on the radio.

Dad said, "You know what happened back there could have turned out a lot differently." Then he lit a cigarette and cracked the window open about1/2 an inch. He said, "I could have cracked the poor nigger's head open, and the cops would put me in jail for assault or manslaughter. That wouldn't make your mother happy." Then, he took a drag of his cigarette, as he drove into a sharp curve on the snow packed road, the rear of the truck started sliding into the oncoming lane.

He said, with a cigarette hanging out of his mouth, "Hold on," then he cut the steering wheel towards the skid, got the truck under control again.

Dad said, "Now, where was I, oh, yeah, the Jungle Bunnies could have shot or stabbed me. Then, Jesse Jackson would get them off the hook, because I violated their civil rights. This, too, would not make your mother happy."

As we started up a steep hill, he downshifted the truck for traction.

I said, puzzled, "But, how is that dangerous for me?"

He said, "I'm supposed to lead as an example, I'm your father."

Then he rolled down the window, and flipped the cigarette out. Then, as the windshield wiper reached its highest point, he quickly grabbed and released the wiper arm off the glass, knocking off the excess ice from the blade. Then he rolled up the window and shifted into fourth gear when we reached the top of the hill.

Dad said, "Your mother thinks that if you see me do things like that, then you'll think that it's okay for you to do the same things. Monkey see, monkey do. That's dangerous."

I said, "I got it, Dad, I'm not going to say anything."

Dad said, "Okay, to anybody."

I said, "I gotcha," looking at him, as if to say, enough already.

As we drove in the snowstorm, we would see a few cars crawling along the road with their hazard flashers on. If we could pass them, we would the first chance we got, because we didn't want to be slowed down going up the hills. Even though the truck had about 1/2 a ton of cargo in the bed, if we were caught behind Mr. Magoo going 10 MPH, we were going to be stuck on the hill. I know why my dad took this route; it was the road less traveled on route 293, most of it, on both sides of the road, was wilderness, and owned by the US Army. If we ran off the road on 293, it would be many hours before we would be towed out, not to mention the expense. But, my dad knew how to drive in the snow; it is everybody else you have to look out for. Once in a while, I would look in the back of the truck to make sure the tree was secure, because we had to tie it down on top of crated tub and toilet.

We ended up behind a 1966 Ford Mustang for about 3 miles, and he was going about 25 MPH. Every time he would go into a curve, he would fishtail almost out of control, and go even slower. My father hated Fords, especially Mustangs because they didn't handle well in the snow or rain. Once we came to a straightaway, dad downshifted, and jumped into the passing lane. The back of the truck swerved to the left as dad shifted into third gear, and we pulled alongside of the Mustang. I looked at the driver, he was in his late 20s, with long brown hair, with a Manchu mustache, and had both hands wrapped on the steering wheel in a death grip, and he looked scared shitless. Once we passed the car, dad shifted into high gear and we pulled into the right lane with about 40 feet of clearance. We could hear the guy now behind us blowing his horn several times, and dad looked in the side mirror.

Dad said, "Look's like the long haired fagot is pissed off, sorry Sweets." Then he said, "Brenda Lee, I love this song," and turned the radio volume up full blast. I liked this song, too, and we both sang along with the song.

Brenda Lee, Rockin Around the Christmas Tree.

After the song was over, dad lowered the volume on the radio, grabbed another cigarette from his pack, and put it in his mouth. He then reached into his pocket, and pulled out his old dented up Zippo lighter. Then he opened it by quickly brushing the top down on his thigh, and then quickly rubbing the flint wheel back up his thigh, lighting the lighter. Then he lit his cigarette, and closed his lighter by hitting the top piece of it on his thigh, and then he put it back into his pocket. I had seen him do this lightning speed maneuver a million times, and I think he thought he was the fastest lighter in the East.

Dad said, as he adjusted his baseball hat, "You know Mitchell?"

I said, "Yeah, Mitch." Mitch was a black plumber's helper, in his mid 30's that worked for my dad. My dad was a master plumber, and a foreman for the company that he was employed by at the time. Mitch was a nice man; he would come to our house, park his old Rambler station wagon in front of the house, and dad and him would drive to work together. Mitch had to be the best plumber's helper, because he worked as my dad's helper, for a couple of years. Mitch was very friendly, and sometimes while he was waiting for my father, he would sit on the front porch and talk to the kids. As he waited, my mom would make him coffee, sometimes mom and him would chat about everyday things. Mitch was married, had six children, the oldest was a girl a year older then me, and youngest was three years old. The whole family rented a house in Monroe. Even though my father never met Mitch's family, you knew that they were good people, because of Mitch's personality. He always had a smile, looked happy, and had great faith in God.

I said, concerned, "What about Mitch?"

Dad said, "Well, you won't see him anymore," then he grabbed his hat, and threw it on the dashboard.

I said, excitedly, "Why? What happened?"

Looking at my father, you could see that he was upset. He said, "Because he's going to the slammer, for burglary."

We started to go down a steep hill, and dad downshifted as we came into a curve. Dad said, "Yeah, him and his brother-in-law pulled a job at a hardware store in West Haverstraw."

I said, surprised, "A hardware store? What did he steal, tools?"

When he came out of the curve, he shifted into high gear. The truck fishtailed and grazed the snow bank, causing a loud scraping noise. My father yelled, "Shit!" Then he got the truck under control again.

Then he grabbed his hat off the dashboard, and put it on his head. Dad said, "Yeah, I should have thought something was up when he showed up a couple of weeks ago with a bunch of new tools. I asked him where he had gotten them from, and he said his brother-in-law sold them to him. They still had the price tag on them. I thought he bought some hot tools."

I said, "Mitch is going to jail because he stole some tools from a hardware store?"

He let out a sigh, and said "Yeah, that's not the whole story." Dad continued, "Mitch and his bro broke into the back of the hardware store at night, clipped some tools, and also stole a safe. Then they packed everything in the back of Mitch's piece of shit Rambler, and then drove it to one of my construction sites. Then they tried to crack the safe open with one of my torches. That didn't work, so they used a sledgehammer, and that didn't work either. So they loaded the safe back in the car, drove to another construction site, and dropped the safe into a pit. A pit where we just installed a new septic tank and leech fields, but we didn't cover it up yet. Then the two Dimwits covered the safe with some dirt, and had planned to come back later, and dig it back up. Then dad took a drag of his cigarette, opened the window, knocked the ice off the wiper bladed again, and rolled the window halfway up.

I said, "Did they get the money?" I looked back at him, waiting to hear the rest of the story.

Dad smiled, and began to laugh, "Noooo, I had the septic tank buried the next day, because we were expecting a heavy rainfall that night." Then he stopped smiling, and said, "Now that I think of it, Mitch asked me a few times why I was covering up the pit, and he said it wasn't going to rain."

I said, "How did the cops find out?"

He took another drag, and said, "I have no idea," then flipped his cigarette out the window. Dad took a deep breath, and said, "I found out when the cops showed up a week ago on the job site looking for Mitch. Then they asked him some questions, went through his toolbox, and found all the hot tools. Then they slapped the cuffs on him, threw him in the police car, and they took off."

The big gust of wind hit the truck so hard it made us drift into the center of the road, he got back to the right side of the road, and dad said, "Take a look at that tree. Is it secure?"

I looked back in the truck, it was still there, and I said, "Looks okay." I said, "Hey, Dad, how did the cops find out about the safe being buried?"

He said, "Mitch's brother-in-law cut a deal, he dropped the dime on Mitch and told them where the safe was buried, for a lighter sentence. And that's not all of it." Then he banged his fist on the steering wheel. He said, "The cop thought that I was involved, because I had the septic buried the next day, and I was close to Mitch because he's my helper. And not only that, my boss Hans has an open account with that hardware store, and I pay cash to the owner of the hardware store once a month."

I looked at him, wide-eyed, and said "What! (Pause) Are they going to charge you?"

Dad said, "No, the cops cleared me of being involved about a couple of days ago, but I had to get a lawyer. Mitch and his brother-in-law told cops I wasn't involved, but they didn't believe them."

As I looked in the back of the truck to check on the tree again, I said, "How much time do you think Mitch will get?"

He said, "Well, he's an ex-con, so maybe he'll get 10 years."

I said, excitedly, "Ex-Con! He was in prison before?"

Dad nodded his head, and said, "Yeah, he did a stretch for armed robbery, he held up a gas station when he was in his twenties. He did 3 1/2 years for that."

I sat there in silence, looking out the window, observing the snow-covered pine trees. I started to think about Mitch's wife and kids. I turned to dad, and said, "What about his wife and kids?"

He said, "I guess they will have to go on welfare. Those kids are so young, and his wife is nice, too. That Mitch really fucked up. He had a nice family. It's a damn shame. I'm taking up a collection for his family at work. That money is not going to bail that asshole out, it's going to his family. He is good as convicted with all the evidence they have."

I could see that my father was really troubled by this, and he felt used and betrayed by Mitch. My dad had met Mitch through the Veterans of Foreign Wars post in Rockland County; Mitch was also a Korean War vet. My dad also knew that Mitch was an ex-con, but my father vouched for him to get the plumbers helper job. Mitch told my father before he hired him that he wanted to get a legit job and go straight. My dad gave him a big break, because he could not have gotten a good job with a record. A good job with a future, because dad had taken him under his wing, and was teaching him the plumbing trade, and Mitch was going to take the journeyman's test in the spring that would have tripled his salary.

Up ahead in the middle of the snow-covered road, stood a big doe and two fawns on the shoulder of the road. Dad quickly downshifted, tapped the brakes, and slowed down to a crawl. Dad said to the deer, "Go on," as he waved at the doe to cross the road. The doe just stood there and looked at us. The truck came to a complete stop. Dad said, "What are you looking at, go before someone hits you." Then he blew the horn. The doe took off like a shot, and the fawns followed. Then Dad put the truck in gear. We started moving down the road slowly with the tires spinning, and then began to get traction again.

He said, "Yeah, my boss Hans, when he heard about what Mitch did, he wanted to bail him out and kill him. Because we had to dig, up that septic system which had a 2-foot frost line. The excavator broke the tank, the leech fields, and most of the pipe, before they got their safe back."

I said, "Are you in trouble with Hans?"

Dad let out a sigh, and said, "No, but because I vouched for Mitch when we hired him, I'm accountable for his actions. I talked Hans into hiring him; even though he had a record." I could not help but think of Mitch's family. How would they face Christmas this year, without their father and no money? We finally got off route 293, and entered route 6 going towards Central Valley. This road was a narrow country road with many sharp curves going down a big mountain. At the top of the mountain, the wind was blowing the truck from side to side, and the storm visibility was near white out conditions. Dad had downshifted the truck when we approached the first curve. He again knocked the ice off the wiper blade. As we went through the curve, the rear of the truck quickly kicked to the center of the road, Dad downshifted to second gear, and tapped the brakes. Then he cut the steering wheel towards the skid, and we now were riding in the oncoming lane. He then shifted to third and eased our way back in the right lane. Suddenly, a big blast of wind hit the truck, and it rocked to one side.

Then I heard the tree thrashing around in the back, and as I turned around, I saw the tree fly out of the back of the truck. I yelled, "We lost the tree!"

Dad yelled, "Fuck!" Then he downshifted, started tapping the brakes, and put on his emergency flashers. As we crawled to a stop, he looks in his side view mirror, and says, "Where is it?" I looked out the rear window, and said, "It's in the middle of the road." We had stopped in the middle of a small straightaway about 250 feet in total length on each end, and there was a sharp curve. The road had about 6 inches of new fallen snow on it. My dad adjusted his rearview mirror, and shifted the truck into reverse. Then he released the clutch slowly, giving it a little gas. The tires spun, and the truck was going nowhere because we were on a hill.

I said, "Why don't we go down the mountain, turn around, and grab it on the way back up?"

He said, "This damn truck will never make it back up the mountain, not with this much snow." Then he said, "I'll go get the tree, you get in the bed of the truck, and I'll hand it to you."

He opened the door, pulled his baseball hat tightly on his head, and got out of the truck. He zipped up his jacket, and he said, "I hope I don't get killed up there, that's a blind curve up there." Then he pointed up the road, turned to me, smiled, and slammed the door. I jumped out of the truck and walked on the snow bank to the back of the truck. I watched my Dad drudge through the snow along side the road, as the howling wind whipped the blinding snow.

Dad turned to me, and yelled, "Get in the bed."

I climbed up on the bumper and into the back of the truck. I bent down and started to unknot the old broken rope. I would look up occasionally, to check on dad's progress up the hill. I got the rope ready, stood up in the truck, and looked to see that dad was about 25 feet from the tree. Just then, I saw a car come around the blind curves at the top of the hill.

I yelled, "Look out!"

Dad saw the car coming, turned quickly, and jumped up on the stone guardrail. The car's ass end whipped into the oncoming lane, and then it whipped onto the shoulder of the road. The car bounced off the snow bank and began to straighten out. Then the car hit the Christmas tree squarely in the grille, and the tree plowed the snow for about 50 feet, until the car slid to a stop. The car was a newer white Cadillac, with a black convertible top and it rested there for a few moments. As I stared at the car from the back of the pickup, I could see my dad was okay, and was making his way back down the hill. The Cadillac's door opened up, and out popped a skinny man with glasses on, who was about in his 50's, and was wearing a suit.

The man yelled, "What the hell are you guys doing stopped on this mountain in a snowstorm? I could have killed some body!"

I yelled back, over the howling wind, "Our Christmas tree fell off the truck," pointing to the tree wedged between the front of his car and the road.

The man walked to the front of his car and looked at the tree. My dad walked up, started looking at the front of the car, and said, "Doesn't look like any damage was done, maybe if you could put the car in reverse, I could un-wedge the tree from the car. Then we could get a better look."

The man nodded his head in agreement, and jumped back into his car. Dad waved to me to give a hand, I jumped off the truck, and walked over to him. The man put the Cadillac into reverse, and started backing up slowly, as his rear tires spun. Dad said, "Grab the tree at the trunk," then he put both his hands on the car hood and began to push the car backwards. I grabbed the tree by the trunk with both hands and began pulling, with my heels dug into the snow and my back arched. As the car backed up slowly, with the rear tires spinning like crazy, I began to be pulled along with the car.

My dad, still pushing the car, turned to me, and yelled, "Pull harder, yank it."

I arched my back forward, placed both feet flat on the snow, re-gripped the trunk, and yanked the tree. Then I repeated the yanking process several times, and finally freed the tree from the car. The man got out of the car. The man and dad removed a bunch of pine branches from the car grille, and looked at the car.

The man said, "Doesn't look like any damage, you and your son better get off this mountain before someone else comes along."

Dad said, "You're right, take care."

Then dad picked up the tree, and threw it into the truck. He and I climbed in the back, tied it down, and then we jumped back into the cab of the truck. Dad started it and we continued down the mountain.

I said, "Wow, that was close, you almost got killed."

Dad said, "Almost and close doesn't count, only in horse shoes and hand grenades."

I said, "Yeah, did you see that big gouge in the tree? I think that tree is toast."

Dad looked in the rearview mirror, and said, "It's fine, just a little bare spot."

I looked at him and said, "Dad, that little bare spot is as big as a Cadillac grille."

He said, with a smile, "We'll put the bare spot in the corner of the living room; no one will notice it there."

I shook my head, and said, "Mom will notice and she'll freak out."

Dad frowned at me, and said, "Look, I'll take care of your mother, and you don't say anything about what happened to the tree to anybody. Got it?"

I shrugged my shoulders, "Okay, I got it!"

A few moments went by as we drove, and then dad said, "One thing I'm not going to do is blow another eight bucks on a fucking Christmas tree."

When we got home, dad backed into the driveway, and we knocked off all the snow on the tree, and put it in the garage.

My father looked over the gaping hole in the tree, and tried to brush the remaining branches to cover the hole; that did not work.

I held the wreath out to my father, and said, "Here this should plug up the hole."

Dad snatched it out of my hand. Then he said in a low voice, "Don't be a wise ass."

Dad closed the garage door. We walked into the side door of the house, and took off our boots.

Dad whispered, "Not a word about the tree."

I nodded my head yes. Dad and I walked into the kitchen and could smell Christmas cookies in the oven.

Mom walked in, and said, "I was worried about you. Did you get the tree?"

Dad said, "Yeah, it's in the garage, it's all wet, I'll put it up tomorrow, it will be dry then."

Mom said, "Dick, I want to put it up today."

Dad said, "I could, but I would have to pull the wet tree through the house, making a big mess. I'll put my muddy work boots on, they're dry."

She said, "You're right, we'll do it tomorrow."

Dad said, "You won't believe who I bought the tree from, Billy Dolan, he was in Newburgh."

While my parents had their conversation, I walked into the living room and watched drag racing on ABC's Wild World of Sports.

The following morning, my father waited until my mother was preoccupied feeding the twins before he brought the tree into the house. Then him and I put the tree in the stand and wedged the huge bare spot into the corner quickly. Then dad quickly scurried around the living room, looking at the Christmas tree from all angles.

He whispered, "See? Looks perfect." I looked at him with my arms folded, with a half smile.

Dad yelled, "Jeanie, take a look at the tree before I string the lights."

Mom walked into the center of the living room, looked at it, and put her finger on her chin. Then she walked to the right side of the tree, and put her hands on her hips. She walked to the left side of the room, and put one hand behind her head. She said, "It looks like its leaning a little to the left."

Dad stood behind her, and said," Yep, you're right. I'll fix it and string the lights. But don't you think it's a pretty Christmas tree?"

Mom said, "Yes, I think its one of the best we've had." Then she walked into the kitchen, and resumed feeding the twins.

Then my father turned to me, with a big smile, and whispered, "It's one of the best Christmas trees ever!" Dad and I fixed the leaning tree and strung the lights. We plugged it in and it truly looked like one of the best Christmas trees we had ever had. However, the real moment of truth is when mom and the kids start decorating the tree. It was late on a Sunday afternoon when we broke out the decorations for the tree. Mom had baked cookies, and put on a Christmas record on the hi-fi. She also poured herself a couple of shots of BlackBerry Brandy, to get her more into the spirit. Dad's job was done; he bought the tree, put it in the stand, and strung the lights. He does not decorate because he is not artistic. Therefore, he would sit in the living room reading his Sunday paper, and field any questions about how the squirrels ate a crater-sized hole in the tree. My mom's first step in the Christmas tree decorating process is to wrap silver garland around the tree. Mom had told me to pull the tree out of the corner enough so I could stand behind it. This would make it possible for me to grab the garland from one side, and feed it to her on the other side. I pulled the tree out of the corner slightly, and squeezed in the back of it. Gina and Ike started opening up the boxes of Christmas decorations, and fighting over who was going to hang what. Mom stood on a dining room chair next to the tree, and started wrapping the garland from the top. As she worked her way down the tree, she would meticulously drape the garland about every 8 inches, and she would direct me on how to drape the garland in the back of the tree. I tried to conceal the bare spot by leaning into the tree, even though the gaping hole was at waist level and twice the width of my body. After she worked her way down the tree, mom jumped off the chair and went into the kitchen to pour herself another Brandy. I peeked around the tree and looked at my father sitting in his chair with the newspaper opened, covering the top half of his body. Then dad closed the newspaper and stared back at me, and then he made a funny face at me. I smiled and began to laugh. I heard mom coming back into the room, dad buried his face back into the paper. I turned my face into the corner, trying to compose myself from laughing. Mom came back into the room, grabbed the chair she was standing on, and pushed it to the side. She took another strand of silver garland and walked over to the tree. She resumed her draping and handed me the garland level to my head. I draped it as she directed and handed it to her from the other side. When working her way around the next time, it was level to my chest. I grabbed the garland, and stepped back from the tree.

She said, "Okay, now drape it….." Mom's eyes bugged out and her mouth dropped wide open, looking at the giant hole in the tree. She turned her eyes on me, and said, "Look at that fucking hole! Didn't you see that?"

I looked at her, wide-eyed, backed into the corner nervously, and said, "It's a bare spot!"

Then she leaned her whole head into the corner, looking at the tree.

Then she stood straight up, turned to my father, and yelled, "Bare spot my ass, half the tree is missing!"

My father dropped the newspaper from his face, and said calmly, "What's wrong?"

She said, "What's wrong is that tree! Didn't you see that?"

Dad got up, threw the paper on the chair, and said, "Let's take a look at it," then he walked to the back of the tree, and stuck his head into the corner. Then, he stood up straight, turned my mother, and said, "It's just a bare spot."

Mom, with a mad face, folded her arms, and started tapping her left foot on the carpet. She yelled, "Richard, you son of a bitch, you ruined my Christmas again!" Then she turned around and stormed out of the room.

My dad followed her into the kitchen, and said, "Jeanie, it's in the back of the tree, no one will even know its there."

Mom yelled, "I'll know it's there, you bastard!"

Dad started to raise his voice louder, and said, "YOU KNOW, A FEW HOURS AGO, YOU LOOKED AT THE TREE FROM ALL SIDES, AND SAID IT WAS THE BEST TREE EVER, AND NOW YOU HAVE A PROBLEM WITH IT!" He yelled at full volume, "BECAUSE YOU'RE CONCERNED WITH A SPOT ON THE TREE THAT NO ONE BUT YOU COULD SEE!"

As I squeezed out from back of the tree, Ike came over, and said, "How bad is it?"

I whispered, "Take a look," pointing to the back of the tree.

Ike stuck his head in the corner, and said, "Holy shit, did you pick this out?"

I said, "No, Dad did."
Ike looked at me with his eye brows raised, and shook his head. Gina went into the nursery to escape the yelling, and to calm down the crying twins.

After about 15 minutes, the screaming and yelling started to die down, with mom and dad hurling insults at each other, both standing in different rooms in 3 to 4 minute intervals. It is during this period of my parents fighting process, where it could become quite comical, and the kids would hear some of the one-liners, and would have to conceal their laughter.

Some examples of the one-liner insults would be:

Mom would be in her bedroom, and yell, "YOU BALD-HEADED MONKEY FUCKING BASTARD!"
Dad yelled his response in the dining room, AH, YOU'RE A BUBBLE-HEADED TOOTHLESS BITCH!"

That it would be silent for 4 minutes, then my parents would be doing something and rotate rooms, never facing each other, and then they would start the verbal dual again:

Mom yelled, "TOOTHLESS? HAVE YOU LOOKED IN THE MIRROR LATELY, YOU PUMPKIN HEADED MOTHER FUCKER?"

Dad yelled back, "MOTHER FUCKER? I WOULDN'T FUCK YOUR MOTHER, EVEN IF SHE WAS THE LAST PERSON ON EARTH!"

Then about 8 minutes later, the bout of verbal insults would resume, but each time taking longer for the next one-liner. About 30 to 40 minutes later, exhausted from fighting, my parents would give up, kiss, and make up.

Once the mauled Christmas tree was accepted as our holiday center of attention, we resumed the tree decorating process. Mom and all the kids would hang the decorations on the tree, some old family bulbs that had been handed down from German generations, recently store bought ornaments, ones from the Depression, and mom's hand made decorations. Once the kids were finished hanging the decorations, mom would rearrange them as her final touch. Then we would light the tree, and suddenly, that Christmas tree became the most beautiful tree on the planet, every single year. The fact is no matter how badly crooked, mangled, or mauled the tree was before the decorating process, and it always turned out to be a masterpiece of a Christmas tree afterwards, every year.

Once the Christmas tree was decorated, that house would be filled with the spirit until it came down. Magically, the fighting over money stopped, even the siblings were civil to each other. It seemed like the whole family was under the Christmas Spirit Trance.

It was this year that I took the money I had earned from my paper route, and decided to buy Christmas presents. This was my first experience with the spirit of giving. My mom had taken me to WT Grants in Monroe, and sent me off alone in the store while she shopped. This also would be the first experience with the mental anguish of buying the right gift. After about an hour, I had settled on leather gloves for dad, lavender and pink ponies on wheels for the twins, a heart shaped gold colored locket for mom, a doll for Gina, and a pocketknife for Ike. At the time, leaving the store, I thought that I had blown a lot of cash, and had buyer's remorse for days afterward. This was the very first time I started to identify what my father had been yelling about all these years. But my biggest angst was that whether the gifts would be truly wanted, prized, and enjoyed, or would they be thrown aside like an old shoe. I would have to wait for Christmas morning for that answer.

On Christmas Eve, after dinner my father had taken a white sheet, and asked me to come into the basement with him. On the table where Ike and I had our Aurora miniature racecar set, there were wrapped Christmas presents stacked on it. Dad knotted the sheet, so it could be used as a sack, and I held it while he placed each present carefully inside it. Then he took the sack outside and put it into his truck.

I said, "Dad, who are those presents for?"

He said, "It's for Mitch's wife and kids. I also took up a collection at work, some guys gave, and most of them didn't. But at least they'll have food and heat over the holidays." Dad went upstairs and told mom that he was going over to Mitch's house and then he left. My mother knew what had happened to Mitch, and had felt that we should try to do something to help his family best as we could. So when dad took up a collection, and came up short, my parents made up the difference to insure that Mitch's kids had presents on Christmas morning, food, and heat for the holidays. As for my father's feelings for Mitch, he never got over the betrayal of trust. However, he did have a final thought, that desperate men do desperate things. It was learned after the Christmas visit at Mitch's family's home, that the reason he pulled the hardware store job was that his wife needed an operation. She had cancer, no health insurance, and no money to pay for the needed operation. But on that Christmas morning, after all that had happened to Mitch's family, there were presents under the tree for each child, food for each mouth, and heat for their home.

On Christmas Eve, all the kids would go to bed early, so they could get up at the crack of dawn and see what they had gotten for Christmas. My mother would stay up most of the night wrapping presents, and dad would have a few drinks and go to bed at 11 PM. Ike and I already knew there was not a Santa Claus at that age, Gina still believed there was one. Which I found confusing considering Gina heard all the fighting about money around Christmas time. Maybe my mother told Gina that dad had to send money to the North Pole before the elves would release the presents to Santa for delivery. But this is only a guess.

On Christmas morning, one of us would wake up the others. My parents standing rule was that it would have to be day light before we could wake them up to open the presents. The other rule was that both parents had to be in the living room while the kids opened their presents. In addition, the first couple of years after the twins were born, it was important not to make any noise that would wake up the little monkeys. As we walked down the stairs on that most exciting morning of the year, the stockings would be filled to the top hanging from the banister; there would be so many presents under the tree that they overflowed to the center of the large living room. We would walk into the living room in amazement, and look over some of the larger toys that could not be wrapped, and shake some to make our best guess of what could be inside. We could hardly contain our excitement, and would bust out and yell something like,

"Wow, I really got it," or "I can't believe it." Then the others would say, "SSShhh, you'll wake up the twins." Then, when we composed ourselves, we would all creep into mom and dad's bedroom, and try to wake them up. We would try to wake mom up first, because she was always willing to get up on Christmas morning to watch the children open their presents. This was the moment to witness the spirit of giving that she worked toward for the last six months, even though she only got four hours of sleep from the night before. We would leave waking my dad up to mom. He was not the kind of man to be awoken by anyone. If anyone woke him up, he would awake startled and swing his arms out in defense. It was because of the Korean War that he had this problem. He would wake up in a second when the Big Ben alarm clock went off. Mom would get up out of bed, and give him a shove, and then jump back out of the way, dodging his swing. Then she would say, "Get up, Richard, it's Christmas," then she would walk into the kitchen and boil some water. The kids would run back to the living room, waiting for our parents to emerge from the kitchen. Once the kettle began to whistle, we knew the time was fast approaching for us to open our presents. My parents would stagger to the living room in their bathrobes, hair all messed up, and cup in hand. Then they sat in their favorite chairs, and gave the go-ahead to start unwrapping presents. Every year, the Kraemer children would go into a present unwrapping frenzy, and the wrapping would go flying everywhere. These kids would dive into these presents like a buzz saw, but always took enough time to fully appreciate each gift. My mom always enjoyed giving us direction on which present to unwrap next, and watched our expressions as we did. My dad sat silently, seeing what gifts we received for the first time. I believe that on Christmas morning, dad had really felt the spirit of giving, watching his children unwrap their gifts, and for that moment, money didn't matter that much. Of course, that feeling would only get so much mileage, and be short lived after he looked at the final bill in January.

After all the children's' presents were unwrapped, the time had come for me to give my presents out. I was nervous as I passed out each one.

My brother opened his up first, and with a surprised look, he said, "A pocket knife," when he opened the blade on the small brown knife, he held it in his hand.

Mom said, "You be careful with that, and don't take it to school." Ike nodded in agreement.

Gina opened her present, her eyes got very wide, and she held the blond doll in her arms. She ran over to me, and said, "Thank you, Dickie, for the beautiful baby," and gave me a kiss on my forehead.

My dad opened his present, and said, "Wow, leather gloves," then he tried them on, and I thought they were a little small. But, dad said they were perfect for driving, and gave me a hug, and said thank you.

Finally, Mom had unwrapped her gift; she looked at the gold colored locket and smiled. Then she opened the locket, and said, "I'll get a picture of all the kids to put in it." Then she took the chain and put it on. She said, "Dick, it's beautiful," held both my hands, pulled me towards her, and she kissed me on my cheek.

Soon after everybody had unwrapped their presents, we could hear Pat and Pam in the nursery, waking up. So the kids cleaned up the mountains of wrapping paper, while my parents changed and fed the babies. Then we brought out the twins to unwrap their presence. At that time, they were 18 months old, and very excited with what was going on around them. One thing they had plenty of was attention, from my parents, and my siblings. After the babies 'presents were unwrapped, Ike and I had put the twins on the ponies. Then we raced the babies back and forth from the kitchen to the nursery. Pat and Pam would laugh hysterically, as my brother and I had made racing them realistic with motor and screeching noises, popping wheelies, and fishtailing, as they rode the ponies. The twins got a lot of mileage from those ponies, and that made them happy.

It was this Christmas that the real spirit of giving and the real spirit of Christmas had been experienced as a young boy, and, "Oh, what a feeling!"

Christmas would not be complete without going to church to Noon mass. In addition, Ike and I would be the altar boys for that Christmas Mass.

Chapter 6 - Archery, Anyone?

My parents were always involved in their children's activities, more so my mother than my father, because dad was working. Mom was a Den Mother for my pack when we lived in Stony Point, and helped with Ike's pack in Highland Mills. She would also get involved with Gina's Brownie activities, baking for cake sales, and fund raising. Mom would help us study for tests, and get involved in our projects. She even helped Ike and I build our slot cars for competition, which would entail taking a block of wood, shaving it down with tools, putting wheels on it, and painting it. This would take hours of work. She was very resourceful, had a mountain of "Can Do Attitude", and lots of energy.

One time, when she was looking at my Boy Scout handbook, she decided that I should try to get a merit badge for Archery. My mom bought a full sized archery set with a bow, a bunch of arrows, and target, as a surprise for Christmas. I was so thrilled with this present that I had to try it out that day. So, later that afternoon after church, Mom and I got dressed, and went into the back yard with the bow and some arrows. We set up the target on an empty box next to the back fence. My mother walked to the back of the house, which was about 50 feet from the target. Then, she took the bow and an arrow, got into position, and placed the arrow in the bow.

She said, "Stand there," pointing to her right side, but slightly behind her. I moved as directed.

As she looked at the target, she said, "See how I place my feet part like this?"

I said, "Yeah."

Then she pulled the bow all the way back with the arrow.

She said, "Look at the way I'm holding the bow, straight up and down."

I said, "Ah ha."

Suddenly, she released the arrow with a whooshing sound, and then a snapping sound as the arrow hit the target just outside the Bulls eye.

I yelled, "Wow, Mom, you hit the target!"

She looked at me, and said, "Of course," and then she smiled.

Mom used to be on the archery team in high school, and had many awards and ribbons. My mother went through all the steps of instruction again, making a few more shots, and every time hitting the target, the last one was a bull's-eye. Then it was my turn, she stood behind me, kicking my feet apart, holding my arms in the right position.

Then she stepped back, and said, "Now, pull the bow back slowly."

As I did, I could feel how hard it was to pull on the bow. Moreover, my arms were shaking because of all the strength it took to pull back. Suddenly, I let go of the arrow, and if flew over the fence into a neighbor's yard, two houses away.

Then my mother said, "Do not pull back so far, and wait for me to tell you to release the arrow."

I go through the same coaching instruction as the last time. I pulled back on the bow, this time about halfway, and held it there.

Mom said, "Pull back a little more, keep the bow straight."

I did, and she said, "Good, hold it, release!"

When I did, with a whoosh, the arrow landed in the snow 2 feet from the target.

She said, "That's good, you almost hit it. Now, let's try again."

I get into position, and go through the same set of instructions. I pulled back on the bow, and held it, waiting for my mother's command.

She said, "Pull back a little more, more."

My arms started to shake.

Then she said, "Hold it," I could not hold it any longer and released the arrow.

I immediately felt great pain my left hand, and the arrow shot to the left into the side of the neighbor's garage. I looked at my left hand, and one of the arrow's white feathers was halfway embedded in my index finger. I dropped the bow, held my hand up with the other hand, in great pain, and let out a big girly scream. Mom grabbed my left hand by the wrist, and then turned her back to me quickly, like a judo hold, blocking my view of my hand, and yanked the feather out. Then she released me from her grip, and I looked at my hand, it was pretty bloody. She then looked around at the neighbor's houses, and realized that their properties were only about 25 feet apart from each other. My mother then concluded that archery practice in the back yard of our house was not a good idea.

So she turned to me, and said, "Okay, let's go in the house, and take care of your finger."
We went inside, and she cleaned and bandaged my finger. Then she promised that later this week we would go somewhere safer to practice archery. Then mom told me to go outside, get the target, and all the arrows. As I entered the back yard, I saw a woman that lived next door bring in her dog, which was tied up next to the garage I had shot earlier. The woman ran in the house quickly, before the next round of target practice began.

A few days later, my mother took me to a state park that was about a 15 min. drive, for another archery lesson. She had selected this large field just off the roadway. We went into the trunk, grabbed all the archery stuff, and walked in the snow that was about 1 1/2 feet deep into the field. We walked for about 100 yards, then mom told me to take the target, and place it on a tree at the opposite end of the field, another 75 feet. She handed me the hammer, some nails, and the hay filled target. I slugged through the snow to a tree she had selected, hammered in a nail, and tied the target to the tree. As I walked back in my tracks in the snow for easier mobility, it began to snow. I reached Mom, as she strung the bow.

She said, "Remember what I taught you."

I said, "Let's go through it again."

She said, "Okay, now watch me and listen." She went through her systematic instruction and then she let the arrow fly. She hit the target, but on the upper left outer ring.

She said, "Let me show you again," and Mom went through all the steps again.

This time, she hit the target just below the bull's-eye. Now was my turn, I took the bow and arrow; she stood back from my right side, and went through the coaching steps. I pulled back on the bow, and released on command. I shot the arrow over the target into the woods, I thought that one was gone forever. I tried again, but this time, I under shot the target, and the arrow went under the snow. My mother gave me instructions after every shot, to correct my errors, as I was trying to hit the target. After about 15 shots, we would run out of arrows, so Mom and I went to retrieve the arrows. As we looked for the arrows, it started to snow harder and it was difficult to find the arrows because they were white. After about a 20-minute search, we had only recovered eight arrows, and it was snowing even harder. We walked to the spot where we were shooting from, and mom had another idea for a training exercise that would not lose any more arrows.

She said, "Dick, watch how I shoot this arrow."

Mom placed her feet apart, and then instead of having the bow in a straight up and down position, she aimed it higher as 75° shooting projection. She pulled back on the bow, and released the arrow into the sky. We both watched it disappear into the snow-filled clouds. Our heads where arched, and our eyes strained looking for the arrow to come back to Earth. Then we heard the arrow slice through the snow that landed about 50 feet from us, standing straight up. I thought, "Wow, this is a good idea, and it will be a lot easier to retrieve the arrows."

Mom hands the bow and arrow to me, then says, "Now, you try it."

I plant my feet apart, I put the arrow into the bow, and then I started to pull back on the bow.

She said, "Bring the bow up higher," I did, as I am pulling back on the bow even more.

She said, "More, more."

Then my arms started to shake, as I moved the bow higher. Suddenly, I jerked the bow above my head, and released the arrow at a 90° shot trajectory. We watched the arrow go out of sight into the clouds in silence.

My mother yelled, "RUN, RUN!" She pointed to the woods at the end of the field. I began running through deep snow.

She yelled, "STOP, RUN TO ME!"

I stopped, and ran towards her, as she ran towards me. She then leaped into the air, and landed on top of me, with a full body slam. She laid there for a second, and then we heard the arrow pierce through the snow, and Mom's body shuddered. Then she moved her head around, and got up to her feet. Mom held her hand out to help me out of the snow crater, created from the body slam.

She walked over to the arrow that almost killed us; it was only 10 feet away and it was exactly where we were shooting from.

She yelled, "YOU'RE NOT SUPPOSED TO SHOOT STRAIGHT UP IN THE AIR, YOU COULD'VE FUCK 'N KILLED US!"

I looked down at the ground, and said, "I'm sorry."

She said, pissed off, "Yeah, go get the target, it's getting late."

We made it to the car, threw the archery set in the trunk, and drove home in silence.

That was my last archery lesson, and I never did get the Archery Merit Badge.

Here's Ike and Dick, hanging out on the front porch trying to look cool.

Chapter 7 - Boys Will Be Boys

As I had mentioned earlier, my brother Ike seemed to make friends a lot easier than I did. In fact, for many years growing up, his friends were also my friends, well, most of them. This would mean, for the most part, that the kids I was friendly with were a school grade behind me, but also I was two years older than they were. I had to repeat the second grade, because the school discovered that I needed glasses and failed the grade the first time around.

The two main friends on Elm Street when we first moved to Highland Mills were John C. and Jimmy O. We found one place in the hamlet that was without adult supervision; the railroad tracks, they were at the farthest end of the village, with no houses by it. A perfect place where we could do country boy things, without our parents saying that it was too dangerous, or you're going to reform school for that.

Ike, Jimmy O, John C, and I used to ride our bikes down to the railroad tracks. Once we got to the small railroad trestle, we would take a drink from a fresh water stream that was along side it on hot summer days. Then, we would do dirt bike stunts on a road along the tracks, on the tracks, and off onto trails. This was a generation before Mountain Biking even existed, and there were no helmets, chest protectors, or shin guards. In addition, we did not have new or expensive bikes, and we worked on our own bikes soup to nuts. There were times we could not figure out a problem with our bikes, and John C would figure it out. John had created his own bike out of a bunch of spare parts. He would work on his bike for hours, trying to make it better, and he did. Simply put, this was a middle-class neighborhood in the late 1960's; most of the families had at least four or five children, a stay at home mom, and a mortgage. Most kids, if they were lucky, got one bike bought by their parents at childhood, and then you were on your own. Therefore, you have to become resourceful, if

---

you wanted to ride, and we were.

One time Ike and I, along with John and Jimmy, were at a gravel pit behind the town hall with our bikes. Each one of us took turns walking our bikes to the top of this huge mountain of gravel and dirt, and then tried to ride down this 45-degree cliff on the other side. John Connelly one of our friends, had this bike that was made of a bunch of spare parts was a cross between an English racer frame, sting-ray handle bars, banana seat, 20 inch front tire, and a extended chopped front fork from another bike. John's bike was so dangerous none of the other neighborhood daredevils would even sit on it, never mind ride. John got ready to go standing on the pedals, pulling back on the handlebars, and went down the dirt cliff, at break neck speed, and he made it with out killing himself. Now it's my turn with a beat up stingray with a leopard-skinned banana seat, and the frame custom spay painted in black by me. I look down this steep dirt cliff, and could see the tiny friends yelling at me to go, and I just froze frightened to death. Just as I was about to chicken out, Ike came from behind me and went over the cliff on his white English racer. As he went down in about the middle of the cliff his front wheel pitched at a 90-degree angel, forcing the English style handlebars into his crouch, and then flipping over the top of the front wheel, and then the bike fell on top of him. We all went running toward Ike, as we reached him he got up, and looked down at his white shorts and saw blood. He immediately unzipped and pulled out his little bloody soldier, and started running in place, and screaming like a girl. This is when being a big brother springs into action, and I say that it doesn't look that bad, and stop acting like a baby. After composing himself a little, we all start walking a couple of blocks home, with Ike holding his tiny bloody stump in one hand, and walking his bike in the other. When we got home, my mother turned pale, started screaming threw my brother in the car and took off for the hospital. The doctor gave him a good scrubbing with peroxide, a couple of butterfly stitches, and a tetanus shot, a couple of aspirin and his pecker would be good as new, or so he says. What a hero. Not only did he take a hit where no man or boy ever dreamed to be injured even in their worst nightmare, but he also saved me from losing face for being chicken and totally distracted that fact from his stunt. Thanks, Ike.

Sometimes, we would ride our bikes to the huge railroad trestle about 2 miles from our entry point. The trestle had about a 75-yard spanning across a gorge that had a state highway, and a stream below, which is about a 150-foot drop to its lowest point. There were wooden planks laid out next to the tracks that gave a 40 inch width walkway, and a flimsy 2 x 4 handrail that was about 4 feet in height. The condition of the walkway across this trestle was not good, there were a few rotted planks, and not all of them were nailed down completely. Given the conditions, width, and flimsy handrail, we could either walk along side our bikes, or sit on the bikes with our feet on the ground and walk across the trestle carefully. Once we crossed this huge railroad bridge, there was a big gravel pit to perfect our bike stunts, and there was the biggest mountain in area, Schunnemunk Mountain, where we would go hiking to the top.

One day, we decided to go hiking on Schunnemunk Mountain, because a couple of days earlier we found out that a single engine airplane had crashed on the mountain. The pilot crashed with his father in the middle of the night. He had broken two legs and one arm, and had crawled down the mountain on his stomach into the gravel pit, where a worker had discovered the pilot the next morning. The police and the fire Department went up the mountain searching for the plane for hours before finding the wreck. They found the pilot's father still alive and carried him down the mountain later that afternoon. The four of us decided that this would be a great adventure to go find this plane, early one Saturday morning. We packed our lunches in our knapsacks and took off to the railroad tracks. As we rode along side the tracks on the rocky dirt road toward the big trestle, we talked about finding maybe an arm or leg, or perhaps we could recover some airplane instruments. When we finally came to the big trestle, we first looked in front of us down the tracks, and looked behind us, down the tracks, to make sure a train was not approaching. Then we dismounted our bikes and put our ears on the tracks to hear if a train was coming. One thing you did not want to happen is to be caught on the trestle halfway across. Because, the trestle walkway was only 40 inches wide, and the train car's ladder overhangs the walkway about half the width. This would give you 20 inches of total width for you and the bike. We also knew that the handrails were flimsy, so you could not rely on them to lean on or over if you needed extra room. Most of all, the train usually traveled at 45 to 50 mph at full freight speed, given the sight distance available to see the train, and running at least 40 yards to safety, it would be impossible to outrun it. The result of being caught in the middle of the trestle and seeing a train coming would be death, or if you're lucky, serious injury. What would your fate be if you were hit by one of the train car ladders at 50 mph on the trestle? You would be thrown under the train, or knocked off the trestle plunging to your death. When we made it across the big trestle, we had to ride a short distance to the gravel pits. Once we reached the gravel pits, we had to be careful not to be seen by any of the workmen, because they would throw us out. We needed to get into the gravel pits in order to get to the trailhead of Schunnemunk Mountain. There would be monster earth moving heavy equipment zipping around these huge gravel pits, and we had to be careful not only to not be seen, but, also, not to get run over. As soon as the coast was clear, we would pedal our bikes as fast as we could to the trailhead. Once we made it to the trail, we would walk our bikes about 100 feet into the woods, and leave them there before hiking up the mountain. The Schunnemunk Mountain trail is a steady incline hike up to about the middle, where then it becomes much steeper as you reach the top. We knew the plane crashed on the side of the mountain we were climbing, but we did not know the site's exact location, or how far off the trail, it was. As we were hiking up the mountain, we were looking for some part of the plane, some medical debris left by the rescuers, or newer blazed trail off the original. We did know that rescuers walked up and down the original trail from and to the crash site. We hiked past the mid point of the trail we found some fresh breaks through the brush, we followed them but the fresh trail would end suddenly. We could only assume the person who had made this new trail doubled back the way they came. This happened to us a few times, as we hiked up the original trail, there were many people on this mountain the day after the crash, and plenty of people blazing new trails. We had been hiking for more then three hours and decided to eat lunch. We tried to figure out the best way to locate this plane, and decided that if we climb to the top of the mountain that maybe we would see the crash site. After lunch, we hiked another hour to the top of Schunnemunk, it was a beautiful spring day, and you could see all the way to Newburgh. Once on top of the mountain, we searched for the highest vantage point to look for the wreckage. The four of us stood up there looking for any kind of sign of a plane or disturbance in the trees or brush. We strained our eyes for 15 minutes, pointing at possible sites that looked different then before, but nothing that we felt compelled to investigate. We stayed on the top of the mountain another 30 minutes just taking in the 360° beautiful view, and taking a rest. We started down the mountain about 1:30 PM; the first part of the descent is the most dangerous because we have to scale down some steep rock outcroppings, and there are many loose rocks. One slip off this part of the trail could land you in the hospital. We always would be spread apart 30 feet on this part of the trail, so we would not knock a rock loose and hit the other hiker. As we made our way down the trail, we had pretty much given up on searching for the plane, and were just settling for a good hiking day. When we were about one third of the way down the mountain, Jimmy O discovered another newly blazed trail. We all stopped on the trail to rest, and drank the last of our water from our canteens. Jimmy O and Ike wanted to follow the new trail in, John C and I did not want to go down one more newly blazed trail. Therefore, they went to investigate, and John and I rested. We sat on the trail for about 10 minutes, and talked about getting started again down the mountain. I got to my feet, and yelled for my brother and Jimmy O. I did not get a response. Then, John C yelled for them, no response. I thought they could not hear us, and maybe traveled out of range of our voices. We yelled again for the two knuckleheads, still not getting a response. John C and I decided to hike down this newly blazed trail after them; they would be about 15 minutes in front of us. As we were hiking, every 5 minutes we would stop and yell for them, and then would continue walking. We hiked for about 15 minutes, and discovered that this blazed trail split in four different directions. At the moment, I had to take stock on what to do next. My number one priority was to find Ike and Jimmy O, who was younger then my brother. My second priority was making sure that I do not get lost in the middle of this forest, also making sure I knew how to get out with John C and the rest of the crew. John C and I agreed that we would have to split up, but we would keep within yelling range by calling each other's names once every minute. At first, when we headed in two different directions, it became a joke calling each other's names every minute. But as we walked farther away from each other, our voices started to fade a bit. Then I yelled John and I heard my name come from a different direction.

I yelled, "Ike," then heard Jimmy O yell, "Dick!"

I yelled, "Follow my voice."

Then I heard, "Dick," I yelled, "Yeah." They came into view in a ravine; I yelled, "Up here," and waved my arms.

They yelled and waved back, as they made it up to me, I could see that they were carrying some empty bandage cartons and soda bottles.

As the two approached, Jimmy O said, "Look what we found."

I said, "Yeah, looks like garbage from the plane crash."

Ike said, "Yeah, we got a little lost."

I said, "If you guys kept walking, I would have never found you"

Ike said, in a sarcastic voice, "Oh, do you know where we are now?"

I said, "I know exactly where we are, so let's go."
Then we started to back track up the blazed trail. I yelled for John C. Then I heard John C yell back, but I could not make out what he said. Ike and Jimmy O yelled back, "What?" Then we heard a banging sound, like someone hitting a metal garbage can. We heard John C yell, "I found the plane!"

Then we looked at each other with excitement. Ike yelled, "Keep banging, we'll follow the sound." And he continued to bang on the plane, as we ran toward the sound.

I yelled, as we ran through some thick brush and branches slapping me in the face, "Slow down and keep in sight."
I didn't want to lose these two again. Suddenly, in a small clearing, was John C standing on the white fuselage of the plane with a big stick.

Jimmy O said, "Cool," as he looked into the cockpit.

I said, "Where are the wings?"

John, still walking on the tail section, pointed, and said, "Over there."
We looked and one of the wings was standing on its side, held up by some big trees.

Ike looked around the site, and said, "Where's the other one?"
John C shrugged his shoulders, and said," I don't know, it could be further up the mountain." This made sense that when

the plane hit the treetops, it probably ripped one wing off first. By doing so, the plane dove into a severe left turn into the trees. We all looked at the cockpit area, the top was completely gone and laying about 20 feet away. It appears that the rescuers had cut it away with a huge can opener. In addition, the doors were cut off and some of the fuselage had been cut with tin snipers, and peeled back like a tin can. My first thought was, "People actually fly around in this flimsy tin can with wings?" I guess if they are about to crash, they just make a quick confession of their sins, and leave the rest up to God. This is providing you have enough time to pray, and judging from the crash, they did not. John C had already tried to take some of the instruments out of the cockpit with the handy toolkit he carried. The jagged metal around the cockpit made it hard to work, without being cut. There was dried blood all over the seats, the dashboard, and part of the windshield. No one wanted to get any blood on themselves, so we used Ike's t-shirt when holding some of the parts. We ended up with an altimeter, a gas gauge, and the steering wheel from the plane. After scavenging everything we could from the crash, we headed for the original trail by backtracking. One of the greatest gifts that God has given me was a good sense of direction, and the training in the Boy Scouts helped. We made it to the trail with little problem, and proceeded down the mountain, with the trophies from our expedition. Once we reached the bottom, we collected our bikes, and started to look at the activity in the gravel pit. In the late afternoon, it seemed to be the busiest for these dirt monkeys, running around in the heavy equipment. We had to wait until they were not in the first two sections of the gravel pit before we could make a break for the railroad tracks. We waited about 15 minutes, and we did not see any trucks or front end loaders. So we broke out of the tree line, and into the open gravel pit, pedaling as fast as our little legs could go. We got through the first section and we entered the second gravel pit, then we heard a loud engine coming in the same direction we were traveling. We quickly drove our bikes behind a huge pile of dirt for cover, then a yellow mammoth sized dump truck appeared and started to slow down. As it drove by the mountain of dirt we were hiding behind, we moved to the opposite sides of it, so the driver would not discover us. Then the dump truck sped off into the pit we had come from. We decided that rather then wait for the driver to get out of the pit; we would make a mad dash to the tracks as soon as the driver started dumping his load of dirt. This way, if the driver did see us, he would have to finish dumping his load before he could chase us. He backed up to the dirt pile, the dump bucket started to rise, and the dirt began to fall out of the back of it. We took off, pedaling even harder down the last 300 yards across the gravel pit. I looked back to see the driver quickly raise his dump truck body full height, reversing the truck and hitting the brakes hard to get rid of his load quicker.

I yelled, "He's coming!"

We were all going as fast as we could, and we were traveling 10 to 15 feet apart. I look back and saw the dump truck gaining on us quickly, with the dump body still in the air. Suddenly, Ike slowed down from the rest of the pack.

He yelled, "My chain broke!"

I slowed down and looked again; the dump truck was still coming. I stopped and turned around to see Jimmy O and John C make it to the tracks.

Then the dump truck driver slammed on his brakes, as Ike, who is now running along side his bike, stops. The driver gets out of his truck, as I rode my bike toward Ike.

The driver yelled, "DAMN IT, BOY, DIDN'T YOU KNOW YOU COULD GET KILLED HERE?"

Ike said, nervously, "No, sir," as he backed away from the driver.

The driver then waited for me to approach, and said, "Didn't you kids see the sign?"

I said, "What sign," looking confused and scratching my head.

The driver yelled," THE 4x8 PLYWOOD SIGN PAINTED RED WITH WHITE LETTERS THAT SAY" KEEP OUT-NO TRESPASSING!"

I said, "Yes, sir, I saw that sign, but I thought it meant over there," pointing to the gravel pits on the far right.

The driver looked at me, and said in a growling voice, "YOU THINK I'M STUPID, BOY?"

I said, in a timid voice," No."

He pulled a dirty piece of paper and pen from his pocket, and said, "What's your name?"
I thought that giving my real name was not a good idea.

I said, "Ed," then looking at my brother.

The driver replied, "Ed, what?"

I said, "Ed Poe, P.O.E., and my brother, Moe Poe."
Then I leaned toward the driver, and put my hands up to whisper to him, and I said, in a low voice, "He's adopted, don't tell him."

The driver looked at me, concerned and said, "Oh, ah, you live in the village?"

I said, "Yes, sir, do you want my phone number?"

He said, "No, you probably would give me the wrong one, I'll look it up. I'm not stupid!"

I said, "No, sir, you're not, well, we have to go home now." We both turned and walked away.

The driver yelled, "DON'T COME BACK, ITS DANGEROUS BACK HERE!"
We waved as if we understood, and kept walking. I jumped on my bike, and rode ahead to brief the crew on what had happened.

After our brief discussion of the counter with Mr. Dirt Bag, Ike had walked up to us, huffing and puffing. Ike asked if we could fix his bike, and after a fast evaluation, we found that, the chain was missing, a joining link and we didn't have any extra links with us. This would mean that Ike would have to walk his bike all the way home, about 3 1/2 miles. The day had become a very successful day, but we were all physically exhausted. We rode our bikes to the big railroad trestle, as Ike lagged behind walking his bike. We went through our safety routine of looking for oncoming trains, and then we walked across the bridge. When we got across the trestle, Jimmy O saw two foxes run over the tracks, and over the side of an embankment, and we rode our bikes quickly to see if we could get one. We jumped off our bikes and into the brush, but the foxes were long gone. We all got back on our bikes, and I looked back to see Ike on the first part of the bridge, he was about one-half a mile away from us. Then I noticed a light in the distance behind my brother on the tracks-at first, I thought that it was those heavy equipment guys coming down the tracks. Then I thought, that can't be, they can't ride on the tracks.

Suddenly, I realized, this was a train, and yelled, at the top of my lungs, "Train," pointing down the tracks.

Jimmy O and John C looked, with their mouths open, and they started waving their hands over their heads.

They yelled, "Ike... Ike..., Train, train!"

I could see him on the trestle, still walking, and not aware of the train that was coming up behind him.

I started pedaling as fast as I could towards the bridge, yelling, "Train..., Stop!"

The train was fast approaching behind my brother, and he was already about one third across. Ike stopped walking, sensing that something was wrong, because we were coming back to him as fast as we could and yelling, but he could not understand what it was about. Then he heard the train, and looked behind him. Then he started running with his bike towards us on the bridge. I realized that he would never make it off the trestle in time, because he had another 50 yards to cover.

I yelled, "Go back..., go back! Turn around!"

I jumped off my bike, and started running towards him on the bridge, waving my arms, yelling, "Turn Around!"

My brother stopped, looked at the fast approaching train, and then pulled his handlebars, taking his front wheel over the tracks to turn in the opposite direction towards the oncoming train.

As I kept running, I yelled, "Drop the bike..., Drop the bike!"

Ike threw the bike on the trestle walkway, he then ran into the direction of the train. I stopped and looked at Ike running as fast as he could, then the train horn sounded, and we could hear the roar of the loud engine, fast approaching. I realized that I had traveled about 20 yards on the bridge, and I turned and started running for my life.

Jimmy O and John C are yelling, "Go... Go... Go!"

I looked back quick enough to see Ike make it off the bridge safely. The train horn blasts again as it gains on me, as I reach the end of the bridge into the arms of my two friends, stopping me. I could hear the engineer yell at us as he blew past us, but I couldn't make out what he said. As the train cars passed us, with a loud deafening sound, I yelled, out of breath, "Did you see Ike get off the bridge?"

Jimmy O yelled, "Yeah."

I looked to the other side of the trestle to see Ike bent over, catching his breath. I felt to my knees, still out of breath, and began to laugh. The laughter started small at first, but as I caught my breath, it became louder.

John C thought I had started to go crazy, at first; I looked at the two of them, as I uncontrollably went into hysterical laughter. As the caboose passed by, the conductor looked out the window strangely at us. I dropped in the dirt, holding my sides, crying because I was laughing so much. The both of them were bent over laughing, as they dropped their bikes. We started to recover from our delirium, and looked at my brother as he picked his bike up from the bridge walkway, then started walking towards us.

Ike yelled, "WHAT THE FUCK IS SO FUNNY," as he continued to walk faster.

We didn't answer, still chuckling, and trying to catch our breath. As Ike got closer, you could see that he was sweating a lot with a scowl on his face.

Then he yelled about 20 feet from me, "DICK, WHAT THE FUCK IS SO FUNNY, ASSHOLE," then he dropped the bike, and ran towards me.

I put my hands in front of me, so he wouldn't hit me, and said, "Wait, wait..., We weren't laughing at you!"

Then, he was in my face, gritting his teeth, and said, "THEN, WHAT ARE YOU GUYS LAUGHING ABOUT?"

I pushed him away with a shove, and smiled with a big grin, and said, "I'm just happy you're alive." He looked at me, puzzled, and he turned to Jimmy O and John C to see them smiling.

Then he said, "Yeah, no shit, I almost got killed."

Then he began smile, and said, "Man, I was so fuck 'n scared." I looked at him, and rubbed his little crew cut head, and said, "Yeah, me, too."

John C said, "Ike, I never saw your fat ass run so quick." Then Ike gave him a little shove.

Jimmy O said, "Ike, you ran like a little girl, with your arms in the air, like this." Then he began to run in place with his arms above his head. We all laughed.

Ike said, laughing, "Yeah, I'd like to see you run for your life, you little twerp."

Looking back on this day, it surely was a brave thing my brother did to save his life. As the train was approaching the trestle, he had to run toward the train to get off the bridge. If he had not and followed his human instinct to out run the train, he would not have survived. I have God to thank, because He was on that trestle that day. Also, reflecting back on this day, the prospect of me telling my parents that Ike had gotten killed, and that I had directed him to run toward the train to attempt to save his life, would not be a pretty picture. My family would automatically make a shrine on top of the piano with an 8 x 10 photo of him, in which he was smiling with a couple of teeth missing, and a bunch of candles. He would be indoctrinated as the family saint, and I would lose my place as the favorite son. Most of all, I would be accused of murder, get beaten to a pulp, and thrown in prison. Yes, God was with us on the trestle that day.

We all walked home that day, talking about our adventure and near death experience.

Sometimes when the Kraemer kids were annoying my father, he would say things like, "Why don't you go play in the middle of the road," or "why don't you go play on the railroad tracks?" He would really mean get lost or go and play somewhere other then there. Looking back on it, my parents did know what we were doing, because they asked us all the time. But, of course, they got enough information to satisfy their curiosity and gain their acceptance. The kids would not give out a lot of information, about the details of what we doing. Giving out too much information could result in my parent's disapproval of our activities where we would be forbidden to wreak havoc on the world, or it would prevent us from killing ourselves. So, when asked by my parents, "Where are you going," or "What we would be doing," we could reply with the truth. But, we would give as little information as possible, and hope that any probing follow up questions would not ruin our plans.

On any typical day, you would find other neighborhood kids around the small railroad trestle. Sometimes we would meet up with them, and do things around railroad tracks with them. On many occasions, we would take coins, put them on the tracks, and wait for a train to flatten them. Then, if we found them, and most of the time we did not we would drill holes in them, and wear them like a necklace. This proved to be an expensive activity, money was scarce, and we quickly moved on to destroying other things. Most of the time, it was an old toy that we outgrew or maybe a sibling's old toy.

There would be other times when we would go down to the tracks, and climb a 35 foot solid rock faced cliff, which had been a huge rock hill blasted by the Erie Railroad. We did not use ropes or other climbing gear, we would climb it hand over foot to the top. There was a lot of loose shale, and you would have to wait for the first person to reach the top, before the next person would start to climb. Otherwise, if a rock hit you on the cliff, not only would you get a nice knot on your head, it could knock you off. Once the gang climbed to the top, we would wait for a train, or we would take a short hike to the New York State Thruway to kill some time. We would walk for about 10 minutes through the woods, until we came to an edge of a 200-foot rock face cliff, overlooking the Thruway below. You could see the cars below zipping back and forth from New York City to Albany. This was the end of the trail for us; we were not crazy or stupid enough to climb down this cliff. However, we did know a couple of kids that had and survived. When we were up high above the tracks, we could hear the train coming a few miles away. Once we heard the train coming, we would run through the woods, to the cliff overlooking the tracks. In those days, there were not a lot of passenger trains, it was mostly freight trains. The name of the railroad today is the Metro-North Port Jervis Line. Once the train came into view, we would take cover to insure that train personnel would not see us. This was a cool vantage point because you could see the train engineer through the windshield as he sped by, and, for the most part, he was looking down the tracks, and not above him at the cliffs. Once the locomotive had passed, we came from our hiding places, and grabbed some good throwing rocks. Let's face it-throwing rocks at steel box or tanker cars was not going to be fun, because you're not going to inflict any damage. Now we start looking for our favorite target, brand-new automobiles and trucks. In those days, Ford had an assembly plant 20 miles away in Mahwah, New Jersey, and I had two uncles who worked there. However, there were other automobile manufacturers that shipped on this rail line also, and we did not discriminate based on brand. Therefore, it was certain that most freight trains would have a few automobile carrier cars in the middle of the steel boxcars being pulled along. Once the automobile carrier cars came into view, we would fire and unload all of our rocks in rapid succession. The timing and aim would have to be precise, because the train was traveling at 50 mph, and at our vantage point, 35 feet above the tracks; it makes for a fast moving target. The Bulls eye target was the windshields of the vehicles. Because of the velocity of the rock being thrown, and the rate of speed the train was traveling at, it was probable that the windshield would crack or break. Sometimes we would get lucky and break the side windows. One thing was for sure, that if we were up on that cliff, there was going to be some damage inflicted on those automobiles. Looking back on all the damage we inflicted on all those classic Mustangs, G.T.O.s, And Barracudas, makes me feel ill. However, it was entertainment, when you're a 12 or 13-year-old boy from the country.

As I had mentioned before, sometimes my brother, our friends, and myself would team up, occasionally, with other kids in the village, to commit other juvenile delinquent acts. I remember on one occasion, Robert P and Mickey M had an idea that had interested us very much. There was a big construction company next to the tracks by the small railroad trestle in our village. An 8-foot chain link fence surrounded the construction yard, it had a big tin maintenance building, and, best of all, the yard was filled with heavy equipment. Mickey M had first hand knowledge of where they kept the keys to the heavy equipment, inside the tin building. On one fine Sunday afternoon, Jimmy O, John C, Robert P, Mickey M, Ike, and I had met at the end of our street, and ridden our bikes to the construction yard. When we got to the locked chain linked gates, we took an old service road that ran along side the construction yard fence, and went deep into the woods, to give us cover. Then we all stopped, ditched our bikes, and crawled under the fence in a place that was dug out earlier by the perpetrators. Once we were all in the yard, Mickey M made his way to the big tin building, while the rest of us started looking over the heavy equipment. This was like playing in a big toy box; we were running all over the construction yard, sitting in the driver seats of cranes, bulldozers, front-end loaders, backhoes dump trucks, and pickup trucks. Suddenly, we heard an engine start, and from the far end of the yard, we could see a red pickup truck speeding in our direction, kicking up a lot of dirt behind it. We all ducked for cover between the equipment. Then, the truck slammed on its brakes, as it made a 180° turn, and made a complete stop at our location in a great cloud of dirt. Some of the kids started diving under the fence, to make their escape. Just then, the dirt cloud started to dissipate, the driver door opened, and out popped Mickey M, laughing as he walks toward us.

He said, "Hey, did I scare you guys," as he was still laughing.

We all laughed nervously.

I said, "Yeah, you scared the shit out of us."

Robert P said, "Half of the little twerps were already on the other side of the fence."

Robert P was a giant compared to the rest of us; he was my age, but 5'11" tall, 175 pounds, and had a five o'clock shadow. This kid could pass for a full-grown man at age 13. Robert P and Mickey M also knew about heavy equipment because their fathers would take them to work sometimes, and let them drive their dump trucks and bulldozers. These guys would come in very handy for this adventure. Mickey M handed a large ring with keys on it to Robert P. Each one of the keys had masking tape on it with the vehicles description on it. Robert P found the key he was looking for, and laid the key ring on the hood of an old truck. The rest of us started thumbing through the key ring.

Then, Mickey M made an announcement, "Don't lose any keys, and park the junk back where you found them. I want to make it look like we were never here."

We all agreed as everyone started up their machines. Robert P fired up a crane, and started to race the motor to keep it running. John C started up a bulldozer and raised its blade. I jumped into a dump truck, and tried to turn over the engine, but it would not start. I called Mickey over to look at it.

He said, "Move over," and he jumped in the driver seat. He pumped the gas a few times, turned the key, while the engine was cranking, he pulled the choke lever out, and it started right up.

He said, "Let it run a couple of minutes and then push the choke back in."

Then Mickey and Jimmy O jumped in the red pickup, and peeled out, kicking up a big cloud of dirt. Robert P took the crane's boom higher and started to swing it to the left. Ike had gotten on the bulldozer with John C, sitting next to each other, and moved it to the center of the yard. I pushed the choke in on the dump truck, pushed the clutch in, and started moving the gear shift around, as the gears started to grind. I finally got the truck into gear, and let out the clutch quickly. The truck jumped forward, stopped suddenly and stalled.

Mickey and Jimmy O raced passed my windshield with the pickup, yelling, "WWWWHHHHOOOOAAAA!" Then they vanished into a cloud of dirt.

Robert P yelled, "Hey, Dick, look at this shit!"

Robert P, still in the crane, had dropped the hook from his boom, latched on to an old truck by its front bumper, and started raising it by its front end.

I yelled, "Lift it off the ground!"

He yelled back, smiling, "The bumper won't hold the weight."

I smiled back, as I started the dump truck up again. Robert P jumped out of the crane, ran over to the dump truck, and got into the passenger seat.

He said, "Push the clutch in, you got it in second, numb nuts, here, put it in first."

He grabbed the gearshift, put it in first, and said, "Now, let the clutch out slowly."

As I did, he said, "Give it a little gas." Then as we started to move, he said, "Put it in second."

I pushed in the clutch, grabbed the gearshift, and it grinded in to second gear.

He yelled, "More gas!" Then I stepped on the gas pedal as I turned to the right, and we were off.

Up ahead, Ike and John C, on the bulldozer, were still in the center yard, and were doing spinning turns, by locking one track and accelerating the other. I was gaining speed, and getting ready to shift into third gear, when Jimmy O passed us on the right in the pickup.

Robert P hung his head out the window, and yelled, "You crazy little fucker!"

I suddenly realized I was in a big cloud of dirt, and could not see anything in front of me.

Robert looked at me, and yelled, "Slow down!"

I put my foot on the break pedal, and then I stomped on it. The back end of the dump truck started hopping from the rear tires, and then both of us lunged forward as we skidded to a stop. A few seconds went by, sitting in this blinding cloud of dirt, until it started to lift. As it did, we could see the bulldozer about 20 feet in front of us, but no one was on it.

I looked around to my left side, and said, "Do you see Ike or John?"

Robert looked on his right, and said, "No, weren't they on the dozer, it's still running."

I opened the driver door, jumped out, and walked around the bulldozer.

Robert got out of the truck, and said, "Dick, they're over here."

I looked back around and the two of them were walking from behind the dump truck.

Ike said, "You scared the shit out of us!"

John said, "Yeah, we saw you coming, then that fucking dirt cloud covered all of us, and we jumped off and ran."

Robert started laughing, and said, "Yeah, you should have been in that dump truck, that was hairy!"

Then we all started laughing.

Robert then said, "You should have seen Dick's face when he hit the brakes!

He made a face with his eyes and mouth wide open, holding his hand out as if he was steering. We all started cracking up, laughing.

Just then, Jimmy O drove up in the pickup, with Mickey in the passenger seat, and they both got out.

Jimmy, smiling, said, "What's up?"

I said, laughing, "You're driving skills suck, that's what we're laughing about."

Robert said, smiling, "Hey, Mickey, didn't you tell this kid not to pass on the right?"

Mickey started laughing, "I was going to tell him, but the little shit passed you too quickly."

We all had a good laugh about each other's heavy equipment skills. After a while, we decided that it was getting late, and it was time to put all the big toys back in their place. Robert took the dump truck back after giving me a few driving lessons. Mickey showed Ike and John how to control the bulldozer, and then back it into place. Then Mickey jumped in the pickup's driver seat, Jimmy rode shotgun, and both took off for their last spin. Robert started the crane, and I was in the cab with him. He first had to lower the junk truck that he had lifted earlier. He first released the lever slowly, and rested the truck on all four tires. However, the hook on the crane was stuck between the bumper and the frame. So we both got out, and walked over to the truck. Then Mickey sped by us, he must have been doing 40 mph. Robert climbed on the front of the truck, took one foot and kicked the top of the hook several times. However, the hook would not come loose, so he jumped off the truck, and grabbed a solid iron rod about 4 feet long. He wedged it between the bumper and the frame, and tried to pry the hook loose. He told me to get on the truck, and kick the hook while he pried. We tried for about 10 minutes, with no success.

Robert said, "Fuck this, I'll get it loose."

Then he started to walk, when Mickey flew by again with a dirt trail behind him, blasting his horn and waving at us. Robert continued to walk to the crane. When we got into the cab, I could see that Robert was pissed off; he just stared at the truck, gritting his teeth.

I said, "What are you going to do?"

He said, "This," and the engine went into full throttle, and he yanked the stick towards himself.

The junk truck jerked up on its two rear tires, we felt the weight of crane boom bouts, making an iron bending sound.

Robert said, "Okay, hold on." Then he thrusted the stick all the way forward, releasing the cable, sending the truck crashing to the ground on all four wheels.

The hook sprang loose and fell to the ground.

I yelled, "You did it, the fuck 'n thing is free!"

Then I slapped him on his shoulder.

He smiled, and said, "I told ya I'd get it off," as he pulled the lever to lift the boom.

Then he pulled the cable lever slowly to get the hook in the original position. As he did, the cabled hook started to swing like a pendulum across the construction yard, towards us, but the hook was too low to hit us in the cab. The hook hit the bottom of the crane, and started to swing away from us. Suddenly, the pickup truck hit the hook at full speed, breaking the windshield. The pickup slid sideways to a stop, in a plume of dirt. Robert I jumped out of the crane, and ran towards the dirt cloud, Ike and John followed. As we approached, the pickup doors flew open. Mickey started brushing glass from his head and face; he had a couple of small cuts to his forehead and cheeks. Jimmy leaned his head forward, and put his hands through his long blond hair, trying to shake out the glass from his hair. Jimmy, too, had a few scratches on his forehead and cheeks. John had gotten a rag and wet it in a nearby stream, to clean the cuts. Jimmy had bruised his knee, he was limping a little bit, and Mickey had banged his shoulder on the steering wheel. After our quick medical assessment, we decided they were okay, and should suck it up. They were instructed, if asked, by their parents what had happened, that they should say that they had been hiking and were caught in some thorn bushes. We covered up the crime scene as best as we could, and Mickey put back the keys, just as he found them. Then we made our way back home that afternoon, and we walked Jimmy, with his bike, because he could not ride with his leg banged up. We were never accused of this crime, because in this town, there were too many suspects. In addition, because of the broken windshield, the construction company got wise, and locked up all the keys. Therefore, we had no more playtimes with big toys.

Even back then, watching 10 to 13 year olds operating heavy equipment in that construction yard that day can only be described in a few simple words; Mayhem, Anarchy, Chaos, and pure madness. Just a thought for you heavy equipment companies out there; "Do you know where your company keys are tonight?"

Chapter 8 - All In The Family

Once the summer rolled around, one thing you could definitely count on was the Ehlers family barbecue. They would have one for Memorial Day, Fourth of July, and Labor Day, but that would not stop them from having a few in between those holidays. The Ehlers were on my mother's side of the family, which consisted of my Nana and Pop-Pop, Bill, Dave, Dick, Pat, Buddy, Sally and my mom, Regina, but everyone called her Jeanie. My grandparents, Nana and Pop-Pop, had 24 grandchildren before they started becoming great-grandparents. I was the oldest grandchild on the Ehlers side of the family.

At least once a year during these barbecues, all the family members would converge all at once at this family gathering. In addition, some other relatives, in-laws, and friends would also attend this family hoedown. The whole neighborhood would know that the Ehlers were having a barbecue, just because of the amount of cars that would be parked on both sides of the street. My father always wanted to get there early to insure that he got a parking space in front of my grandparent's property.

My Nana and Pop-Pop had owned an old fieldstone Cape Cod house in Garnerville, New York. All of their children were born in that house, starting in the late 1920s. They had an old garage in the back that needed either a torch, or a bulldozer to knock it down, but Pop-Pop couldn't decide which was better, and the grandchildren were not allowed in it. Pop-Pop also had a 30-foot wooden archway, in which he grew grapevines over, directly out his back door.
Pop-Pop used to make his own wine with the grapes, and it was a good source of shade for barbecues.

During those barbecues, the grandchildren would be outside playing, or conversing in the back yard, or the side lot that my grandparents also owned. Most of the men would drink beer and catch up with each other on what was happening in their lives. The women would all cluster together and talk about feminine things.

One thing that the older male children would do, including me, would be to sit in on the men's discussions. This is where I would begin to realize how the world worked. I would sit there and listen intently about politics, and about the work place. I would find out how my uncles felt about unions, hippies, black people, management, the war, and anything else they would throw out on the table. Sometimes, the conversations were about to change for an adult only crowd, and either my dad or my uncles would tell me to go outside, or see what the other cousins were doing. In short, they would tell me to get lost, when it came to adult only conversations. When I say adult only conversations, I do not only imply talk about sex, drugs, gambling, and alcohol. But also, conversations that young impressionable minds should not hear. Some examples might be talking about any other adult unfavorably, religion conflicts, opinions on education, or someone getting a payoff. When I was young, I really got pissed off when they used to tell me to get lost. However, it was not until I was an adult that I realized how important it was for me not to hear those conversations. As an adult, I have seen the damage parents have done by letting their children listen to their no holds barred conversations and the effect on their children as they grew into adults. My parents and my adult relatives talked to the children as children, not as adults. The order of respect is you are the child, I am the adult, and you will speak to me that way. In our family, the parent, aunt, uncle, adult, or child would communicate to you with respect, within the respective social order, No Exceptions. There were not parents of 14-year-olds having adult conversations consistently, as though the child was a friend or a peer. The parent and child peer communication trend happens to be a big modern day fad for parents for the last 30 years. My point is that this family made a conscious decision to exclude children from any adult conversations and to let children think and speak like children. There was no reason to speed up the growing up process, and they would learn to be adult when the time came.

Once the men's conversations got a little stale, most of the men would turn to gambling for entertainment. My grandparents had a huge dining room table, so anyone who wanted to get in, could. This was a men only game, even though sometimes some of the women would try to charm their way into the game. But the women would not last long trying to muscle in on the game and would quietly watch the game, or would most likely retreat back into the kitchen with the other women. The men did not want the women around watching how much money they were gambling with, and wanted to avoid their wives from nagging them about how much they had lost. Poker was the name, and five-card stud was the game. Sometimes even Pop-Pop would play poker for a short time, and then Nana would nag him so badly, he would have to stop. My Nana did not approve of gambling, and depending on her tolerance level at the barbecue that day, would determine how long the poker game would go on. Most of Nana's sons were the ones who had instigated the game to begin with. Therefore, she would go after them first to stop the game. If the nagging got bad enough, they would move the poker game outside to the picnic table. My Nana thought that gambling around the grandchildren would leave the next generation with gambling problems. To my knowledge, none of the grandchildren ever had a gambling problem.

My uncles of Irish/German descent were, for the most part, tough guys. Pat and Buddy were blue-collar foremen, Dick was self-employed, Dave was a corporate marketing executive, and Bill was a career naval officer. My Aunt Sally was married to an Uncle Andy who was a Korean War veteran, and a Border Patrol officer. My Uncle Andy was best friends with my father. My father, for the most part, regarded Pat, Buddy, Dick, and Andy as his own brothers, and not just brother-in-laws. They all had a close bond for many years, and had many good times together.

About halfway through the barbecue, it would never fail that the men would run out of beer, and would have to make a beer run. The men would all jump in one car, and take off for about an hour. Just enough time to shoot a quick game of pool, and have a shot of booze. If they took any longer than that, they would get some flack from the women.

All during the barbecue, the yard was filled with people in their lawn chairs, most of them under the huge shade trees that encompassed the backyard. There would be so many kids in the yard that it would be hard to navigate around them. So the parents would send the kids to the large side yard next to the house. There, you could play badminton, baseball, football, or throw a Frisbee around.

Pop Pop was the barbecue organizer and he would be constantly in motion. He would do most of the cooking with some help from his sons or son in-laws. He was a good man, and he always reminded me of Jimmy Stewart, the way he carried himself and talked. He always took the time to talk for hours to the grandkids, and had a gentle side to him.

Nana was the barbecue Sheriff in town, she would be the enforcer, and she made sure everyone, adult or children, behaved themselves. When you have a gathering this size and magnitude, there has to be someone that carries a big stick, Nana was just that person for the job. No one wanted to get on the wrong side of Nana, because it could lead to big trouble for you and anyone that was directly connected to you. Therefore, everyone knew the rules; break them if you were brave enough. My Nana was a nice lady, but she wasn't a warm person. She would engage in conversations with her grandchildren, and made sure she spent time with each one. I guess in her heart she loved each one of her children, and grandkids, but it was hard for her to let it shine through at times. My personal experience and relationship with my Nana was that I was the firstborn grandchild and the favorite.

However, the disagreement about the joint venture of my parent's home and my grandparent's investment left my dad and Nana as archenemies for life. Because of the animosity that my dad and Nana had for each other, this caused her to unconsciously or consciously dislike me because I grew up to look just like my father, a carbon copy clone. I had noticed Nana's attitude change towards me, but I never questioned it, and I just accepted it.

The women would each bring the potato, macaroni, and other assorted salads from home. It was a tradition that everybody brought something to the barbecue, and that meant that with a get together of this size, there was always plenty of food to go around.

As it got later during the hot summer afternoon, Pop Pop would fire up the grill, and would cook for hours with the help of other men until dark. They would first cook the hamburgers, and hot dogs to feed the first few waves of children. Then eventually they would start feeding the adults. This feeding cycle would go on for about 3 to 4 hours, with different cooks at the grill. However, for the most part, Pop Pop was the Pit Master.

When it became dark, my Nana would fill a coffee urn, and break out the cake and cookies. The last hour or two, everybody would gather again in the dining room, where the parents would sit and talk, while their children hung around them and started to whine about going home.

Then each family would leave, one at a time, always making sure they said goodbye to everyone, and repeat previous plans to meet in the future. Then a lot of people would walk the departing family to their car or to the sidewalk.

Those Ehlers family summer barbecues were deeply missed, as I got older. The family unity, the love and friendship those people had for each other, was something I would never forget.

Of course, I would be lying if I told you that during the Ehler's family reunions they all departed with love in their hearts for every relative they met during the barbecue. That would be a story of childhood Fairy Tales, unicorns, and pink ponies. I believe that every one of my uncles, including my father, had their turn to be voted as most scorned, during these barbecues. Sometimes there would be a close second, third, forth, and fifth door prizes, for the scorned. But there could only be one first prize for the most scorned. The prize would be judged and awarded by the Sheriff of the barbecue, and the most scorned would be deemed by how unruly that person was. In the later years, my father had won the most scorned first prize more than a few times.

THE KRAEMER FAMILY VISITS

On my father's side of the family, the Kraemer's family visits had been much lower key than the Ehler's barbecues. Grandma Kraemer, Freda, and Grandpa Dick had five children, Carol and Helen, who were both housewives, Dick, my dad, Ike, an auto plant worker, and a college student, Albert. Grandma Kraemer and Grandpa Dick had a total of 14 grandchildren. We would visit the elder Kraemers on Sunday's, maybe once a month; we would get there usually around noon and would stay until about 4 PM. Most times, my grandma would prepare lunch for us; she would have prepared a German cold cut platter and cold pasta salad with tuna fish, celery, carrots, and onion. All of the vegetables were homegrown in the gardens that my grandparents had.

Both my Grandma and Grandpa Kraemer had immigrated to United States in the early 1920s from Germany. Grandma Kraemer, Freda, had a heavy German accent and she could speak the language fluently, and so could my Grandpa, with no hint of an accent. However, none of their children spoke the German language. When their children were born, it was important for my grandparents to teach only the English language as the primary language they spoke. There were two primary reasons why the Kraemer children never spoke German. First, they wanted to insure that their children did not get confused by a second language while being educated in America. In addition, my grandparents wanted their children to speak, read, write, and think only as American citizens, without any cultural confusion. Second, because of all the turmoil that Germany was going through while they were raising their children, my grandparents thought it best to blend into an American culture, and hide their German heritage. When America sent Japanese Americanized citizens to interment camps during World War II, it sent a clear message to German Americanized citizens that they could be next.

During our visits to my grandparent's home, Grandma Kraemer would some times start talking in German to my grandpa Dick, and he would respond in German. Then he would realize that we couldn't understand them, and tell my grandma to speak English. I believe my father understood some German, but only bits and pieces.

After lunch, we would go to the gardens outside. My grandpa Kraemer had a white brick ranch and a large yard at the end of a dead end street. He worked for hours and days on end on his lawn and gardens. My grandpa certainly had a green thumb, and he would love to show it off. The shrubs and trees were meticulously maintained, the mulch under each plant was neatly raked and free of any debris. A blacktop sidewalk ran from the driveway to the concrete and slate patio area in the back yard. On the large patio, my grandpa Dick had built a slate barbecue pit and small walls on each side of it. From the patio, a pure white gravel path led to the center of the backyard. The white gravel path would lead around a huge circular slate garden where he had grown thousands of yellow flowers. As you looked over his dark green lawn, you did not notice one blade of grass out of place. In the back of the property, he had a fenced-in vegetable garden and a lawn shed.

The only rules my grandpa Dick had about the backyard was do not touch the plants and do not walk on the grass. If you did, he would yell at you, and then give my father hell about it. Therefore, if you stayed on the path and did not touch the plants, you were in the good graces of grandpa.

My grandma Kraemer would keep the inside of the house in immaculate condition. In this house, there wasn't anything out of place. They had handcrafted doilies under all the lamps and family photos on the dust free coffee and end tables. The curtains were neatly pressed and pleated. There was not one stray piece of paper to be found. There was not one speck of dirt with in 100 yards of this home.

There wasn't many times that other uncles or aunts would visit when we came to visit. But it was mostly by design of my grandpa Dick. My grandpa was not a happy man, and I don't ever remember him ever laughing or even smiling. He couldn't or wouldn't relate with children, and having a whole bunch of kids over at one time would send him over the deep end. He could relate with adults pretty well, but children, he really had no tolerance. However, that does not mean he did not talk to us, he did, when he had to communicate to us. If we came over to my grandparent's home, we kept very quiet in the TV room, or the enclosed porch, while my parents would talk to my grandparents in the kitchen. My siblings and I did not run around making a lot of noise and tearing things up, that would get us thrown out quickly.

My grandma Kraemer was a happy person who loved to laugh and smiled a lot. She loved children, and would always talk to us, and ask us about kid stuff. Every time the kids used to visit, she would give us Pecan Sandy's cookies from the old breadbox she had on her counter. Often during the visit, she would enjoy joking around with my parents and the children. My father looked forward to seeing his mother, and they would stand in the kitchen and talk. You could see the love my father had for his mother, and the relationship that they had. My mother loved Freda, I believe that she idolized her, and she fashioned a lot of grandma Kraemer's homemaking as her own.

But, once my Grandpa Dick's presence was known in the room, it was as if a cold breeze had just swept through the room. Everyone's demeanor would change when grandpa would enter the room. If everyone was laughing, smiling, and joking, they would all seem to change to a serious, subdued state of conversation. It really was quite creepy.

There were times when my Grandpa Dick would be on the outs with my father or the rest of his siblings. Many times, dad and his siblings would be forbidden by Grandpa Dick to come and visit, because he was feuding with one, some, or all of his children. Depending on the circumstances, these feuds would last weeks, months, and even years. Sometimes during the feuding periods, my father would call my grandma Kraemer, and find out when Grandpa Dick wouldn't be home, so dad could see her. When dad visited grandma under family feuding circumstances, he mostly went alone and during the workday. But there was a few times I went along for the ride, but always waited in the truck while he visited. On those visits, it was my grandma's request for her to see her son. After the visit, when my father was leaving, grandma Kraemer would wave good by from the screened in porch. On one of those visits, I tried to get out of the truck, and give her a kiss and a hug good by, but my father stopped me, and told me to get back in the truck. When we pulled out of the driveway, and drove off, I asked why I could not get out of the truck and say good-bye to grandma. My father said that her face had been bruised, and then she felt embarrassed and ashamed to have her grandchildren see her that way.

It was then that I knew that my grandpa Dick was a wife beater. In addition, most of the family feuding was mostly about the treatment of my grandma, at the hands of

Grandpa Dick. My dad and his siblings all begged Freda to leave grandpa, and come live with them. She refused because Freda felt trapped, and afraid that if she did leave what grandpa might do. All these visits with Freda had to be kept secret, and she was forbidden to have any contact with her children, including phone calls. Freda and her children were scared to death of what grandpa might do if these secret phone calls or visits were discovered. Because those communications had been discovered in the past and grandma Kraemer had paid the price.

A few years after the on again, off again visits, grandma Kraemer suffered a massive stroke, and was unable to walk or speak. When we came to visit, the children would sit with her in the TV room, and watch Women's Roller Derby together, she loved watching it when she was well. But, for the most part, she was just a shell of the lively woman she once was. Sometimes I would turn to her, and I could see that she would begin to cry. Many of us hoped and prayed that grandma Kraemer didn't have a thinking, emotional, and functional brain due to the stroke, as my grandpa claimed. My father and his siblings begged my grandpa Dick to let them take Freda and care for her in their homes, but grandpa refused. Instead, Grandpa Dick took care of her in their home, with the help of nurses and aides. Albert, the youngest uncle, had graduated from college, worked for IBM, and was living with my grandparents. I did not see very much of Uncle Albert, he was always working or off doing something while we visited. Once grandma Kraemer suffered her stroke, we visited as often as we could, and the feuding had stopped. It pained my father greatly to see his mother that way, and I believe that he would have taken her in our home if given the chance. I knew it troubled him greatly that his mother, was unable to walk, talk, and take care of herself, and was now totally dependent on Grandpa Dick, her past abuser.

A few years later after Freda had her stroke, the Lord had mercy on her soul, and the ones who loved her, and she passed away from pneumonia.

Chapter 9 – Life In Highland Mills

If there was ever a place that you could now step back in time in 2011, and go back to Norman Rockwell days, it would be this small hamlet of Highland Mills, New York. I had recently revisited my boyhood hometown, which had inspired me to write this book about my life, and the people I had been blessed to know on my journey to adulthood. The hamlet has most of its original look very much as it did when I was a boy; it is almost like the Twilight Zone. Most of the buildings uses have changed, but those building look exactly as they did 40 years ago. I had recently walked down the street that I grew up on, and to this day, the neighborhood looks like it did in 1968. In addition, most of the family names still own those homes to this day on Elm Street.

Sometimes, when I had some money from my paper route, Ike and I would go to Gary's Pharmacy at the end of the block. They had an old-fashioned soda fountain with eight stools. We would order maybe a chocolate egg cream or a milk shake, sit there quietly, and drink them. Mr. and Mrs. Gray were in their 70s at the time, they were friendly business people, but somewhat cranky. So if you were to buy something there, you bought it, consumed it, and then your ass hit the door. There was no hanging around Gary's Pharmacy for kids, and when you were there, you had better behave as though you were in church. This would be the main place for adults to Hob-Nob and gossip. The Gary's had a big parrot in the back of the pharmacy that used to say, "Pretty lady," and "No Sale." We used to try to talk to it after our drinks, and it would always say, "No Sale," and shortly after Mrs. Gary would kick us out. I believe that pharmacy had not changed since Herbert Hoover was president. The Gary's had lived above their pharmacy all those years, and preserved a great American mainstay, The Country Pharmacy.

A good example of a good neighbor business, in those days, was Beatties Esso gas station. This was an old-fashioned Esso with two bays, two gas pumps, and a full service gas station. The owner was Mr. Beattie, and his sidekick, Jim H, was a mechanic. Mr. Beattie employed a couple of high school kids to pump gas, which would free up the mechanic's time to work on cars. In addition, they would take a younger kid from the neighborhood under their wing, teach them some mechanics, and to help around the shop. One of those kids was a friend, Robert P. Robert was a big kid at 13 years old, weighted 180 pounds and who stood 5'11" tall. He could pass as an adult with his five o'clock shadow. The other kid was my brother, Ike, at 12 years old, with an average weight and height. Jim H took a liking to my brother, when Ike started to hang around the gas station, interested in cars. As Ike started hanging around more at the gas station, Jim H and he bonded as best friends. There was a time that the gas station and Jim H consumed all of Ike's free time. After school, weekends, and even a couple of summers, Jim H and he would be at the gas station. I used to tease him that he was a Little Grease Monkey, but to be honest, I was a little jealous at times. My brother did pickup a lot of knowledge from Jim H and that gas station. He learned everything, from changing oil to engine rebuilding. They taught him how to drive, rig a car on a tow truck, and put a car on a lift. Jim H was a short, heavyset, happy go lucky guy about 28 years old, always had a smile and a joke to tell. My brother really worked as a mechanics helper for Jim H, and Jim would throw him a few bucks and buy him lunch. Occasionally, I would drop by the gas station, just to see what was happening. I would always see Ike in the grease pit, banging on tail pipe, or pulling parts off an engine. My brother would be covered with oil, dirt, and grease, from head to toe. He also wore an old orange T-shirt with the sleeves cut off. Ike would drive my mother crazy, because she was a clean freak, and to see her son, so dirty, walking through town, made her want to crawl under a rock. When Ike would get home after being at the gas station all day, she would make him strip down to his underwear in the basement, before she would let him in the house. This was a good experience for my brother, growing up. It gave him the exposure at a young age, to the hard work ethic. In addition, what it took to make a living.

The Boy Scouts had sponsored a fund raising campaign that would help send it's scouts to summer camp in 1969. The more merchandise the individual scout sold during this fund drive, the less money he would have to come up with to go to camp. The merchandise we sold had been useful household items like fire extinguishers, flashlights, and cooking utensils. I had an advantage over the other scouts because I already had a customer base from my paper route. So, the next time I collected money from my paper route customers, I dressed up in my Boy Scout uniform, and pitched the merchandise. I sold a lot of stuff to my paper route customers, and I was one of the top selling scouts in my troop. The end result was that I raised almost enough money to pay for the entire summer camp, and my parents kicked in about $15 of the remaining balance.

The Boy Scouts Jamboree in the summer of 1969 at the Beech Mountain camp in upstate New York was my first time away from home. I do remember being home sick a little, but I didn't start crying to the scoutmaster about it, I sucked it up. I also remember being part of a relay race, against other troops at the camp. My part of the relay race was to swim out in the lake, retrieve a watermelon covered in Vaseline, and bring it back to shore. I swam out to the watermelon in no time flat. However, the slick melon was too slippery to hold on to, every time I tried to grab it, the watermelon would shoot out of my arms. After a few long minutes straggling with Big Green Slimy I became exhausted, and started to fear that I could drown. So, I decided that drowning for Vaseline covered watermelon was certainly not worth my life, so I swam back to shore empty-handed. Once I reached land, I fell to the beach exhausted, coughing and gasping for air. Some of my fellow scouts ran over, started shouting insults and telling me how I let down the troop. I felt bad about it for a while, but then I thought that at least I am still alive to feel the shame.

Early one sunny summer morning at the Boy Scout camp, the scouts of my troop were walking to the chow hall for breakfast, when we came upon a crowd of boys by this big dumpster. As we got closer, I see two older boys holding long wooden branches and poking inside the dumpster, and the boys were trying to get these animals to walk up the branches. I made my way to the dumpster, looked inside, and sure enough, there were two raccoons in one corner of the dumpster with about four or five empty boxes. Every time the big branch would come close to the raccoons, they would attack it with their claws and teeth, making them madder. I decided to back away from this scene, sensing danger.

As I backed off, I heard a man's loud voice, "What's going on here?"
I turned and looked at this fat Scoutmaster from another troop. He had on a Smokey Bear hat with a strap around his chin, a green sash across his chest with more than 100 merit badges, medals, and ribbons on his green uniform shirt. He also had matching shorts pulled up to his chest, and green knee-high socks with tassels. I thought he might have been a General in the Boy Scouts, if they had such a thing. He was quickly briefed of the situation by two Eagle scouts that accompanied him.

The Scoutmaster said, "Everybody, get away from the dumpster."

Then he said, "I don't understand you boys, don't you know that raccoons are wild animals and they cannot be coaxed to walk up those branches?"

He went on," Move back further, keep going," holding his hands up in the air.
Then, he went to the dumpster, pulled the branches out, and threw them to the side. He then moved a milk crate next to the dumpster, and stepped onto it with both feet. He bent from

the waist into the dumpster, reaching for the raccoons. Suddenly, there was a loud thumping inside the dumpster, from the bodies of the raccoons trying to get away from the Scoutmaster. We then heard the raccoons making growling noises. Immediately after, we heard bloodcurdling screams from the Scoutmaster, both his feet have left the milk crate, his legs were waving in the air, and his body was seesawing on the dumpster edge. Quickly some scouts had grabbed him from the dumpster, his hands and arms were gushing with blood from his elbows down. Someone came running with a first aid kit, and started bandaging his hands and arms. As the ambulance arrived, two scouts had tipped over the dumpster on its side. Then, about a minute later, the raccoons ran out of it, and dashed off into the forest.

There is always moments in life when you say, "Now, that was stupid, and I don't want to be that guy," this was one of those times.

Chapter 10 - Crime & Punishment

Occasionally, we would be caught in our juvenile delinquent acts or violating a family cardinal rule and the punishment would fit the crime. In the 1960s, it was very common for children to be punished By a Good Old-Fashioned Beating. Both of my parents were brought up under similar parental corporal punishment discipline, but more extreme. My mother's and father's upbringing in the 1940s was strict. My father and his siblings would be taken to the woodshed and would be beaten bare assed with a hickory stick. As the children got older, their father used a barber's razor strap, my father and his siblings were stripped naked during the punishment.

My mother's parents would use a man's belt doubled over to beat the bare bottoms of their children. As the children got older, my grandparents simply used the same belt, but used the buckle end to connect with their target, but the children would be fully clothed. After talking to my parents as an adult about their corporal punishments as a child, my mother felt that for the most part the offense fit the punishment in all cases, but my father felt that although the offense fit punishment, my grandfather Dick went way beyond the call of duty in most cases. I will leave it to your imaginations about what my father meant, believe me, you do not want to hear the details.

Corporal punishment in the Kraemer family had been generous, and extra doses of beatings were always available. My parents were great believers of the old saying, "Spare the rod, spoil the child," and the Kraemer children were a lot of things, but not spoiled. My parent's main corporal punishment tool was a man's belt, and the children were fully clothed during the act, growing up. Sometimes during the punishment, there could be a few slaps, kicks, or punches, as we got older, because we were trying to deflect either the belt or trying to get away. Because my mother was, for the most part, a stay at home mom, she would be at the home front, and would know first hand of our offense, most of the time. Therefore, she would get the first crack at disciplining the children. My mother took disciplining the children very seriously. However, she would get very emotional during the process. As a kid in my household, the breaking point was reached with my mother when there would be silence; followed by her light blue eyes bulging out of her head, and she would grit her teeth. My body temperature would go up to 110°, and the kids that were not involved in the offense would scatter like mice. However, the kids that knew they were the target for discipline would freeze in place, knowing that running for cover would only bring more pain, once my mother caught up with them. Once it was established that you were going to get a beating, my mother then took a few steps towards us with hands propelling forward, and opening them up as though she was about to choke you to death, but she would never make contact. Then, she would yell at the top of her lungs, some examples, "You little son of a bitch," or "You little bastard," and end with, "You're going to get it now!" Then, she would turn, run for her weapon of choice, and then she would start swinging in a frenzied state, until she was exhausted, and would start crying. As I mentioned before, the belt was the main discipline tool when we were young. However, as we got older, my mother had a full arsenal available at her disposal. There was a paddle that use to have an elastic cord with a ball on it, which was used until it broke on someone at age 11. Then she upgraded to the ½-inch thick wooden yardstick, which gave her more range, and could be used with two hands for more leverage. The yardstick gave my mother flexibility like a ninja warrior. If you used your hands and arms to deflect the blows of the yardstick, that hurt more than the beating itself. Yeah, she got a lot of mileage from that yardstick, until it broke at age 13. Finally, the most coveted weapon of choice for mom was the 1-inch thick wooden breadboard. After the first two discipline tools failed her in the heat of the battle, the breadboard stood the test of time in close combat until I reached 16 years old; she broke it on my backside and then threw the broken pieces at me.

When it came to corporal punishment sessions, they could be one on one, or group beatings. As far as group beatings, usually Ike and I were the offending parties, and Gina, being three years younger then I, would seldom receive the standard punishment, she might receive a couple of slaps. In addition, Gina was a girl with special needs at the time. The term "retarded" was used a lot, and for the most part, she was a good little girl.

The most memorable corporal disciplines were group oriented, and the two sons were the major offenders. On one occasion, I do not remember what offending act Ike and I had committed, but I do remember the result as clear as day. My mother was in the kitchen, getting dinner ready, Ike and I had just entered the opposite side of the kitchen. Words were exchanged, and suddenly, it was silent. My brother and I started to back out of the kitchen into the hallway. My mom gave that look of, "It's ass whipping time," and started to move towards us with her hands reaching out.

She yelled, "You Little Fucker's!"
Then she grabbed a fork from the table and threw it at us. Suddenly, Ike looked down, started screaming and running in place. The fork was lodged in his leg just above his right kneecap. My mother changed from battle mode to, "I can't believe I did that" mind set in 2 seconds flat. She started to run towards Ike with her hands covering her mouth. She said, "Hold still," then she reached down and pulled out the fork. As Ike continued to cry, mom told him to take his pants off, and told me to get the peroxide, gauze, and tape. When I returned with the supplies, my mother patched him up, and told him to put his pants back on. She then told us both to go to our room until dinnertime. I helped Ike up the stairs; he

was still in some pain. It was quiet in the house until my father got home, and he was briefed on the fork-throwing incident.

> My dad came in our room, looked at Ike's knee, told him to bend it, and said, "It will be sore for day or two, but you'll live."

Then he said, "After dinner, you both go right to your room, no TV tonight," and walked out.

I knew that my mother felt guilty for years about the Great Fork Throwing Incident. However, it never stopped her from corporal discipline in the future.

As for my father's part in corporal punishment, he was the escalated version of the next level. My mother was the first line of discipline, if she felt the offending party needed an extra helping of ass whipping, which was 90% of the time; it would be forwarded to my father. Once my father had the corporal punishment request on his shoulders, he would make a decision whether or not to follow through with the proposal.

The following had been my father's deciding factors for corporal punishment:

A. If my mom got to us first with a beating, my father would not give us a second thrashing 9 times out of 10. However, if the offense was bad enough to warrant a second round bout, he was up to the challenge.
B. If he felt the offense did not warrant corporal punishment, he would issue other discipline like taking away privileges, grounding you, going to bed without dinner, no TV, or foregoing something that meant a lot to us.
C. If the offense were serious enough, he would rise to the occasion and perform his parental duty.

Unlike mom, dad would never show emotion during the act of corporal punishment. Don't get me wrong. He would get really pissed off, and he would show it. However, during the punishment, he always had a clam demeanor. There was always a cooling off period for him between the time he got mad, and actual execution of the beating. He would send us to our rooms first, and then he would follow a few minutes later. I believe that because of the brutal beatings my father had as a child, is the reason for his pause and reflection. I also believe because of his upbringing, he needed to communicate purpose to his children for applying the punishment.

One occasion is a perfect example of how my father approached corporal punishment. My brother and I had sibling rivalry since we left the womb. When we were young, we were always fighting, arguing, and trying to out do each other. My parents endured this back and forth bickering and fighting for years. This would be easily remedied by my parents warning us, and smacking us in the back of the head. Until one day, Ike and I were in our room, that we shared, and we were beating the crap out of each other. This was an all out brawl; bodies were hitting the floor and walls. The beds and the rest of the furniture were moving across the hardwood flooring. My parents were in the living room below us, listening to the racket, watching the dining room chandelier swinging, and the plaster dust falling from the ceiling. Finally, my father had enough; he walked up the stairs quietly, opened the door of our bedroom, and stood in the doorway with his arms crossed, observing his two sons duke it out. At first, we did not know he was there, but when we did notice his presents, we continued to beat the shit out of each other. We figured that he had come up the stairs as a spectator. In addition, it was up to us to show him who the toughest son was, and who would be the victor. Ike and I continued smashing into furniture, punching each other, and then wrestling to the floor, as dad looked on for about 5 min. Once we were on the floor, I ended the fight by punching my brother a few times in the face, and he conceded. When I got up off the floor, I looked at my father still standing calmly with his arms crossed, in the doorway.

As Ike picked himself up off the floor, my dad asked, "Are you done now?"

I looked at him, and said, "Yeah."

Then my father said, "Good, I want the two of you to sit down." Then he sat down on my bed, my brother and I sat on the bed opposite my dad.

He said, "I stood there watching the two of you fight, and how you fight each other. I came to the conclusion that you both really hate each other, and that troubles me."

Then dad said, as he looked at me, "Do you really hate your brother that much to beat him that way?"

I looked at him, puzzled, and not sure, what the right answer was. I said, "But he started it!"

Dad said, "I don't care who started it, that's not what I asked you."

I said, "No," as I looked down, ashamed of myself.

My father looked down at Ike, and said, "Do you hate Dick that much the way you beat him?"

My brother looked at my father, and said, "No."

Dad said, "Good, because you and your brother should love each other, and you'll never have anyone closer than your own brother in your lives."

Then he stood up, and said, "Do you understand what I'm saying?"

Ike and I both said, together, "Yes."

Dad said calmly, "Good, now I have to punish you both, so you understand."
As he pulled his belt from his pants, and doubled it over, we started to back away from him, totally surprised that we were going to get an ass whipping.

Ike started to scramble to the corner of his bed, screaming, "No, no, no!"
I stood, frozen in shock, between the two beds.

My father said, "This is going to hurt me, more than it does you."

Then dad started swinging his belt from above his head, as I dropped to my bed, he connected with my legs and ass a few times. Then, he turned to Ike, and gave him a few lashes, as Ike screamed for mercy. Then, he switched back to me, holding one of my arms to keep me in range as he swung the belt several times, whipping me on the back, ass, and legs. I, too, was crying and begging for mercy, and the only relief I got was when dad turned his attention to my brother. Watching my brother get beaten was disturbing; my father did not cut him any slack because he was two years younger than I was. Dad would switch his attention from one son to the other several times. The whole corporal punishment session lasted about 5 min. When it was over, Ike and I laid on our beds, crying. My father stood over us for about 30 seconds. Then as he walked out of the bedroom, he turned and looked down at me, without saying a word. It was that last glance of my father's face that day that really burned into my memory. He looked disappointed in me, and I think that it really did hurt him more than it did us.

My father handled punishment in a similar manner all through my childhood; it had to be calm, clear, and with a purpose. Ike and I, after that day, still had fights, knock down, and drag out beatings. Nevertheless, we kept the fighting low key, and tried to keep my parents unaware of it, because a repeat performance of this memorable ass whipping was not desired.

The reflection of this day, and my relationship with Ike has been close and I love him, and he is the closest male person in my life. We do not beat each other up anymore, and he is still a pain in the ass sometimes.

I feel the need to clarify my parent's positions on discipline and corporal punishment for their children. They both felt they needed to apply punishment, thoughtfully, and with purpose. My mother applied corporal punishment with a lot of emotion during her sessions, most of the times crying during and after the event. My father kept his emotions in check during corporal punishment applications. They always kept their objective of teaching a lesson when punishing the children. They never applied corporal punishment under the influence of drugs or alcohol. In addition, they never beat their children because they had a bad day. There was always a purpose in order to discipline their children.

Chapter 11 - The Run Away

There was not one time I was punished; I can recall now, that I did not deserve everything I had received. However, I do remember one time that I thought I was wrongfully punished, and it turned out bad. One time when I was 13 years old, I started smoking cigarettes with my friends. My mother caught me when she would notice that I would go out to the garage a little too often, to sneak a smoke. She had finally caught me red handed in the garage, and sent me to my room until my dad came home. Once my father came home, my mother called me down stairs for a family discussion at the kitchen table. My dad first asked where I had gotten the cigarettes from, and I told him that I bought them myself. My mom interjected, and said that I had stolen some cigarettes from her because she found the same brand butts on the garage floor. She then placed the cigarette butts on the table. I then admitted to stealing her cigarettes in the past, but had my own pack now.

My dad said, "You stole from your family?"
I sat back in my chair, bracing for the smack, as my father slapped me in the back of my head with his left hand. The left hand was always the worst because he had a heavy gold wedding band on it, and it left a little knot on the back of my head.

Dad then turned to mom, and said, "Where in the garage did you find the cigarette butts?"

Mom stood up glaring at me, with her arms folded, and said, "Next to the acetylene tanks!"

Dad looked in my eyes, and said, "Yeah, both of those 250 pound tanks are full!" He continued, "Do you know what 500 pounds of acetylene would do if you ignited it?"

I said, nervously, as I waited for another slap, "Cause a lot of damage?"

Dad turned to mom, and said, "Look, Jeanie, we have a fuck 'n genius on our hands."

Then he turned to me, and said, "Yeah, you'll cause a lot of damage, you'll blow up half the neighborhood, killing you and your whole family, you stupid son of a bitch!"

My mom started frantically pacing back and forth; as though she was visualizing this horrific disaster scene unfold.

She stopped, and yelled, "Are you a fuck 'n idiot," as she held her hands out about to choke me.

Then mom pointed at me, turned to dad with her face red as a cherry, and yelled, "He smokes, he steals, and he almost killed all of us!"

Then she turned to me, and said, "You've got to beat the shit out of the little bastard!"

My father sat at the kitchen table, cool as a cucumber, with his arms folded, and looked up at mom. Dad said, "Now, Jeanie, beating this dummy is not going to do anything!" Besides, it wouldn't be kind to beat someone with a mental problem."

I immediately got defensive, and said, "I don't have a mental problem!"

Dad turned to me and looked me straight in the eyes, and said, "No?"

He paused, and then he continued, "So, it was smart to smoke next to the acetylene tanks? You fuck 'n moron."

Then he shook his head, looking at my mother, and exhaled loudly.

My father got up from the table, and said, "You're grounded for two weeks, go to your room."

As I walked up stairs, I could hear my mother begging him to kick my ass, and him rejecting the idea because I was too stupid.

After that family Pow Wow, I sat for a long time on my bed, looking out my window onto the street below, thinking about what had just unfolded. Surely, smoking was wrong for a kid my age, I did steal a few cigarettes, and broke one of the Commandments, "Thou shell not steal", which was a big deal in my family. Being a thief in my family was the lowest organism on the planet. However, what troubled me most about that day was that my parents confirmed something I suspected all along; I was Stupid, a Moron, and a Fuck 'n Idiot. I started to put the pieces together in my mind. I reflected on what had happened in school and at home. My eyes turned from light blue to green over night at age 5, threw my parents into a panic, and they ran to a few doctors to discover that I was okay, or so they said. Then I was left back in the second grade, after they discovered in the middle of the school year that I needed glasses. Then, there was the never-ending struggle with my schoolwork. When I was called on in school to read aloud, I would stammer and trip over every single simple word, making a fool of myself every time. My defense was to become a class clown, and refuse to read aloud anymore. Because it took me four times longer than anyone else to read a chapter, I fell behind in my homework assignments so badly, that I hid it from my parents. My mother would spend countless hours helping me with my homework. I still got some C minuses, but mostly failing grades. All that time my mother spent helping me with my homework, had become fruitless. Now she seemed a lot less interested in helping me with schoolwork.

Finally, as I sat on my bed, had an "Ah-hah!" moment. Earlier that year, my parents took me to a psychologist, because I used to say, "I forgot," a lot. My parents would ask me to do something or remember something, and my old comeback if I did not do it or remember was, "I forgot." Therefore, they set up a bunch of appointments with a psychologist, and ran a shitload of written tests on me. Then every Wednesday for about a month, I would meet with Dr. Knucklehead, and he would ask me stupid questions like:

"Do you love your mother?" Or "What's today's date?"

He would hold up an ink blotter, and ask, "What does this look like?"

I used to answer the last question with, "Butterfly", all the time just to fuck with Dr. Knucklehead. After the series of visits with Dr. Knucklehead, my parents did not say anything about the test results. I waited a couple of weeks after the psychologist visits, and I decided to ask my parents individually about the test results.

Once I cornered my mom, and asked, "Do you have the results from that Psycho Dude?"

As she was standing by the sink, she immediately stopped what she was doing.

She then turned to me, "Oh, ah, the doctor said you're perfectly normal."

Then she forced a smile and hugged me.

Then, about a day later, my father was in the back yard and I asked him the same question.

He said, "Yeah, the doctor," then he stopped and turned to me.

He rubbed his baldhead, and said, "Ah, the doctor said you're okay, just try harder in school."

Of course, at the time, I bought their answers, but after reflecting on my parent's responses, I knew they were hiding something. Then it hit me like a ton of bricks! The results of those tests Dr. Knucklehead gave me were scientific evidence that I was Stupid, a Moron, and an Idiot, all rolled in one. This really made me mad that my parents had been lying to me all along, and that they had evidence that I was a numbskull, and tried to hide it from me. Then, I also realized that I would no longer be trusted as the oldest son, and I would have to relinquish all my responsibilities. In addition, hearing about my asshole brother being known as the smart son, who he is not, was too much to bear.

It was at this time in my life that my parents discovered that I had dyslexia, which is a psychological disorder that affects a person's ability to read, spell, and write. In addition, a person with dyslexia has a severe loss of short-term memory, which would affect many things including reading comprehension. A person's defense mechanisms would kick in with dyslexia, in fear of discovery. Some examples of psychological defensive mechanisms-a person would prefer to be a loner, trouble with relationships and making friends, and being disruptive in a classroom environment. These defensive mechanisms were used to cover up their inabilities, and a way to manipulate others to read, spell, and write for them. As mentioned earlier, I had not discovered that I had dyslexia until I was 44 years old. In addition, the public school system in the late 1960s had little resources, if any, to teach children with dyslexia, and private schools were cost prohibitive for my parents.

Just a note; at the time I did know that acetylene was an explosive gas, and could be ignited by a lit cigarette. I just forgot.

So there I sat on my bed, looking out the window, putting all the pieces together, after the verbal smack down, which by the way, hurt more then any ass whipping I ever had. I was pissed off at my parents. I felt sorry for myself, and needed to do something about it.

This was when I had decided to run away from home the first chance I got. Besides, my family would be better off without me. They wouldn't have to worry about me blowing up the neighborhood and killing my family in mass destruction. In addition, they did not need to cover up the fact that their oldest child was a Dumb Bell any more. I'll just pack my bag and go, the very first chance I get. But, where would I go? I thought about that for a while. I did not have anyone that I could stay with, and the few friends that I did have lived with their parents. Then it dawned on me that there was a vacant house at the end of the village. My friend, Michael B, and I had broken into this two family house a few times. The place had some beds, other furniture, and running water, but the electricity had been shut off. This was a perfect place to run away to, I thought. I called Michael B the next morning and he came over to my house, so we could plan my escape. Even though I had been grounded, I was able to have friends come to the house to visit. Therefore, we plotted that the next time my mom needed me to go to the store I would make my getaway. This would give me enough time to get to the vacant house and set up shop, before my mother would come looking for me. I asked Michael to get some blankets and some candles, and to store them in the house. I would get the rest of the supplies at the store during my escape. Sure enough, the next morning my mother needed a few things from the Grand Union. I slipped out the side door with a paper bag of some clothes and some Playboy magazines, and I took off. I took my money, some cash mom had given me, and I bought a lot of soda, cup cakes, Ring Dings, Funny Bones, and little fruit pies. Then I rode my bike to the edge of the village where the house was. I looked around to make sure that none of the neighbors saw me, and then I rode my bike up the driveway, and stored the bike in the barn in the back. I looked around again to make sure no one was around, and then I ran to the upstairs apartment of the house, and jimmied the door open. I was safe at last, concealed from the rest of the world. Home sweet home, I laid on the bed drinking a soda, and read my Playboy magazine, it was still midmorning. I decided before my mother starts driving around looking for me, that I should go tell Michael that I had made my escape. He only lived a short distance from where I was, so I drove my bike to his house. I knocked on the door, and his mother answered.

I said, "Hi, Mrs. B, is Mike home?"

Mrs. B yelled, "Michael, your friend is here."

Then he ran to the door, looked surprised, and said, "You did it?"

I said, "I did it, let's go."

Mike yelled, "Mom, I'm going out, see you later."

Then we drove our bikes back to the house, and hung out all day. Mike had brought a battery-operated transistor radio that we jammed to, as we bullshitted. We also drank a shitload of soda, and filled up on junk food all afternoon. I tried to talk Mike into running away with me, and he rather liked the idea, at first, being foot loose and fancy free. But as the day wore on, he didn't want to run away, he had it too good. He came from a family with a lot of kids, and he was one of the youngest of the litter, and had it pretty good. Therefore, he thought he had no reason to run away. I agreed, why run away if there was no reason to. He did not know the real reason I ran way, he just knew that he was just helping a friend in need. Occasionally, I would look out the window from the top floor apartment, looking out for my mother's car. I did spot it speeding by a couple of times. I couldn't help but think that if she or my dad had gotten hold of me, I would get the worst thrashing of my life. It was getting around dinnertime, and Mike had to leave, but promised that he would be back with something to eat. I laid on the bed, smoking cigarettes, listening to the radio, and thinking about what my parents were saying. Maybe something like, "Well, maybe it's because Dick was too stupid to find his way home why he's not back yet." Alternatively, "Maybe he got run over by a car, and it dragged him to the next county."

It was almost getting dark, and Mike came with a plate of fried chicken, corn, and potatoes. As I started to scarf down the food, he told me that my mom had called his house, and talked to his mom. Mike said that his mother remembered seeing a blond boy with glasses this morning, going out with Mike, but she had not seen him all day. Mike's mom asked him when the last time he saw Dickie Kraemer was. Mike replied, "We rode our bikes to the Grand Union, and that was the last time I saw him." Mike's mom had called my mother, and informed her of the update. Mike had lied for me, what a true friend, and he brought me dinner, too. I guess that with all of the activity in his house, he could sneak a plate of food after dinner, and get away with it. I commended Mike on his loyalty, and smoked a few more cigarettes, and we bullshitted some more until the streetlights went on, and it got dark. That was his cue to go home, and he said that we would meet again in the morning with breakfast. I had lit about three candles in the kitchen/living room area where there were a couple of beds, and a table and chairs.

As the summer night wore on, I could hear the crickets outside, making a racket, and the old house started to make creaking noises. I would look outside, and I could see a low fog mist rolling in across the street where there was a cemetery. I turned up the radio to drown out the noises, smoked another cigarette while I flipped through the Playboy magazine. Then I started to think about what was going on at my home, and that no doubt, either mom or dad was out looking for me. The radio started to make static noises. I got up, moved the antenna around, and moved the tuning knob to get better reception. As I did, looking out the window, I observed that it was a full moon, and through thickening low fog, the gravestones in the cemetery across the street were illuminated.

After screwing around with the radio, I got a rock 'n roll station, and the first song was,

"Bad Moon Rising" by Creedence Clearwater Revival.

At this point, I had been spooked, and had totally forgotten about the cemetery across the street, until now. I lit up another smoke, and turned up the radio full blast, to ward off evil spirits. Then, I walked through the hallway on the top floor to the front part of the house, holding one of the candles. I made it to the front bedroom, and looked out the window, for a better look at the graveyard, and it looked even scarier closer up. Suddenly, I heard a door slam downstairs.

I yelled, "Hello is there anybody there?"

I was shaking so badly that the candle light almost went out. Then I ran down the hallway to the top of the staircase, and held the candle light down it.

I said, with a shaky voice, "Is there anybody there?" No reply, I could just hear the loud music in the kitchen.

I backed away from the staircase, down the hall to the kitchen and turned off the radio. The only thing I could hear was the crickets, and I walked toward the hallway.

I yelled, "I got a bat, Mother Fucker," as I grabbed it next to the door.

There was silence, and I thought that the wind most have slammed the door. I walked back to the table and grabbed another bottle of soda, and took a couple of good belts. I threw the bat on the bed and sat at the table. As I sat there, I started to think that this whole idea of running away was dumb. In addition, my parents probably had called the police, and they were out looking for me, too. Maybe the cost of a good beating, and being labeled the family Idiot Stick was worth the price of admission back into my home. Then, I dismissed that vision, and walked over to the radio. I stopped, about to turn on the radio, and I thought I heard a noise down stairs. I stood motionless and listened carefully. There it was again, it sounded like someone walking on the hardwood floors. I ran to the bed, grabbed the bat, then ran to the counter and grabbed the candle.

I yelled, "Okay, you fucking asshole, you asked for it," and ran to the top of the stairs.

I held the candle out over the stairway into the darkness below. I could only see the bottom step of the stairway, and reflection of the moonlight on the bottom hallway floors. Suddenly, I heard the footsteps coming closer. I ran to the kitchen, put the candle on the counter, grabbed my paper bag, and blew out the candle. Then I stood frozen with the bat in one hand, and the bag in the other. Just then, I heard a door slam upstairs. I grabbed the kitchen doorknob, yanked the door open, and ran down the outside staircase. As I hit the bottom stair, I tripped and fell to the ground. I jumped up quickly, picking up my bag and bat, and ran to the barn. Once in the barn, I turned and looked at the top floor of the house. I then threw down the bat, jumped on my bike, and pedaled as fast as I could down the driveway to the main road. Once I hit the highways, I pulled a wheelie, flying right into the center of the road. Suddenly, I heard screeching tires and saw car headlights on me as I flew across the street in front of the graveyard.

I stopped and looked at the car and a man's voice yelled, "I could have killed you, you stupid fuck!"

I looked into the headlights and yelled," I'm sorry, mister."

He yelled back, "Go home, you little moron, and stay off the road," as he drove off.

I stood in front of the cemetery for a moment, and thought, "Yeah, that's me, the Stupid Fuck, the little Moron, he must have been talking to my parents, it's a small town. But, at least, I'm alive." Then I slowly pedaled my way home , wondering what my parents had in store for me.

I reached the front of my house on the sidewalk, about 11:00 PM. I could see that the porch light was on, and the whole downstairs was lit up. I rested my bike on the porch steps, and opened the front door. As I did, my mother quickly appeared in the kitchen, and ran towards me in the doorway. I could see that she had been crying for a while, as she approached, and then she hugged me so tightly that my spine was cracking. Then she started crying again, as my father came into view. He then placed his hands on my blond little head and rubbed it lightly.

A few moments went by, and then mom grabbed my shoulders, and looked at me and said, "Where were you, we looked everywhere?"

I replied, "I was in an abandoned house, up on 32 across the street from the cemetery."

Mom said, as she wiped away her tears, "Why?"

I said, "I wanted to run away."

Mom said, "Why would you want to run away," as she released me.

I moved back a step, and said, "Because." Then I paused, and looked at both of them as I started to cry.

Then my father grabbed one of my shoulders gently, and said, "Why?"

I looked at him, with tears rolling down my face, and said, "Because you think I'm stupid, and you don't love me anymore!"

Then, my mom dropped to her knees, and grabbed me by the shoulders. She said, as she began to cry again, "We love you, honey, and you're not stupid."
Dad shook my shoulder firmly, I looked up at him, and you could see a tear roll down his face.

He said, "Dick, we love you, and you're not stupid." Then he leaned down and gave me a kiss on my forehead. This tender moment of parental love was always there in my life, and also for my siblings. So even though they didn't always say the words, my parents always showed the love, sometimes it was a little to hard to see, but it had always been there. After the tender moments of the reunion, my parents had asked if I had eaten. I said I had, and was not hungry, and they sent me to bed. As I walked up stairs, they instructed me that after I was done with my newspaper route, to come right back home because I was still grounded for two weeks.

The following morning was a beautiful sunny summer morning. I had finished my paper route, had eaten a bowl of Capt. Crunch cereal, and had been working on my Little Red Wagon dragster model. All was right with the world. I did not care that much about being grounded, and besides two weeks would go by quickly.

As I worked on my model, I looked out the window and noticed Mike had ridden his bike into my driveway. So I ran downstairs, then as I got into the kitchen, I heard him knocking, and I went to the side door. I opened the side door; Mike dropped his bike, jumped back in the middle of the driveway with his eyes popping out of his head and his mouth wide open.

I said, "Mike, what's wrong?"

Mike started to move his mouth, but nothing was coming out.

I walked toward him, closing the door behind me, and said, "What is it?"

He said, as he held his hands on his face, "I thought you were dead!"

I said, "Dead," smiling and started to chuckle. "What are you talking about?" Thinking that maybe he thought my parents had murdered me.

Then he grabbed me by the arms, and said, "The house burnt down last night!"

I said, "What house?"

Mike said, "The house you were in last night, burnt up!"

I stepped back in disbelief. I looked to the kitchen window to see if it was open, so my mom would not hear us. I put my finger to my lips for silence.

Then I whispered, "You've got to be shitting me, right?"

He whispered, "No, the fuck 'n cops were at my house this morning."

My eyes got very wide, and I said, "The fucking cops, how did they find you?"

He said, "They found my ID bracelet up stairs on one of the beds! The cops said the whole up stairs is totally burnt out, and couldn't tell if there was a body up there!"

I whispered, "What did you tell the cops?"

He looked at me, held out his hands, and said, "I had to tell them everything, my mom made me. I thought you were dead!"

I looked down at the ground, and said, "Do they know my name?"

Mike said, "Yeah, and where you live. I didn't mean to rat you out."

I looked at him, put my hand on his shoulder, and said, "I know you're not a rat, you had to." Then I said, "Listen-you better get out of here before the cops come, you don't need any more trouble."

He said, "Yeah my mom is going to beat the shit out of me for lying to her."

I said, "Blame it on me, and tell her I made you do it, I'll back you up."

As he got on his bike, he said, "Yeah, I'll try it, let me know how you make out. Okay?"

As he rode off, I said, "Yeah, sure." Thinking that I was truly fucked, and how that would be worded to him in a letter from Sing Sing.

As I came in from outside, my mom asked, "Who was that outside?"

I said, "That was Mike, he had to go home."

I looked at the clock; it was 11:30 AM. I walked slowly up the stairs into my bedroom, and closed the door. I went to the edge of my bed, and looked out the window overlooking the front of the house to the street below. I figured that the police would be here any minute, and there was no reason to tell my mother what happened to that house. She would find out soon enough, that the house burnt down, why upset her now? Besides, all I wanted was peace and quiet, to be left alone. As I looked out this same window many times before, I had never been in so much trouble in my life. The only safe place for me was sitting on the edge of my bed, looking out onto the street, waiting for the police to take me away. I could not run away, I burnt down my last alternative. I visualized how this would all go down. The cops would come to the house, ask some questions, slap the cuffs on me, and take me to jail. Then my parents would visit me on Christmas and Thanksgiving, and give me clean underwear and a toothbrush as presents until I reached 25 years old. Wait-maybe, I could plead Stupidity and get off with a warning. All I needed was Dr. Knucklehead's report, and my parents to testify that I am truly a Moron, and, of course, they would present evidence of me almost blowing up the neighborhood. But wait a minute, maybe the court will find that I am too dangerous of an Idiot to be on the loose, and commit me to the Looney Bin. I guess I would take the Looney Bin over jail, I may have to fake being a little bit more of a numbskull that I am now. However, I might be able to pull it off. Then I started thinking that my parents were going to take back what they said last night. Today, they might say, "We love you, Dick, but you're dumb as dirt. But that's okay because you're too stupid to help yourself." Yeah, that's how it's going to end, I thought. I sweated my ass off, in that bedroom all afternoon, waiting for the police to come. The only time I came out of my room was to go to the bathroom, and drink some water from the faucet. I returned to sitting on my bed, and thinking that I would truly take the biggest ass whipping of my life, over going to reform school, or the Loony Bin. Then I began to pray, I asked God to forgive me for being so stupid, I asked to be smarter, and asked for guidance. Suddenly, the police car pulled up in front of the house. I said to myself, "God must have certainly acted quickly." As the officer got out of the car, and put on his hat, it seemed that the temperature in the room got to 200°. I could see that he was a young police officer as he walked to the house. The moment had finally come; I got up from my bed and tucked in my T-shirt. The doorbell rang, and I could hear my mom walk across the floor. I open my bedroom door to hear what was going on.

Mom said, "Yes?"

The officer said, "Hi, are you Mrs. Kraemer?"

Mom said, "Yes."

The officer said, "My name is Deputy Blue, ma'am, do you have a son, Dick?"

She said, nervously, "Yes."

Deputy Blue said, "Ma'am, we're investigating a fire, and we think your son could help us."

She said, "Yes," then she yelled, "Dick!"

I yelled, "Yeah?"

She yelled, "Come down here!"

As I walked downstairs, she said, "You don't think my son was involved, do you?"

He said, "No, ma'am, just following up an investigation."

I reached the bottom of the stairs. Mom turned to me and said, "This is Deputy Blue, answer all of his questions." I nodded yes.

The Deputy said, "Hey, son, do you know where the Highland Mills cemetery is on route 32?"

I said, "Yes, sir."

Deputy said, "Well, there was a fire last night in the house across the street, it was the old Smith house. Do you know where that is?"

I said, "Is that the white two family house with the barn in the back?"

He said, with a smile, "Yes, that's the one; there was a bad fire there last night."

I took a step back, made a surprised look, and said, "There was?"

The deputy stood up, with a straight face, adjusted his belt, and said, "Do you know Michael B?"

I said, Yes, sir, he is my friend," as I looked puzzled by the question.

He said, as he tipped his hat back, and leaned forward, "He said you and him were in that house last night. Is that right?"

I looked down to the floor, and said, "Yes, but Mike went home before it got dark."

Then the Deputy tapped me on the shoulder and I looked up at him. He said, "Son, what were you doing in that old house so late at night?"

I looked at my mother, who had her mouth wide open, and I said, "I was running away from home, I guess.

The Deputy then knelt on one knee and said, "The electric was turned off in that house what did you use for light?"

I looked at him in the eyes, and said, "Candles."

The Deputy then looked at my mother, and said "Ah.",

He looked back at me and said, "We also found cigarettes in the house, too. Were you smoking in the house?"

I said, "Yes, sir." Then mom gasped a breath of air.

He said, "This is important, son, did you blow out all of the candles before you left?"

I stood there with a blank face, trying to think if I had blown out all of the candles.

I said, "I think I did....But, maybe I didn't....Wait a minute, I blew one out... But not the others."

The Deputy then stood up, and said, "You didn't blow them all out, I see." Then he smiled.

My mom had her hands on her face and she said, "How bad was the fire?"

Deputy Blue said, "Well, ma'am, the whole top floor was gutted, the fire was so hot it incinerated everything, and we were not sure if there was a body up there."

I said, "Deputy Blue, I thought I heard footsteps and doors slamming in there."

He turned to me, and smiled, "Maybe it was just the old house creaking, but I'll put it in my report."

Mom said, "What will happen now?"

The Deputy put his hand on the doorknob, and said, "I'll write up the report, give it to the Chief, we'll talk about it, someone will be in touch."

He opened the door, and said, "Nice to meet you, Mrs. Kraemer," he tipped his hat, "Dick," and walked out to his patrol car and took off.

My mother closed the door, and said, "You were fucking smoking again?"

I knew not to respond, and just stepped back a couple of steps. I could see that mom was having one of those meltdown moments. She stood there with her arms fully extended to her sides, looking up at the ceiling, and stomping her left foot. Then she held out her arms as though she was going to choke me to death.

She said, "Do you know what's going to happen now?"

I stepped back, thinking that she is going to end my life, and shaking my head no.

She continued, "You don't. They are going to throw you in reform school, and there's nothing we can do about it." Then she lit a cigarette, and started to pace up and down the hallway. I started to walk up the stairs slowly.

Then she stopped and looked up at me on the stairs.

She then yelled, "THE PEOPLE THAT OWN THAT HOUSE, THEY'RE PROBABLY GOING TO SUE US! DO YOU KNOW WHAT HAPPENS THEN? WE LOSE OUR HOUSE, AND WE WILL BE IN THE STREETS!"

Then she said, as she began to cry, "Wait right there," then she ran into the nursery. I did not know what she was doing, but it was scaring the shit out of me. My mother ran back with Gina by the hand, and my little sister was crying.

Mom said, sobbing, "Why don't you tell her why she is going to lose her house?"
As I stood there, looking at the two of them crying, I started bawling myself. The reason I was crying was for my family, not for me. I felt sorry for them, I felt sorry for screwing this whole thing up. I could see that they were the real victims, that they had been the bystanders of my own destruction.

I replied, as I cried my eyes out, "I'm sorry".

Mom said, "You're sorry? Tell her," pulling my sister forward. I could not take anymore-heartbreaking conversation, and walked up to my room and closed the door.

My mother yelled, "Just wait until your father hears about this!"

As I returned my bed overlooking the street I thought to myself, "This was an accident. How can it be that a boy like me could be so stupid and not blow a candle out, and change the whole course of his family's future? How could it be?" Maybe the outcome could have been a little different, if I had died in the fire. At least, I would not have to see my parents lose their home. Why didn't God take me that night? There must have been a reason why God had chosen me to live. But, what was it? I knelt down beside my bed, and rested my head on my hands, I prayed for my family, and I threw in a good word for myself. I prayed to God to make me smarter, and to make this whole situation go away. I promised that I would be good, and not to get in any more trouble. I had a time for reflection before my father got home and I used it.

That evening, when my dad got home, mom debriefed him first, then we had the family Pow Wow at the kitchen table. As I ran through my story a half dozen times with only the truth, I could see that my father was shaken by the prospects my mother had painted for him. We also went through a rerun of mom's previous dramatics from earlier that day. My father called the police, and set up a time that he could meet with them. The evening meal was so quiet, you could hear Pat and Pam fart, and they were about a year old. As I went to my room, dad yelled, "Dick, your still grounded." I replied, "I know." Like that was my only problem.

The following day my father spoke to Deputy Blue and the Chief. My father said we would have to wait and see what happens. After a few weeks went by, I had asked my dad what was happening with me, and that house I had accidentally burnt up. He said it was taken care of, and don't worry about it. The relief of that statement was as if the weight of the world was lifted off my shoulders. My prayers were all answered. And some say there is no God.

Chapter 12 - The Career Change

After being a newspaper boy since the fall of 1968, waking up at 4 AM everyday, delivering over 100 newspapers in all kinds of weather, and earning almost $20 with tips weekly, I began to weigh my employment options. I needed to work smarter, not harder, which didn't mean doubling my route to deliver 200 newspapers to double my earnings. Which was suggested by a pimple faced college kid that worked for the newspaper, and came by once a week to pick up the collection money.

I decided to quit the newspaper route for a few more reasons:

1. Making less then $20.00 a week was not very 'lucrative'. Once I turned 14, in a few short months, I will be able to get my working papers and make at least twice as much with another employer.   .

2. The idea of getting two more hours of sleep before going to school was very appealing.

3. The prospect of missing the bus could result in my mother igniting into a fireball, due to spontaneous human combustion, thus causing a bigger problem.

4. Chicks don't dig paperboys.

The target date for quitting my route was January 20, 1970, because during Christmas I would get tips for the year, a windfall of about $60. On my last morning, I set my alarm clock to 3:00 AM, got dressed quickly, and ran into the garage. I then grabbed two 2X4's that I cut 2 feet long and had hammered as many ten penny nails in them as I could, the day before. I ran down to the end of my street which was two houses down from my house, placed the 2x4's horizontally about 2 feet apart on the right side of the road on the corner. I then shoveled snow over the 2x4's and reviewed my work. I realized that I was working under a bright streetlight on the corner, then looked around in a panic, and hoped no one had seen me working my devilish deed. There's nobody awake in my neighborhood at 3:15 AM, but that feeling of being in the spotlight had made me paranoid. I started to study this pile of new shoveled snow in the road, and thought that, even though the road was snow packed, this new pile of snow at the end of the street didn't blend in with the rest of the setting. So I quickly started shoveling more snow into the street; time was running out, and it would be my luck that Scumbag would be early. I then started frantically patting down the snow with the shovel, so it would blend into the street corner. I stopped, took a good look around again, and then I looked at the booby-trap, and it looked more natural. I ran back to my house and waited.

It was now 3:45 AM, as I waited impatiently for Scumbag, which seemed like a lifetime. I started to reflect on what I was about to do and how this little scheme will turn out.

The following scenarios played out in my head in those final minutes:

A. Scumbag gets one or two flat tires, thinks the 2x4's fell off a truck, and he would be stuck for the rest of the morning. The desired result.

B. Scumbag gets one or two flat tires and figures out that I did it, he comes to the house and wakes up the family.

I started to think about the "B" result and how that would play out. Scumbag would come to the door and bang on it. He would say, "I see you in there, you little bastard!" Then he would say, "Go get your father!"

The whole family would wake up, the twins would start crying, and my mother would start screaming for my father to go to the door. My father would grab his gun, and run to the door and shoot him or listen to what the man had to say. Whether my father shot Scumbag or listened to him was not my biggest concern. First, there would be one of the worst ass whippings I ever had in my life; I reflected on that for a few moments. Second, there would be a police investigation, there would be fingerprints on the 2x4's, and I would go on trial, he found guilty, and get sentenced to reform school. I knew a little bit about reform school, my parents used to tell me when I did something really bad in the public crime sector that I would go to child prison. But, also, I learned about reform school from the magic of TV. There was a series that was produced in the 1940s and 1950s called, "The Bowery Boy's". The movie series was about a gang of juvenile delinquents-the main characters were Slip Mahoney, the tough guy leader of the gang, and Horace Debussy, "Sach" Jones, the clown of the gang, also, not that tough. In one episode, they go to reform school, they are beaten pretty regularly, and Sach, the character that I had identified as myself, ends up in the hospital on his deathbed. This is not painting a pretty picture of my future. I looked at the clock, it's 4:20 AM, and I ran up to my bedroom to see if I could get a better view. All I could see on the corner was the red illumination of his tail against the snow packed road. I went back down the stairs, the house is completely dark, and it was very quiet. I sat on the couch in the living room, waiting for Scumbag to come knocking on the door. I looked at the clock again and now its 4:45 AM, if I wait any longer I would not get my route done in time, but then I thought maybe I wouldn't deliver all the papers that day, and still make it to the bus stop on time. Then I thought, if I didn't deliver all the papers, the newspaper would get complaints and connect me with the crime. So, I decided to deliver the papers, and could not wait any longer. I quietly opened the side door, got my sled, and peeked around the corner of the house to make sure he wasn't out there. Then I slowly walked to the bundles of papers on the sidewalk, tied them to the sled, and started walking up the street in the opposite direction of the crime.

Then, all of a sudden, I heard a loud voice scream, "Hey, kid!" I turned, It Was Scumbag, standing under the streetlight at the end of the street. I froze right in my tracks, with my mouth open, and just stared at him in fear.

Then, he yelled, "Hey, kid, come here."

I thought about running, but I was too scared. I yelled back, "Why?"

Then Scumbag yelled back, "Come here, I want to talk to you," and he started walking toward me.

I yelled, "What for?"

He is getting closer. He is now about 10 feet away from me, and he said, "I need to use your phone."

I said, "Why?"

He said, "My van has two flat tires, and I have to call my job for some help."

I said, "My family is asleep, and they do not let strangers in the house."

He started to smile, with his yellow teeth, and bent over to look me in the eyes, and said, "I'm no stranger; I'm your newspaper delivery driver."

I said, "My dad would be really mad if he had to wake up for you to use the phone. There's a pay phone in front of the police station in town." And I pointed towards town.

He said, "Thanks, kid," and started walking towards town.

I quickly delivered the newspapers to everyone on my street and then turned the corner where the van was jacked up, in the rear. The passenger rear tire was off, and one 2x4 was stuck on it, and the spare was already mounted on the axle. I looked around the van looking for the other flat-it was the passenger front tire. I thought for a moment, how that could have happened. But, more importantly, what happened to the other 2x4? I went back to the corner and, lo and behold, the other 2x4 was still buried in the snow. Looking at the van's tire tracks; he just missed it by an inch. I grabbed the 2x4, kicked the snow around a little to cover up the crime scene, and I took off.

I finished my paper route on time for the last day, and when I went to the bus stop, Scumbag and his van were gone. I learned that revenge was sweet, but only if I do not get caught.

The Hot Shoppes

In the spring of 1970, I was talking to a few kids in school, and found out that there was a place that was hiring for the weekends, and during the summer vacation. The only requirement was to be 14 years old, have working papers, and be on time. My birthday was in May, and after school that same week, I got the working papers, and scheduled my interview. I hitchhiked down route 32 South to route 17 South to a town called Sloatsburg, New York. Then I walked a short distance through the woods to a rest stop called the Hot Shoppes on the New York State Thruway interstate route 87. The whole trip from my house to the Hot Shoppes was 17 miles one-way. I had filled out an application and given them my working papers. The manager looked over the paperwork, told me that I would be a bus boy, and said that I would be at the new snack bar where I would be cleaning off tables and taking out the trash. The manager laid out some ground rules like being on time and no horseplay. In addition, I would need a uniform, which was a white shirt, a black bow tie, a black pair of pants, and black shoes. Then he introduced me to my supervisor, Stewart Gary, and he walked me around. Then Stewart asked when I could start, and I said this weekend. He said that I could start this weekend if I had my uniform, and the parental permission slip signed. I reassured him that when I showed up at 11 AM Saturday, I would have both. We shook hands on it and he walked me out the door.

As I made my way back to the highway, I felt like I had just won the lottery. I was going to make $1.60 an hour, and in a month, I would get a raise to $1.85 an hour, a windfall by my standards. What I could earn in one day at the Hot Shoppes, would take me almost a week on my paper route. In addition, I would be scheduled to work Sundays, too, and almost double my old paper route income. Yes, indeed, I am certainly in the chips now. As I hitched up 17 N., I was thinking about the uniform, I already had black shoes, and white shirts, but I needed to buy a pair of black pants and a black bow tie. I thought that would be no problem, I have money saved from the old paper route.

I had gotten home and told my mom the good news. First, she was shocked, because I never told my parents that I applied for the job, and that this job was 17 miles away. In addition, my parents knew that I was hitchhiking, but did not realize the distances I was traveling, which concerned them. I was a resourceful young boy, and had a great desire to earn money. My mother wanted to approach dad about my employment before giving the okay. Later that evening, my parents sat down with me and discussed my new career as a bus boy. When I had the paper route, they never got involved with me delivering newspapers; I was responsible for the whole thing. Now that I would have to travel 17 miles one-way and be there 11 AM to 7:30 PM, on Saturdays and Sundays parent transportation would be required. They both questioned me about alternative employment options, but there was not much available. If there were jobs, most of them would be after school, which my parents thought would interfere with my homework. After about 15 minutes of my parents trying to figure out who was going to drive me back and forth to work, they agreed to my new employment. However, there would be a few conditions, I would have to get passing grades, go to church before work, and continue to do my chores. In addition, if there was a family function, that I was required to go to, I would not be able to work that day.

My parents wanted me to work at an early age, to teach me the principles of the hard work ethic, and the value of a dollar. What they did not know was that they had created a

Capitalist Monster, and, later in life, I would be severely infected with the Workaholic Disease.

My first day of work was Saturday on the Memorial Day weekend. The new Hot Shoppes Snack Bar would open up at 11:30 AM. The location was on the New York State Thruway Interstate 87, about 45 miles north of New York City in Sloatsburg, New York. The major destinations were the Catskill Mountains, Albany, Buffalo, Niagara Falls, Woodstock, or just to get out of the city.

Stu, the manager, and Russ, the short order cook, were college students in their early 20s. They, too, would work full time during the summer and go back to school in the fall. The rest of the snack bar crew was between 14 to 18 years old and in school. The Hot Shoppes Snack Bar was a small business unit compared to the much larger cafeteria business unit in the same building. The Snack Bar was a new pilot business concept for the Hot Shoppes, and the first of its kind on the New York State Thruway. The Snack Bar crew was just a team of school kids who ran this small fast food business.

Before we opened the snack bar, we would empty all the garbage cans around the patio area, and we would hose down all the picnic tables and the huge concrete patio. Then we would go inside the snack bar, fill the napkin holders, catsup, mustard bottles, and the salt and pepper shakers. This was done with only two bus boys, within 30 minutes, and we hadn't even opened the doors yet.

Once the doors opened, the people came streaming in and formed a line 50 feet out the door. The hamburgers and hot dogs filled three full sized grills, Stu, the supervisor, and Russ, the short order cook, were working that. The French fry guy had six deep fryers going, splashing oil everywhere. The soda fountain girls had poured at least 100 small and large paper cups of soda. A heavyset girl cashier was itching to ring up the first sale. Suddenly, the hamburgers, the hot dogs, and French fries were ready, and people started grabbing for anything they could get their hands on. The crowd filled the stand up counter space in front of the pane glass windows inside the snack bar, and they overflowed onto the concrete patio. The sun was blazing hot and it was 92° with no wind. They gave me a little broom and a dustpan on a stick, and told me to start picking up anything on the patio deck, and on the snack bar floor. If they spilled something, I would go get a mop and clean it up. If someone didn't pick up their garbage after eating, on the tables or the counter, I would throw the junk away and wipe the space clean. Then the garbage cans would get full almost every hour, and I would empty them. In the meantime, people would tell me to get them napkins or straws. About every half hour, Stu would come out, and direct me to do something else that needed attention. It was so hot that day that I had sweated through five paper hats, my white shirt was drenched, and my new black double knit polyester pants felt like they had melted on my body. After about three hours of working my ass off, I took a moment to assess the current situation, and stood out of sight of the other workers. I could see that behind the grill was pure mayhem, Stu and Russ were running around, grabbing buns and yelling at the other workers to go faster. They were flipping burgers and rolling hot dogs with one hand, and throwing French fries in the deep fryer with the other. There was a nice looking red headed girl about my age frantically filling soda cups, and as she turned to put Cokes on the counter, I could see that she was crying. The cashier was arguing with a customer over change and becoming unglued. The bus boy partner of mine was mopping up another spill, and just got rudely shoved aside by a customer. This seemed to me to be chaos, no organization, everyone fighting to keep pace with the mob of customers on the other side of the counter. The customers were pushing and shoving; their children were screaming and crying. Some people thought they didn't need to stand in line, but now that line was 75 feet outside the door. They walked inside the snack bar, went underneath the rope dividers, and cut into the front of the serving line. Then people started yelling at the line cutters, two men and two women picked up paper dishes of French fries, and threw them at the crowd behind him. One big guy that had his family pelted with the fries, grabbed one of the men line cheaters by his collar, and punched him in the mouth, sending him to the floor. As the big man stepped on the cheater's hand, another small man cheater, about 5 feet tall, jumps on the big man's back. The big man stood up straight, as the small man was choking him from behind, with the small man's feet dangling about 2 feet off the ground. The crowd of people all jammed the exits, trying to get out. Stu, the manager, 5'7" tall and about 160 pounds, comes running out to stop the fight. As Stu approached the two men fighting, the big man quickly turns, making the small man's legs swing in midair, hitting Stu and sending him into the rope divider and falling to the floor.

Stu quickly jumps up, and yells, "Call the police!"

Russ ran to get help. Then he said, "Stop, stop, I'm calling the police!"
The big man, red in his face from losing oxygen, staggers to the eating counter, turns, and thrusts backwards into it, smashing the small man's spine into the counter. The small man yelled in pain, released his grip, and fell to the floor in agony. The big man was bent over coughing and gasping for air. The crowds of people were now outside peering into the plate glass windows. The big man's wife and children had surrounded him, crying. Stu handed the big man a cup of water, and turned to attend to the small man, still on the floor. Just then, two State Troopers arrived, one knelt next to the man on the floor, and the other started to aid the big man. The Troopers called for an ambulance for the man on the floor, and escorted the big man outside.

Stu turned around, and said, "Okay, let's get busy," then he yelled, "I need a bus boy to clean up these fries."
I ran over with my dustpan and broom, and started picking up all the fries off the floor. Stu ran around, picking up and realigning the rope dividers.

Then, he walked over to me, and said, "You stand right here by these ropes, and don't let anyone jump the line."

I looked at him, and said, "How am I going to stop them?"

Stu said, "If anyone jumps the line, you just say politely to them that the line begins back there," then he pointed to the end of the 75 foot line.

I said, "What if they don't listen?"

He said, "Then just come and get me, I'll take care of it, okay?"

I nodded my head, and said, "Yeah, okay." I thought to myself, "Yeah, just like you handled this incident that turned out well."

Stu then went to the door, and said, "Okay, folks, everything is fine now, come on in."
People streamed in like a herd of buffalo, pushing and complaining about the snack bar not having any air conditioning. The ambulance crew arrived a few minutes later, and put the small guy on a stretcher. As they were taking the man in the stretcher out the door, they bumped into an old woman, causing her to spill a large Coke on the man's chest. I could not help but think how crazy it was to have a real WWF match in the snack bar, when in one minute; it could have broken out into a riot. Then the next minute, we resume feeding the carnivores as if nothing ever happened, and it's back to business as usual. As I paced the length of the line, guarding the roped in hungry humans, I saw a woman dart under the rope and wedge her way into the line. People started yelling, and I walked over to the woman. She had looked behind the counter, and tried to act as if she didn't notice me approach her.

I said, "Excuse me!"

Then she looked down at me. She said, "Yes?"

I said, "The line starts out there," as I pointed outside.

She said, with an indignant voice, "I know, I've been in line for over 30 minutes."

Another woman, who was a few people back, said, "That's bullshit, you cut the line, bitch!"

I said, "I saw you cut the line, and so did others. You'll have to go to the back of the line."

The woman looked at me as if she was going to burn a hole in my forehead with her stare. Then she stomped her feet on the floor, got out of the line, ducked under the rope, and walked out the door. A few people began to clap; I turned and lifted my paper hat. Then I ducked under the other side of the rope, and resumed walking my post. I thought to myself, "Gee, I guess adults will obey orders from a 14-year-old dork with glasses, amazing, I Got The Power!"

I fielded a few more rope jumpers, emptied a half dozen more garbage cans, and filled a dozen napkin dispensers. At 4 PM, the crowd had died down, and Stu sent me on my 30-minute break. I got two cheeseburgers, fries, and a large Coke for free, and went into the air-conditioned break room upstairs. I thought I was in heaven. I was drenched in sweat, my feet hurt from being on them all day, and I was starving. After I was done eating, I began to get cold the A/C must have been on 60°. I walked out side to warm up, I looked at the temperature outside, and it was 98°. My clothes dried quickly in the heat, and I went to the dessert bar in the cafeteria part of building, grabbed a piece of lemon meringue pie, and ate it quickly. I reported back to work, I did not need to watch the line any more because there wasn't a huge line of cattle out the door, so I resumed my normal duties. The crowd started to build again at 6 PM, and things went crazy busy until we closed the doors at 8 PM. When Stu locked the door, the whole snack bar crew began clapping, throwing their paper hats in the air, and cheering loudly in celebration of ending the day. At first, people would knock on the doors and windows to let them in, like a bunch of hungry road-weary zombies. The snack bar crew found great pleasure telling the animals that they were closed. Then a crewmember would direct the travelers to go to the cafeteria part of the building.

Then they would make a comment low enough, so only the rest of the crew could hear, like:

"Please, don't eat the young."

"Feedbags are on the right side of the door."

"Please, don't drool on the children."

"The dessert trough is by the cashier."

Everyone was just happy to finally close the door on the day, clean up, and go home. I mopped the snack bar floor, wiped down all the counters, and emptied all of the garbage cans. As I punched my time card, Stu called me and the other bus boy over.

Stu said, "Well, you survived the day, you guys did okay today. But I expect the both of you to know what needs to be done without being told what to do all the time."

I said, "You mean we didn't do a good job?"

Stu said, "I mean that you did an okay job, but as you guys get used to the job, you should empty the garbage cans when they get full, and fill the napkin holders when they're empty, and all that other stuff without being told by me. Okay, you get that, right?"

I nodded my head, and said, "Yeah."

The other bus boy did the same. Stu said, "Good, I'll see you both tomorrow at 11 AM, okay?"

I said, "Yeah, okay, Stu."

The other bus boy said, "I'm not, I don't like this job."

Stu said, "Okay, give me your time card, and I'll send your check in the mail." The bus boy walked over to the time clock, grabbed the card, and gave it to Stu.

As we both walked out of the break room, Stu said, "I'll see you tomorrow, Rich."

I said, "Okay."

As the other bus boy and I walked over the pedestrian bridge to the southbound side of the Thruway, the bus boy pulled his shirttails out of his pants, and threw his black bow tie in the garbage can. He said, "Hey, I can't believe you're coming back to this hell hole tomorrow."

I said, "I need the money, man."

He said, "I don't need the money that badly, they're a bunch of slave drivers."

I said, "This job is a cake walk, compared to delivering newspapers seven days a week."

He said, "Delivering newspapers is for suckers, man."

I said," Yeah, the Hot Shoppes is paying double what I used to make."

As we walked into the parking lot, he said, "My parents made me take this job, wait until I tell them I quit, they're going to shit a brick."

I saw my mom's car waiting in the employee's parking lot.

I said, to the bus boy, "See Ya."

I got into the car, and mom said, "How was it?"

I pulled off my bow tie and unbuttoned my shirt, and said, "It was hot."

As I turned up the A/C dial to full blast, mom said, "Do you like it?"

I looked at her, and said, "It's okay, but they worked me hard."

As we drove, I explained what I did as a bus boy, and left out the part about the fight that broke out in the snack bar. I left the brawl part out because, if she knew about it, I was afraid that she would make me quit. When I got home, I looked at myself in the mirror. I realized that I had sunburn on my arms and face. In addition, there was a white band around my forehead where I had worn the paper hat. I smelled like a mixture of garbage and body odor. So I soaked in the tub for about half an hour to get the stench off me.

On Sunday, the following day, I started to get a handle on what my job responsibilities were, and because they hadn't replaced my bus boy partner, I was doing the job for two people. Occasionally, Stu would come out and help me keep up. But he knew what I was up against, being down one bus boy. At the end of the day, Stu said that I had started to get the hang of the job, and by next weekend, he would have another bus boy partner for me to work with.

When my school summer vacation began, I worked for the Hot Shoppes snack bar full time. My parents had given me the okay to hitchhike back and forth to work sometimes, because it was burdensome to drive me five days a week. They did drive me back and forth on the weekends, at least.

We worked hard all summer in that un-air conditioned snack bar, and we were not only coworkers, we also became friends. Yeah, we did work hard, but after we locked the doors for the night, and began to clean up, we joked around, and engaged in some horseplay.

At the end of the summer, on Monday of the Labor Day weekend, the snack bar crew pooled our money together and threw a little party after work. We had some cake and soda, sat around, and talked about our plans for the future. It was somewhat sad, in a way, because after this summer, most of us would never see each other again, even though we became friends. I personally made better friends that summer than I had ever made at school. Those old friends from the snack bar that summer, it would turn out that our paths would never cross again.

Once the snack bar closed for the summer, the Hot Shoppes hired me as a bus boy for the cafeteria on the weekends during the following school year.

Chapter 13 - Junior High

When I started junior high school in the Fall of 1970, the bus stop was in front of the police station/town Hall. We used to wait across the street in front of Frank's Meat Market, and wait for the bus to arrive. Frank was a nice Italian butcher that moved from Brooklyn with his wife, Dolly, and their two sons. They bought the market building and lived up stairs. Frank's Meat Market was a neighborhood convenience store with a butcher shop in the back. All the neighborhood kids waiting for the school bus in front of the Meat Market was a good thing and a bad thing for Frank. The good thing was that in the morning almost all the kids would buy something from him, which was good for business. The bad thing was that sometimes having many kids hanging around your store is not always good for attracting adult business. Sometimes he would have to disburse a crowd of kids from his doorway, to make sure adults could come and go from his store without navigating around a bunch of kids. However, most of the kids knew that Frank was a good person, and he liked kids. In fact, sometimes he would have some of the kids work for him around the store. He would even ask some of the larger kids to disburse the crowd at times. In the wintertime, it would be very cold out, and he would let the kids stay inside the store until the bus came, but they would have to yield to any adult customers. This would be a small price to pay, to stay warm until the bus came.

There was also an unwritten rule in my neighborhood that you do not steal from anyone, especially from the local businesses. I was raised to believe that a thief was the lowest scum sucker on the planet, and anyone caught stealing in my family would be severely punished. The other families in the neighborhood seemed to embrace the same view on stealing. The kids in my neighborhood would be enforcers of the Golden rule, to the point of kicking your ass for thievery, or dropping a dime on you.

Local businesses supported the neighborhood and their children, and looked out for their welfare. There would be, on a number of occasions, where local business owners had informed my parents about what we were doing in town, those eyes were always watching. Sometimes I would ask my parents how they found out about things that I thought would never be revealed without an informant, and their response would be, "I have eyes EVERYWHERE!" I thought that answer was somewhat creepy.

When I started junior high school, I had made some defensive choices about how people would treat me in the future. As I had mentioned before, in regards to my reading and writing disability, I had decided to refuse any public outing of my stupidity in a classroom setting. Refusing the teacher's request to read aloud or write on the black board in front of the class, had given me the reputation of being an uncooperative juvenile delinquent. Which in turn landed me in the vice principal's office and detention more than a few times.

In addition, I had made a conscious decision to change the name that everyone called me by, to a short version of my first name. The reason was that being named Dick in the late 1960s and 1970s, brought about too many wise cracks, which would lead to fist fights, and some that I had lost. Leaving me feeling like a victim of the name I was given, in which I had no control over. Having fights over the name everyone calls you, and winning these fights would be a victory. But losing some of those fights over the name everyone refers to you by was twice as painful mentally. I was not a sissy kid, and I was not a tough or bully type of kid either. I would be a regular middle of the road type of kid, I would not be one to back down from a fight, but I would never go looking for a fight either. After having too many fights over my name, Dick, it seemed to me that I was always asking for a fight.

Therefore, I decided to change my name one-step at a time. Every time that I had an opportunity to be introduced

176

into a new environment, and meet new people, I would have people call me Rich or Richard. When I started to work at the Hot Shoppes Snack Bar, no one knew me from school, and it was a perfect place to start my new identity. The first day that I started junior high school, I was insistent that everyone call me Rich. Changing my name with people that knew me had proven more difficult. First, I had to convince my siblings to call me Rich, which was a challenge. Any time that I was in the company of Ike or Gina, they would slip and call me Dick. Gina really complied quickly, because she knew how important it was to me, even though she slipped from time to time. Ike, on the other hand, was slow to learn, and would slip, then correct himself. Ike and I would be standing around with other people, and he would slip like this: Ike would say, "Hey, did you see what Dick was...... Ah, I mean Rich was doing?" Then I would look at him, as if he needed a slap up side his head. Then the other people standing around would be looking at one another, and realizing that I was Dick, and that we were both hiding it as if the name was a family secret. Then I would feel awkward, and act as if my brother had brain damage. Sometimes Ike would call me Dick in front of people intentionally, just to piss me off. This would lead to me kicking Ike's ass, but it never did any good.

My parents never complied with my name change request, although I did ask several times. My father, Big Dick, refused because I was named after him, and he felt that if I ran into anyone that didn't like the name, that I should just beat the shit out of them. My mother had a little more sympathy for me. She told me to reason with the assholes for making a mockery of my name. I thought to myself," How would that script be written?" I guess it would go like this: a pinhead would say, "Hey, Dick Kraemer, you fuck 'n penis head, how's it hanging?"

I would respond by saying," Hey, I really don't appreciate you calling me a penis head. That makes me sad and hurts my feelings. Do you know that the most respected Dick in the country is the President of the United States, Richard Milhous Nixon?" Then I would envision getting my ass kicked all the way down the street. Reasoning with people that make a mockery of my name, was not on my to-do list. My family rule was, if anyone would honor it, was to call me Dick at home, and call me Rich outside the home.

The first day in junior high school, I had met some kids that knew me. When they would say my name, Dick, I would say, "From here on, I would like to be called Rich, okay?" The results where mixed at first, some would laugh, or would be surprised, or asked if they could call me Pecker Head instead. But as I became more insistent and stuck to my resolve, my new name began to stick. Of course, there were some non-compliant assholes, and I knew that I would have to deal with that, but it was well worth the price.

The last fight over my name transformation, I'll never forget, it was with a friend, Pat M, we were friends for about a year, but over the summer, our interests differed, and we went our separate ways. When we went back to school, he had an ax to grind over our past friendship. Therefore, when he found out that I was insistent about people calling me Rich, he made it a point to start fucking with me about it. I really didn't want to fight this guy, because he could take me, but I could not let this ridicule go on. So we set a time after school, and the place, Memorial Park, to duke it out, a lot of people knew about it, and there would be plenty of spectators. One thing that I was not looking forward to was a public beating, but if I didn't show up, the bullshit would never stop. In fact, if I backed down from this asshole that everybody hated, the crowd would never let me live it down. Then I would be just a stupid Dick.

Pat M. was a wise ass, and most of the kids hated him, he was a controlling, over indulged, big mouth bully. I didn't want to be friends with him anymore, because of those innermost personality traits. So this was a showdown of ex-friends, and the burying of a friendship.

I arrived at the Memorial Park with kids from my neighborhood trailing behind me. There must have been at least 25 kids in the park, which was a great turnout for a hamlet of this size. I was surprised that there were so many kids that showed up, and wondered if they were going to start selling tickets. Pat M., standing in the middle of the small park, began to warm up, sparring with himself, and throwing a few jabs and uppercuts in the air. As I walked into the park, Pat M. started to show boat his performance, by bobbing and weaving, like a professional fighter.

Pat M. said, "Okay, Kraemer, you Dick, ready for your ass whooping?"

I looked at him, and put my left foot in front of me, turning my body slightly to the right, and extended my left hand and motioned my fingers toward myself. I said, "Come and get it, you fagot." Pat M. charged into me, as he came, I punched him in the right side of his head, and then the left side of his head. Then he punched me in the left side in the lower rib cage, and then followed up hitting me on the right side of my mouth. He hit me so hard that I fell on my back. Pat M. then sat on my chest and began to punch me in the face with a flurry of left and right punches. As he sat on my chest, he knelt on my right arm pinning it to the ground, and I had only the use of one arm to defend myself. As I laid there, which seemed to be forever, trying to defend myself, Pat M. used my head as a speed bag, my life started to flash before my eyes. Suddenly, it stopped. I looked up, and Pat M. is still sitting on my chest, but his arms are waving in the air, and there was someone throwing a series of punches to his head. Then the person jumped over my head, and then landed a good shot to Pat M's right side of his head. Then he jumped off my chest. When he got up, I got up quickly.

I heard my brother Ike say, "You leave my brother alone, Douche Bag!"

Then Pat M. started to run towards Ike. My brother was too quick for him and ran about 50 feet, and stopped, standing on top of a stonewall. Because Pat M knew that he could not catch my brother, he turned and walked towards me.

Pat M. yelled, "What's the matter, Dickie, you need your little brother to fight for you?"

I said, "Fuck that, let's go again, you pussy."

The crowd was rooting for me, and begging me to continue. Pat M. looked around him and knew that the crowd wanted to see him get his ass kicked. I could see that his face was beet red, his left ear was bleeding, and he was gasping for air. He turned his head and looked at my brother, and Ike responded by flipping him the bird.

Ike yelled, "Fuck you, Moron!"

Pat lunged towards Ike about 2 feet, and Ike jumped off the stonewall, ready to run. My brother was two years younger and much smaller than I was. Ike knew that Pat M. would make short work of him.

Then, Pat M. turned to me and walked up to me. He yelled, "Had enough, Kraemer?"

I leaned forward, and yelled," No, come on," as I raised my fists.

Pat M. took a step back, and yelled," You're not worth it."

Then he turned and walked out of the park, as the crowd jeered him. My head was hurting and my mouth was bleeding, I pulled my glasses out and put them on. The crowd yelled for me to continue fighting and go after Pat M., but I let him go. I was embarrassed, because I clearly got my clock cleaned, and my little brother jumped in to stop it. In addition, I had lost my courage to continue fighting. I walked home with my brother and some of our friends.

I said to Ike, "You shouldn't have jumped in, man."

Ike stopped, turned to me, and said, "Okay, next time, I'll let you get your brains beat in."

I didn't say anything, and continued to walk. I knew he was right, if my brother had not stepped in, I would be in worse shape than I am now.

Ike, then stood in front of me, and said, "How about a fucking thank you, asshole?"

I looked at him, and said, "Thank you."

I reached my house and sat on the front porch steps. Ike went inside, got a wet washcloth with some ice in it, and gave it to me. My lip was cut, and had begun to swell. I placed the washcloth on my mouth.

Ike said, "You should have seen that fucker's face, when I did that rat a tat on his head."

I laughed, and said, "Yeah, he looked surprised, you're lucky he didn't catch you."

Ike said, "Fuck him."

I said, looking him in the eyes, "He might come after you, Ike."

He said, "Let him, I'll take care of him."

I said, "No, if he comes after you, I'll fight him again. You'll tell me, right?"

Ike said, "Yeah, alright. But I want to be there. Okay?"

I stood up and looked at him, "Okay, just don't jump in.

He smiled, held his hand up, making an OK hand sign.

It was then that I realized that my little brother was surely willing to get his ass kicked, for the sake of his older brother. The kid that I lived with all my life, and had fought with since we were in diapers, had put his ass on the line for me. In the back of my mind, I knew that he would stand up for me, as I did for him, but this brawl rather sealed it for me. From this day forward, I had newfound respect for Ike, and there was a new sense of brotherly bonding. We also did not fight with each other as much as we did in the past.

The next day, the swelling of my lip went down to normal, all I had was a little cut on my lip and a small scrape on my forehead. I went to school that day, and I passed Pat M. in the hallway between classes. As he approached in the opposite direction, I noticed that he had sunglasses on. He looked at me, and said, "Fuck you, Kraemer," as he passed by. A teacher stopped him in the hallway, and told him to take off the sunglasses. I turned around, and looked down the hallway at Pat M., as he took off the shades. Pat M. had a huge black eye and it was partly closed, due to swelling. As I looked at him, he turned and looked at me. Then the teacher told him to get to class.

This one junior high school was composed of several small towns, villages, and hamlets in the Woodbury school district. Therefore, when the word got out with 25+ kids spreading the word that Pat M a high profile blowhard, had a black closed eye, due to a fight about him calling me Dick, everybody knew it. Pat M. would tell people that he kicked my ass, and was japped by my brother, who gave him the black eye. His story, for the most part, did not bode well for his image, looking like a Cyclops, seeing that I had a small cut on my lip and forehead, and Ike was much smaller than he was, and two years younger. When people asked us who gave Pat M. the black eye, I would claim I did it, and Ike would claim he did it.

Ike and I would debate for years about who gave Pat M. that shiner, that argument was never settled. But, whoever did it, I benefited greatly from that trophy that lasted for about two weeks on the face of a high profile asshole like Pat M.

After that fight, my new name, Rich, stuck, and everybody knew that I was willing to fight for it. My brother really didn't realize how much he helped me acquire my new name, and was only looking after his big brother.

As for Pat M, after all the ribbing he got about this fight, he chose to be more willing to forget about it, and leave the past behind him, rather than vindicate himself by fighting me again, or going after my little brother. I think he thought that if he did try to vindicate himself, it could make him look like more of a fool than he already was.

This would be my first year at the Monroe Woodbury Junior High School. I was looking forward to going to school that fall because for me elementary school sucked and I thought Junior High School had to be better. I thought maybe I could make some new friends, have new experiences and do some cool things. I thought that maybe I could get a girl friend, and that would be nice.

My first week was a little chaotic, because all the students had to change classes or go somewhere eight times a day, by the prompting of a deafening school bell in the hallway. This was a real challenge for me because of my Dyslexia, I have short-term memory loss, and I am also audio sensitive to loud noises. So when the bells would go off, my brain would freeze. Once the bells stopped, I would forget what and where my next class would be. At this point, I would have to put down all my books on the hallway floor, look at my class schedule and the map of school, while hundreds of students passed by me through the hallway. Because this brain disorder is hypersensitive to multiple stimuli, i.e. people pushing, shoving, yelling, and talking loudly, I would find it hard to concentrate and focus on the task at hand. Then as the crowd of kids would thin out, and go to their classrooms, I would then get my bearings and rush to my next class before the bell would ring for the second time, to signal the beginning of class. Most of the time, I was late for class, which made me look stupid or like I didn't care, to the teacher. I finally had memorized the schedule after about two weeks, but the damage was already done.

Because Dyslexia is a learning disability even though I didn't know it at the time, where it impedes a person's ability to read and write, I had decided to hide it. I did this because it was very embarrassing in elementary school to read aloud or write on the board. When I did, most teachers and students would ridicule me, and make me feel stupid in front of everyone. So in Junior High School, I wanted to turn over a new leaf, and was determined not to be made fun of anymore. The most effective defensive measure was simply refuse the teachers request to read aloud or write on the board. This landed me in the vice principal's office more than a few times, where he became more familiar with my name, not a good thing. This would start the troublemaker and bad boy image in school and follow me for years. I started to make new acquaintances in school, and they were called the Bad Company. The Bad Company I was keeping in those early years were mostly not friends, and not enemies, but kids that carried the bad boy image. If we met together, it was only by circumstance, like smoking in the boy's room.

This brings me to one of my earliest memories of being in trouble with the vice principal in junior high school. It was during our lunch period around 12:45 PM and I had just finished lunch, and I was waiting for my next class to begin. I decided that I would smoke a cigarette in the boy's bathroom and take a leak. The most preferred boy's room would be the farthest from the lunchroom where most of the activity and the teachers would be. Once I reached the boys bathroom, I could see that the door was open about 6 inches and a pair of eyes had been staring back at me. This would be the lookout assigned to the bathroom, and he would open the door for me. Once inside the bathroom, the air was filled with cigarette smoke, and filled with about eight boys. There were the usual suspects, Danny D, Odell C, Billy R, Larry S, and a few other regulars. They would be hanging out in the back of the bathroom, at the last toilet stall. One guy would take a drag of the cigarette and pass it to the next boy. This smoking process would be pretty similar to smoking a joint, take a toke and pass it along. As the cigarette would burn down with all the little juveniles toking on the same smoke, the red hot ash could get at least an inch long. Then they would lightly hit the cigarette on the stall wall. The lookout would be at the door in the front part of bathroom, the smoking was done in the back part of it. If a male teacher or the vice principal were walking down the hallway towards the bathroom, the lookout would yell a warning and close the door. Then anyone would ditch the cigarette and assume an innocent position, I. E. belly up to the urinal, close themselves inside the stall, wash their hands, or walkout. The penalty for smoking in the bathroom was three days suspension, and, talking to others in the crew, it would be followed up with a good beating from their parents, including myself. So the stakes were high for being caught. So the Bad Company security had to be tight.

On this day, I walked to the back of the bathroom and waited for my turn to take a drag of the cigarette. When I got a couple of tokes, I started to bullshit with Billy R who was a good friend of mine. As we spoke, Danny D and Odell C had been by the sinks and trying to yank a 12 foot mirror off the wall. Billy R and Larry S thought that it would be a great idea to rip the mirror off the wall and joined the party. I looked at my watch and saw that at any minute the bell was going to sound to begin the next period. So, I walked up to the urinal, pulled out Mr. Happy, and began to take a piss. Looking over my shoulder, I could see that the Wrecking Crew was making progress and then I turned my eyes back to the wall in front of me. Suddenly, I heard a great crash behind me, and I turned around to see everyone running out of the bathroom over the glass-covered floor. Then the bell sounded for the next period. I could not move from the urinal, because I was in midstream and was stuck there. The bathroom door opened, and I turned to see who it was. The vice principal walked in and looked in amazement at the broken mirror all over the sinks and the floor. It would figure that he would be the first at the scene because his office is about 30 feet away. He was a big man about 6 feet tall in his early 40s with a crew cut his name was Mr. Stoddard. He said, with a stern voice, "What happened in here? I looked at him with my Little German in my hand, and shaking it off, I turned back to the wall and said, "I don't know." Then I zipped my pants and turned around.

He said, "Okay, Mr. Kraemer, go to the administration office and wait for me." Then he held the door for me. I walked out into the busy hallway with a lot of kids looking at me. An overweight woman teacher, Mrs. Tubby, ran up to Mr. Stoddard.

Mrs. Tubby said, waving a chocolate donut in her hand, "Ed, after I heard the crash, I saw about five boys run out of the bathroom," then she took a bite from her doughnut and pointed it down the hallway. Then she said with a full mouth, "That way."

Mr. Stoddard said, tapping me on the shoulder, "To the office." I walked through the crowded hallway to the administration office, and sat down on one of the chairs. As I sat their waiting for the vice principal to arrive, I thought that he might work me over with a rubber hose. Because he appeared like, he could do it. In addition, I know my parents would have approved.

My mom once said to my third grade teacher, in my presence, "If he gets out of line, you have my permission to knock the day lights out of him." The teacher never did, but she did have that option.

Then, as I was waiting, thinking of my fate, I heard a knocking sound on the hallway plate glass window behind me. I turned around in my seat to see the whole Bad Company crew looking back at me as though I was a caged animal at a zoo. They knocked on the window smiling, and making faces at me as though I was in big trouble. Danny D put his finger to his lips and then he slammed his fist into the palm of his hand. Danny D was the biggest troublemaker, but the smallest one of the bunch; he would also be the leader of the gang. I figured that if I fought Danny, then I would have to fight the rest of them, not a good thing. I took Danny's hand jesters to mean, if I rat, I'll get my ass kicked. Now getting into a fight with a kid that small is not a problem, taking on some of the rest would be. The warning pissed me off, because I don't rat, and that has never been the way I roll, even to this day. I stood up and turned around, then looked back at him, as if to say, "Go fuck yourself". Then they spotted someone coming down the hallway and took off.

I sat back down on the chair.

Mr. Stoddard walked through the door, and said, "Friends of yours?"

I looked up at him, and said, "No!"

He said," Come into my office." as he stood in front of me pointing in that direction. I walked into his office; he followed and closed the door behind himself. He said, "Sit down, Mr. Kraemer." I sat down in one of the chairs in front of his desk.

Then he walked in front of the desk, leaned on the edge of it, and looked down at me. He said, "So, what happened to the mirror in the bathroom?"

Looking up at him, I said, "I don't know, I was going to the bathroom and it broke."
Mr. Stoddard then put his fist to his mouth and stared at me for a moment. Then he rested his hand on the desk and leaned over me.

He said, "Did you ever hear the song, "The Games People Play?"

I looked at him, and said, "Yeah."

He said, "Do you know the words?"
I was thinking about it for a moment. Then I thought I hope this guy doesn't think I'm going to recite the lyrics of the song to him.

Looking confused, I said, "I know some of the words."

He straightened his back, still leaning on the desk with both hands on it. Mr. Stoddard said, "I'm talking about you and me, and the games people play."

I looked at him, and thought, "Yeah, but do you know the rest of the song?"

He said, "Mr. Kraemer, I think you're playing a game with me."
I slid back in the chair as Mr. Stoddard leaned over me again.

I said, nervously, "Okay, some kids ripped the mirror off the wall. But I didn't do it, I was taking a piss."

Then he smiled, and said, "Good, now we're getting somewhere. Who are they?"

I looked down at his brown penny loafers and green Argyle socks.

I said, "I don't know, I was facing the urinal wall."

Mr. Stoddard then stood up, walked around to the back of his desk, and looked out the window with his hands on his hips.

He said, "Richard, I don't think you're telling me the truth!"

I said, "Mr. Stoddard, I really don't know who they are."

Then he turned to me, put both hands on the desk, and leaned forward.

He said, "How about the boys in the hallway, you know them, right?"

I said, looking innocent, "Yeah, I know them, but they didn't do it!"

He smiled, and said, "How do you know? You were facing the urinal wall."

I just looked back at him, knowing that he knew I wasn't going to drop the dime on the Bad Company. He knew it was the Bad Company, but he needed a witness because Mrs. Tubby could not positively identify the boys running away from the scene of the crime.

Mr. Stoddard folded his arms, and said, "The Games People Play."

Then he wrote on a pad on his desk for a few moments, and ripped a page from it.

Then he walked over to the door, and opened it, and said, "Agnes, come here a moment."

The secretary, Agnes, came to the door, and said, "Yes."

He handed her the piece of paper, and said, "Here is a list of boys I want pulled out of class, and have them wait in the administrative office."

Then Mr. Stoddard turned to me, and said, "Okay, I'll play the game. Wait here."

He walked out of his office and closed the door.

I thought that the vice principal was up to something, but I just couldn't figure out how he was going to play the game. About 10 minutes went by, the door opened.

Mr. Stoddard said, "Richard, come here a moment."

I got up, turned around, walked to the doorway, and stopped. Suddenly, I realized that the whole Bad Company gang was staring back at me, about 3 feet from the door. A few moments went by in silence.

Then Mr. Stoddard pushed me back inside his office, and said, "Okay, have a seat." Then he closed the door, leaving me alone again. I thought that I was really fucked now. The Bad Company is going to think I finked on them and I'm going to be beaten to a pulp. I stood there amazed at how Mr. Stoddard had turned the tables on me. The vice principal walked into the office and closed the door. He walked behind his desk with a folder in his hand.

He said, "Were they the boys that broke the mirror?"

I looked at him for a moment, and he looked back at me as if he had me in a checkmate.

I said, "Nope," looking back at him defiantly.

He looked at me sternly, and said, "Okay, we play on." Then he opened the folder, and said, "I have your folder here, I'm putting down that you were involved in this incident, and if I see you in my office again for anything, you'll be suspended. You got that, Mr. Kraemer?"

I said, "Yes," looking down at the folder, trying to see if there was anything else in it.

Mr. Stoddard said, as he wrote, "Good now get out of here. I'm done playing games."

I turned, walked to the door, and opened it.

He said, "Oh, one more thing," I turned and looked at him. He said, with a smiling face, "Those boys are not your friends!"

I said, "I told you that already." Then I walked out and closed the door behind me.

As I walked down the hallway to my next class, I thought that the vice principal really fucked me. He fixed it so even though I didn't rat on these guys; they're going to think I did. I needed to face these guys as a gang, as soon as possible. Telling my story to one guy in the gang would not do, it would have to be all of them together, so they could think as a group.

It wasn't until the next day, at lunchtime, that I spotted them sitting on the grass on a hot fall day, behind the school. As I walked up on them from behind, one of them yelled, "There's Kraemer!"

Then they all got up together, and Danny D ran up to me about 10 feet and shoved me. Danny D yelled, "You fuck 'n ratted on us!"

I put my hands in front of me, and said, "I didn't rat on you guys," backing up as the gang surrounded me.

Danny D, with both hands open palmed, pushed me in the chest again, and said, "How did they get our names?" I fell backwards against one of the members, who then pushed me forward.

I said, "I don't know. All I know is that I took the rap." Danny D then went lunging at me again, and Odell C and Billy R held him back by his arms.

Odell C said, "Danny, he took the rap. We didn't get in trouble, did we?"

Danny said, "Ya, not yet!"

Then he shook their hands off, put his finger in my face, and said, "If you do fuck 'n rat, I'll fuck you up."

Odell leaned down to Danny D, and said, "Wait and see." Then Odell C looked at me, and then he looked at Danny as though he was a spoiled little brat.

I said, "I would never rat, you guys should know that." Then I turned and walked away from Bad Company, hoping no one would jump me from behind.

I knew that most of those guys would never be my friends nor did I want their friendship, especially after this incident. Leaving me there with my dick in my hand, literally, and have me take the rap. I thought what valiant souls they were. I wondered if they would ever drop a dime on me, if they had to. I think most would, and those are friends I do not need. As the school year went on, I discovered that the Bad Company was never a gang at all, but just a group of individual kids that by circumstance met in the bathroom to smoke. The gang element comes into play when they commit a crime together, and then try to escape justice by any means possible, as a group. In this case, letting me take the rap was an easy sell for them. I learned a lesson of guilty by association with this incident, and I was very careful about who my friends were, and who could be trusted.

As I mentioned before, for the most part, I was a loner. Most of the friends, at this point, were really friends of my brother, and all were at least two years younger than I was. In junior high school, I had no previous friends going to the same school. So, even though I was a loner, I always longed for a good friendship. Just a note of reference; a dyslexic person's personality traits are to isolate themselves so that they would not be discovered as a moron. Even to this day, I find great comfort with being alone. But the human social need is always there, and needs to be satisfied.

Soon after the Sing-A-Long with Mr. Stoddard, and confronting the not so Bad Company, I met up with Billy R, and he turned out to be a good friend. We did many things together, like hang out at the Bowl-A-Fun bowling alley, raid our parent's liquor cabinet a few times, and hitchhike everywhere. We had to hitchhike to meet each other because he lived about 10 miles from me on the far side of Monroe. The junior high school was about the mid point as far as mileage between of where he lived and I lived. My mother would occasionally drive me, 1 out of 10 times, but for the most part, the transportation resource was my thumb. There was no public transportation between towns. Sometimes we could get on each other's school bus after school, if the bus driver didn't catch us and throw us off. My parents were not crazy about the idea of me hitchhiking, and there were no other alternatives, but for them to drive me. So, it was more convenient for them, and easier for my mobility. In the late 60s and 70s, in this rural area, it was fairly safe for teenagers to hitchhike.

As for Billy R, he has a brother a year younger then he, his name was Danny R. Their parents were getting divorced, they lived with their mother and their father was in the Air Force, stationed somewhere in the Midwest. His mom worked full time, and that gave him a lot of freedom to do what ever he wanted.

Billy R and I looked alike. We both had blond hair, wore glasses, and were about the same size. His hair was much longer then mine and he wore hipper clothes than I did. There was no mistaking him for me, or vice versa. We would mostly meet after school in Monroe, because Highland Mills really did not have much to do there. The Bowl-A-Fun was in the center of Monroe, we used to meet there, bowl a couple of games, and hang out. Sometimes we would not have any money, and we would hang around a while until someone would throw us out for not bringing in any business. Then we would go through Mill Pond Park, and chase the geese as we made our way to the other side of the village. There used to be a head shop, above a bar next to the railroad tracks, called the Collage. This store was much more than a head shop; it had posters, imported rugs from India, pot pouches, Army shirts, suede fringe jackets, bongs, and other Hippy stuff. This place was one stop shopping for the cultural changelings of the day. You could walk into this place as a straight-laced red-blooded American, and walkout as an Anti-Government Radical Doper Hippy type in one shopping trip. We could spend as much time there as we wanted, and no one would hassle us. We would buy some stuff there, but it was expensive.

The owners were Anti-Government Radical Doper Hippy types, but most of all, Capitalist Marketers. The bar below the Collage was a blue-collar hangout for the working class. Sometimes in the summer, they would leave the front door open, some of the guys in the bar used to get drunk, and yell at some of the adult hippies that used to walk by. However, the owner of the bar was also the owner of the building. He would throw the drunken troublemakers out, because the owner wanted to keep on
receiving the rent payment from the Collage. Next to the bar, there used to be an entrance stairway to a series of underground tunnels, similar to a subway passageway. The steep concrete stairway would lead under the railroad tracks, which were at ground level. This would allow pedestrians to walk under the railroad tracks to access the street on the other side, without physically walking over the tracks. Occasionally, we used to get a bottle of wine and drink, down in the tunnels.

There was not that much we did together other than hitchhike together from town to town, hangout, smoke cigarettes, and talk. We really did not get in trouble. We were constantly in motion, always going some place, searching for something to do. I guess the most important part for the both of us was our friendship, and someone to talk to.

The most memorable event that I could remember was when I was invited to my first coming of age teenage party, i.e. a chance at love, and alcohol. A heavyset girl, Donna L, was going to have a birthday party; Billy R and I were invited. I was excited to be invited because I liked Donna L, and was most interested in the little lumps on her chest, breasts. I wanted to make a great first impression, so I wanted to dress to impress. I wanted to buy a new pair of pants before the party. Therefore, I hitchhiked to WT Grants it Monroe, and bought my first pair of party pants. The pants were white bellbottoms with a multi colored Paisley trim that ran from the hip of the outer seem all the way down the side of the pants. In addition, the pants came with a matching multi colored Paisley sash. I also purchased a brown short sleeve Nehru shirt that I would tuck into my pants, so I could show off my sash. The party was on a Friday night, and I convinced my mother to drive me because it was at night, and I was not allowed to hitchhike after dark. Before I left, my parents got their first look at my new duds. My father thought that I looked like a cross between an India/Mariachi band player, and then I should complete the outfit with a pair of maracas or a sitar. My mom thought I looked "mod", and that I looked good. However, both said I could wear this outfit to the party, but not to school. In those days, my parents thought that if I dressed like a hippy, it would promote illegal drug use. So about 7:00 PM, my mom dropped me off at an auto repair garage on 17 M in Harriman, where Donna's parents had a trailer in the back. I walked down the steep driveway, where I met Billy R, and a bunch of other kids hanging outside the trailer. They had some China lanterns and balloons strung over the deck. The record player was playing some music; there was a cake, and a pitcher of Kool Aid on a table. I looked around and noticed that there were a lot of guys at the party, and about three girls. I looked at Billy R, and said, "Where's all the chicks?"

He said, "I think they must be inside the trailer."

I said, "Well, let's go!"

I wanted to find Donna, the birthday girl. We walked up to the door, and knocked, and Donna answered it. She looked nice with a cheesecloth peek-a-boo blouse and blue jeans.

She said, "Hi, Rich, nobody is allowed inside, I'll see you later." Then she closed the door.

I looked at Billy, and said, "There's no chicks in there, just Donna." He looked at me and shrugged his shoulders. He knew that I was interested in Donna. He also knew that having all these guys around was not good for me. We walked over to the table, poured some Kool Aid in a Dixie cup, and tasted it, hoping it was spiked.

Billy drank some of it, and said, "Kool Aid!"

I said, "Who is bringing the wine?"

He said, "Jamie T, and maybe Larry S."

I looked around, and said, "Hey, there's Jamie!" We made our way through a bunch of guys smoking cigarettes, and Billy tapped Jamie T.

He turned, and said, "Hey, Billy!" Then they did the bro handshake by grasping each other's thumbs.

Billy said, "Hey, man, did you get any wine?"

Jamie shook his head, and said, "No, man, my mom was home, and I couldn't cop a bottle."

Billy said, "Did Larry get any?"

Jamie said, "Nope, his brother stole his bottle."

Billy looked at me, and said, "Bummer."

I looked at him, and said, "No booze, and hardly any chicks."

He said, "Yeah, this is totally fucked up!"

So Billy and I mingled together in the crowd, smoking cigarettes, drinking Kool Aid, and bull shitting with the rest of the guys. Donna L came outside and started talking with all the other guys throughout the night. I finally got a few moments to talk to her, but she kind of blew me off in about 2 minutes, and continued to work the crowd of boys. My mom arrived about 9:30 PM, and I felt it was a long wait. I was totally crushed that this girl had no interest in me whatsoever. She did appear to have many boys to choose from. Donna L did express interest in Billy R, but she was not Billy's type. The only reason I was invited was that Billy R was my friend.

This would be my first brush with female rejection, but would certainly not be my last. After about two days, I had gotten over my first female rejection, and looked forward to many more rejections, determined to find a girl that truly liked or loved me for who I am.

Walter "Ike" J. Kraemer

Pat & Pam kissing the neighbor's kid, Gina plays match maker.

Chapter 14 - The Babysitter

During my junior high school years, my parents had felt comfortable with me watching over the flock of Kraemers, and had entrusted me with the high honor of babysitting. They started me off small at first, when I would have to look after the little knuckleheads when mom would go food shopping. When my mother found the children still alive after her shopping trips, I would graduate to my next level of responsibility. I took my given responsibilities very seriously; I truly wanted my parents trust and respect as the eldest son. I had full authority over the children when my parents were away, Gina complied, and Ike complained about equal rights.

One time, my parents needed to go to a wedding, and would be away for several hours. Mom left me a whole list of things to do, then she told Ike and Gina to listen to me, and that I was in charge. The first hour went smoothly; Gina was assigned to amuse Pat and Pam, in which she did gladly. Ike was assigned to clean the downstairs bathroom, while I cleaned the upstairs bathroom. Then, we had lunch, and fed the babies. I had instructed Ike to clean the lunch dishes. In response, he told me to go fuck myself and flipped me the bird. I realized that I could not have dissension amongst the crew because I feared there would be a mutiny; I thought it would be wise to punish the mutineer. Therefore, I slapped him in the head a few times, to snap him out of his insubordination. In turn, he hit me with a few body blows, and then retreated to the nursery. Ike thought that this would be a safe harbor for him, because we did not want to upset the twins with violence, and start the little buggers crying. I asked my brother one more time to get in the galley and wash the dishes, as his captain ordered. The scalawag again raised his middle finger in a full bird salute, and then said that his commanding officer should have intercourse with himself again. Knowing that I needed to control this situation in front of the rest of the crew, I walked toward Ike as he started to cower behind one of the cribs in the corner of the room. I quickly picked up an official NFL football from the floor, and threw it at my brother with all my might. Suddenly, he ducked behind the crib, the football hit his shoulder, deflecting it, and sent the ball crashing into a rear bedroom window. The glass broke into a thousand pieces, falling to the bedroom floor, only about 6 inches from where Ike was squatting. Pat and Pam started crying, Gina started to panic, and wanted to call my parents, and Ike started to defer all the blame for the broken window to me. At this very moment, as a 14-year-old boy, I knew that it was my responsibility to bring this sense of chaos to an immediate halt. I first grabbed the telephone receiver from Gina's hands, and unplugged it from the main phone base. Then I talked her down from her hysteria, and asked her to help calm the babies down. As we started to get them to stop crying, Ike started to try his alibi script on me on what he was going to tell my parents. I looked at him, annoyed. I sent him out of the room, and he complied. Once we got the babies calmed down and happy again, I needed to plan my next move. I looked at the broken window, and pulled the shards of glass from the pane. I called my brother in the room, and told him to get a dustpan, broom, and trash can. We started to carefully pick up the glass, making sure nobody cut themselves. Now, the time was 1:30 PM, my parents would not be home until 6:00 PM. I went into the basement, and got a measuring tape. As I walked toward the nursery, I grabbed a pen and paper. I started to measure the length and width of the windowpane, about three or four times.

Ike asked, "What are you doing?"

I said, "Wait a minute," as I wrote down the measurements.

Then I walked into the kitchen, grabbed the phone book, and started thumbing through it. I found the closest hardware store was Smith and Strebel's in Monroe, about 7 miles one-way. I reconnected the phone receiver, and dialed the hardware store.

A man answered, "Hello?"

I said, "Hi, is this Smith and Strebel's?"

He said, "Yes."

I said, "I need to fix a broken window, do you have glass?"

He said, "Yes, we have glass and we can cut it to any size you need. What kind of window is it?"

I said, "It's an outside window, 28 3/8" by 31 1/4."

The man said, "Yes, we could cut that size."

I said, "How much will it cost, and what time are you opened until today?"

He said, "It should cost about $7.50, and we're opened until 5:00 PM."

I said, "I'll be there this afternoon, thanks," and hung up the phone.

I turned around and there was Ike, listening to every word.

Ike said, "Are you fuck 'n nuts, how are you going to get to Monroe?"

I said, "I'm going to hitchhike," as I walked into the nursery.

My brother followed behind me, and said, "You can't leave us alone!"

I turned, and said, "Listen, Gina, I'm going to Monroe to get some glass for the window. Ike is going to be in charge, and you do what he tells you."

I turned to Ike, and said, "Ike, you're big enough now to be responsible for Gina and the twins. Do not do anything stupid while I'm gone and stay in the nursery."

My brother looked shocked that I was going to leave him in charge.

Then, he said, "I'm in charge now?"

As he smiled, I could see that he liked being in charge for the first time, whatever the cost.

I said, "Yes, until I get back, do not call anyone, and stay in the nursery. Gina, you listen to Ike until I get back," she nodded her head yes, but she looked a little confused.
I then ran upstairs to my bedroom, grabbed a $20 bill out of my drawer, and put on a baseball cap and a windbreaker. I then ran downstairs, told Ike to change the babies diapers and to wash the dishes. Then, I walked out the door into the pouring rain

I walked through town to the only traffic light in the hamlet, walked about 40 feet on route 208, and stuck out my thumb to all the passing cars. The rain started to slow a bit to a drizzle and at this point, I was already drenched. I waited for about 10 min. for a ride, until a woman picked me up. She had a 61 Ford Falcon just like my mom had once. She asked where I was going and I told her that I was going into the village of Monroe. She said that she was going right down Main Street, which was perfect because that was where the hardware store was. Just as she pulled up to the hardware store, it started to rain hard again. When the woman let me out, I thanked her for the perfect ride, and ran inside the hardware store. There was a big man with glasses in his mid 50s standing behind the counter.

He said," Hi, can I help you?"

As I took off my sopping wet hat, I said, "Yes, I called before about the glass."

He smiled as he came around the counter, and said, "Well, you sounded a lot taller on the phone."

Not sure how to respond, I said, "Yes, do you have the glass ready?"

He said, "I didn't cut the glass yet, we don't take orders over the phone."

As I wiped the rain off my glasses with my wet T-shirt, I said, "Okay, could you cut it now?"

He said, with a smile, "Sure, if you got the money, I have the time."

I put my hand in my pocket, and yanked out the wet $20 bill, and said, "I got the cash!"

He said, "Then, let's get busy."

Then he went into the back room, and I could hear him whistling and banging around. Then he reappeared with a huge sheet of glass, and set it on the table in the back of the store.

The man said, "So, son, where do you live?"

I said, "Highland Mills."

He said, "Did your mom or dad take you here?"

I started to shuffle my feet nervously, and said, "No, I hitchhiked."

He said, "As wet as you are, I thought you swam here," as he clamped down the glass to the table.

Then the man said, "What were those measurements again?"

I took the wet piece of paper out of my pocket, and read, "28 3/8 by 31 1/4."

As he looked over his glasses, he leaned over the table with a straight face. He said, "Are you sure, because there are no refunds on cut glass?"

I said, "Yeah, I measured the inside of the bedroom window, the length and width, I measured it about four times."

Then the man stood straight up, and said, "Sounds like you measured it right."

He put his hand to his mouth, looked to the ceiling, and said, "Broken bedroom window, ah?"

The man leaned over the table again, and looked over his glasses, with a smile.

He said, "Do your parents know you're here? How did the window get broken?"

I took a step forward, looked into his eyes, as he smirked.

I said, "I broke it with a football, and I need to fix it before my mom and dad get back."

He stood straight up, and began to laugh. As he continued to laugh so loud, it echoed throughout the empty store. Then he took off his glasses to wipe away his tears from his eyes, as he started to calm down. I smiled back at him, thinking to myself that I didn't find this situation quite as funny as he did, and wondering whether he might be over medicated.

Then the man said, "Okay, I'll help you, have you ever fixed a window before?"

I said, "Nope," shaking my head.

As he put on his glasses, and picked up the measurements, he said, "Okay, first we have to cut the glass." He picked up a metal yardstick, and placed it on the glass. Then he notched it with a glass-cutting tool in several places, and put oil along the marks he made. He then clamped the metal yardstick to the table and ran the glasscutter along the length of the glass twice. Then he lightly tapped the edges of the glass, as he held the outer part of the glass and the remains snapped off cleanly into his hands. He repeated the same process for the width. He grabbed some newspaper, and wrapped and taped the glass.

The man turned to me, and said, "You're going to need window putty and window pins."

I nodded my head in agreement and followed him in the store. He grabbed the putty and pins from the shelf, and said, "Do you have a small hammer, and putty knife?"

I said, "I have a small hammer, but I haven't got a putty knife."

The man said, "Okay, first you have to place the window in the frame, and make sure all the old glass, putty, and paint is out of it. You could run an old butter knife along the frame to do that. Then you place the glass into the window frame from the outside. Do ya got that so far?"

I nodded my head, and said, "Yep."

He said, "Good, now the glass is in place, you're going to press the window in place with your left elbow, and with your left hand you take a pin and place it in between the window and the glass. Then tap the pin in to each corner, but be careful not to hit it too hard because you could break the glass. You got that?"

I said, "Ah ha."

He went on, and said, "Good, once you hammer one pin in each corner, then start from the center and hammer a pin in the pane every 2 inches all the way around. Then take the putty and run about a quarter inch bead along all sides of the window. Then I use a butter knife to smooth out the edges. To finish it up, you could take a wet rag, and with one finger, run it lightly over the putty, to make it look professional. You got any questions?"

I said, "It seems a little tricky holding the glass in place, holding the nail, and hammering."

He said, "Yeah, do you have someone to hold the glass in place?"

My eyes opened wide, and I said, "Yeah, my brother!"

He said, "Good, he could hold the glass while you hammer," as he walked toward the counter with the stuff. He added everything up, and said, "That will be $10.56 with tax."

I handed him the money, then he returned my change, put the pins and putty in the bag, and he said, "Here you go." I picked up the bag, put it in my pocket of the windbreaker, and took the wrapped glass from the counter. I said, "Thank you very much, you helped me out a lot!"

As I walked towards the door, he said, "Yeah, about that." I stopped and turned around. He continued, "You didn't tell me about your parents not knowing about the window, okay?" Then he smiled.

I smiled back, and said, "Okay."

He said, "If you do exactly what I told you, maybe they'll never know!"

I opened the door, and said, "Yeah, that would be nice, thanks a lot," as I walked onto the sidewalk into the hard pouring rain.

When I made it to the highway, and started to thumb a ride, I started to think about the concept of completely getting away with this incident, without my parents knowing. I thought, at first that would be impossible, because Ike and Gina would spill their guts as soon as they got home. The best I was shooting for was that the broken window would be fixed by the time my parents got home. Now I was thinking that it would be really cool if my parents did not even know the window was broken. I walked in the rain for about 20 minutes, and an old man stopped in a red pickup truck. I open the door and the old man said, "Where ya going, young feller?"

I said, "Highland Mills, sir."

He said," I'm going that way. What is that you got there?"

I said," Glass."

He got out of his truck, pushed his seat back forward, and said, "Put it back here."
I placed the glass behind the seat, and we both jumped into the truck and closed the doors.

The old man said, as we took off down the road, "It's raining like hell there, boy. What brings you out in this nasty weather?"

I said, "Well, I broke a window, and I wanted to fix it before my parents got home."

He said, "Break a window and make it as though it didn't happen. Too bad you couldn't do that with everything in life."

I said, as I took off my hat, " Ah ha."

The old man looked at me, and said," I thought you were my son standing in the pouring rain."
Then he turned his eyes back on the road, and began wiping the water off his face with his hand.

I looked at him, and said," You have a son my age," thinking that he was old enough to be my grandfather.

He said, "Oh, no, he must be near 25 years old by now."

At this point, I thought the old codger might have lost his marbles.

I said," Oh."

Then the old man pulled a cigarette from a pack on the dashboard, and lit it with a Zippo lighter.

He said, "My son gave me this last year," holding it between his thumb and forefinger.

The lighter had an Army insignia with corporal stripes on it.

I said," Looks nice, where is he stationed?"

He took a drag of his smoke, and looked in the rearview mirror. He put his eyes back on the road, and took another drag.

He said, "Arlington, it's beautiful there, his friends are there, too." Let's see, there's Davis, Billings, Smith, and his best friend, Taylor. There are a couple more, but I can't remember all their names right now."

I said, "Yeah, was he ever in Nam?"

He smiled, "Oh, yeah, he got a few medals, he even killed a few Viet Cong. My Timmy boy, he was a fighter."
He took a deep breath; the smile went away, and he took another drag from his cigarette.

The old man said, "But, the communist fuckers cut him up into little pieces, and sent what was left of him home in a box, along with his friends."
I was shocked at what the old man said about his son with great composure, and I was thinking, maybe I'd get out here.
The old man threw his cigarette out the window.

He said, "Arlington is a cemetery for war veterans, kid. I didn't mean to lead you on. I have friends there, too, from D-Day in WWII."
Then we approached a very narrow curve a little too fast, and as we went into the curve, the rear tires slid hitting the gravel shoulder, and the sound of rocks hitting the tin fenders had

made a scary racket.

The man shouted, "WWWWHHHHOOOOOO," then he wrestled the truck back under control.

I said, "Yeah, that's a bad curve."

He said, looking annoyed, "Thanks for telling me." He rubbed his face, as he said, "Now, where was I? Oh, yeah, WWII, that was hell on Earth, damned near killed me. What was I thinking, talking my only son into joining the Army?"

Then he looked at me, and said, "You look a lot like him, you know."

I said, nervously, "I'm sorry about your son, mister."

He let out a big sigh, "Yeah, me too, I would do anything to have my son back. I wish it could be as if it never happened, as if he never died, kind of like you fixing that window, like it didn't happen. You know?"

I said," Yeah, I see what you mean."
We approached the traffic light in Highland Mills.

I said, "You can let me off at the light."

He said, "Kid, its still pouring. How far is it to your house?"

I said, "I live right down the block, it's not far really."

He said, "I'm going to Newburgh. Can I take you any further?"

I said, "Yeah, you could drop me off in front of that store," pointing to Frank's Market.
He pulled in front of the store, we both got out, pushed the truck seat forward and I took the glass out of the truck. The old man jumped back in the truck and closed his door.

I said," Thank you very much for the ride, you helped me out a lot," as I grabbed the handle to shut the door.

The old man said, "Kid, you helped me more than I helped you, and I thank you."

I said, "Ah, okay, take care."
Then I closed the door and held my hand up, as a goodbye. As he took off, I turned and walked down my street, carrying the pane of glass by my side in the down pouring rain. While I

was walking, I thought about the old man and how he seemed to blame himself for his son's death in Vietnam. I thought that maybe I would pray for the old man, because I think his son was the only thing he had left in this world. I would have to attend to that later, because the clock was ticking and I needed to get this window fixed before my parents got home.

I got to the driveway door of my house and went inside. As I entered the kitchen, my wet sneakers slid on the linoleum floor, and I almost fell. I regained my balance, and put the glass on the kitchen table. I could hear the kids playing in the nursery. I looked at the clock; it was 3:45 PM. I quickly went into the nursery to check in on the kids. I said, "Is everything all right?" As I looked around the room and made a quick head count, I saw that all crewmembers were on deck. I thought it was amazing that they were all still alive. Ike turned around with a plastic bowl on his head and a teddy bear in his hand.

He said, "Yeah, Gina wanted some cookies, and I told her that she couldn't have any."

I said, "Did you change the diapers?"

He said, "Yeah, Pam had a dump, and Pattie only peed."

Gina said, "Dickie, can I watch TV? She sat on the floor with one of her dolls.

I said, "Not right now, I need you to watch the twins, and Ike is going to help me."

My brother took the bowl off his head, dropped the bear, and said "Now what?"

I said, "Get mom's little hammer, a butter knife, and meet me in the kitchen."

Then I quickly ran upstairs, went into the bathroom, threw my soaking wet windbreaker, hat, and T-shirt on the claw foot tub, grabbed a towel off the rack, and dried the top half of my body. Then I ran to my bedroom, and grabbed another T-shirt out of the drawer. I ran back into the bathroom, got the putty and pins from my jacket, and raced downstairs. Ike was waiting in the kitchen with the hammer and butter knife in hand.

He said, "You know you're not going to get away with this."

I looked at him, and thought for a moment, that I would punch him. I then thought I needed his help, and maybe later I would have to deal with him.

I said, "Just shut up, and help me, we are both in trouble."

He said," I didn't break the window, you did," pointing the hammer at me.

I said, "Look, are you going to help me, or am I going to do this myself?"

He said, "I'll help you, but I'm not taking any of the blame."

I picked up one of the kitchen chairs, and said, "Yeah, fine, follow me."

I walked to the side door, and said, "Open the door." Ike opened the door, smiled and pointed the hammer outside. I walked outside, walked to the back of the house where the broken window was. The rain had stopped, but the back of the yard was still mushy from all the rain. I placed the chair in front of the window, stood on it, grabbed the window screen, and pulled it off its hinges.

I said, "Ike, take this, and put it against the house." He dropped the hammer and the butter knife, and took the screen from me. There were shards of glass on the windowsill.

I said, "Get the garbage can, dust pan, and brush, but first give me the butter knife."

He gave me the knife, and walked back into the house. I ran the knife along the inside edges of the window, stripping out the small pieces of glass, the old putty, and paint, just like the man in the hardware store told me. Ike had returned with the stuff I had asked for.

I said, "Ike, get all this crap off the windowsill, and put it in the garbage can. I'll be right back."

I jumped off the chair ran into the house, and unwrapped the glass. Then I carefully carried the pane of glass to the back of the house, and set it down next to the chair against the foundation. I told my brother to get another chair from the kitchen, and he returned moments later. I set the chairs next to each other in front of the window. Then I put the pins in my T-shirt pocket, placed the hammer on the windowsill, and climbed up on one chair. I told my brother to hand me the pane of glass. Ike handed me the glass, and I placed the bottom edge of the glass into the window frame. I moved the glass slightly to one side, so it would fit into the frame. I looked at both sides of the frame, as I eased the glass into the window. Then the glass would not go any farther because there was a piece of old putty still in the frame.

I said, "Ike, take the butter knife and get on the other chair."
When he got on the chair, I told him to scrape out the small piece of putty. He worked the knife carefully on the spot, and chipped away the old putty. Then I resumed pushing the glass into the frame until the glass was fully in place. I placed my hand in the center of the glass holding it in place, and looked at how the glass fit into the frame. The bottom looks good, the left side looks good, the right side looks good, and the top-holy shit!-The glass has a 1/4 gap where the glass meets the frame on the top!

I yelled, "Mother Fucker!"
Ike said, "What's wrong?"
I said, "I measured the window wrong, I should have measured from the outside."
Ike smiled, and said, "See? I told you that you couldn't fix it."
Holding the piece of glass in place with one hand, I took my free hand, and shoved Ike off the chair, and he fell onto the wet ground.

He jumped up, and kicked my chair, and yelled, "You asshole, I'm all fuck 'n wet!"

I said, "Take it easy, you'll make me break the glass. Then I'll have to kill you."

He said, "It's not going to work anyway!" Then he walked back into the house.

I stood on the chair giving a lot of thought about the amount of time and money I put into this project. I was not about to give up just yet. Then, it started to rain again. I thought about what the man in the hardware store told me about putting in this window. Then, I had a great idea! I told Gina to get Ike and tell him to come out side.

My brother came outside, and said, "I'm not helping you, Jerk Off, it's raining out here."

I said, "I'm sorry I pushed you, I have an idea that's going to work, hold the glass."

Ike looked at me for a moment, and I said, "I can't do this with out you."

That statement sold him on the idea that I needed him, and he climbed on the chair next to me.

I said, "Hold the glass in the middle were my hand is." When he did, I removed my hand from the glass and grabbed the hammer. I pulled a pin out of my T-shirt pocket, and placed it in the right corner of the window frame next to the glass. I began to hammer the pin lightly into the frame. I lost a few pins at first, and I finally got the first pin in. Then I ducked under Ike and carefully hammered the left pin in. I repeated the pin hammering process up each side of the window. When it was time to do the top, the end of the pins barely covered the glass. I told Ike to let go of the glass, and find out what time it was, and get a rag on his way back. Then I popped the top on the putty, and started to apply it where the glass meets the frame. I took big globs of it, at first, and spread it like peanut butter along the bottom of the window, and then I scraped most of the putty off and tried again. Ike came out and said it was 4:50 PM. I told him to start cleaning up inside, before mom and dad came home. I continued to apply the putty quickly knowing that my parents were due home in an hour. When I puttied the bottom and both sides of the window, I caked the top with 1/2 inch bead of putty, covering the 1/4 inch gap. I then jumped down off the chair, and put the rag in the puddle. I jumped back up on the chair and ran the rag lightly along the putty on all ends. After I was finished, I stood on the chair and inspected my work. I thought to myself, "Hey, this looks pretty good," and I started to admire my craftsmanship. I took all the tools off the windowsill and wiped off the excess putty on the window frame and sill. I grabbed the screen, placed it back on its hinges, and closed it shut. I jumped down from the chair and looked at the window. Looking at it, you would never know that it was broken. I placed all the stuff on one chair and carried it to the side door, and grabbed all the stuff off the chair and put it in the house. I ran back outside, grabbed the chair and brought it into the kitchen. I told Ike to get the other chair from out side. As he did, I put away all the stuff we used and ran up stairs to change my shirt, pants, and socks. I came back downstairs; the time was 5:35 PM. I wiped down the wet muddy chairs and the kitchen floor with a towel. I then sat on one of the chairs, exhausted from this crazy day. Then I started to think; did I forget anything? Is everything in place? Did I do everything my mom told me to do? I got up and started to look around in every room of the house. Every single room left the way my parents had left it, perfect. I walked into the nursery. Gina was still playing with the babies after all these hours. I walked to the now fixed window, looked it over carefully, and the floor under it-perfect.

I said, "Gina, I need you in the kitchen for a minute."

She said, "What's up?"

I said, "I need to talk to you, just go in the kitchen."
She got up and went into the kitchen. I walked into the living room where Ike was watching TV. I said, "Ike, I need you in the kitchen."

He looked at me, pissed off, and snarled, "What is it now? I'm not doing any more cleaning!"

I said, "I don't want you to clean anything, just come to the kitchen."

In a huff, he got off the couch, walked in the kitchen, and I followed. Gina was sitting at the kitchen table with her doll in her arms, Ike turned around with his arms folded.

I said, "If you look at that window, you would never know it was broken."

Ike put his hands on his hips, and said, "Yeah, right!" He then walked into the nursery and looked over the window, and I followed.

He said, "I see putty here, here, and there," pointing at little specks of putty that were not that noticeable.

I said, "Mom and dad wouldn't notice that unless they studied the window real close."

My brother turned around wide-eyed and said, "You're not asking me to lie to mom and dad, are you?"

I said, "Let's go back to the kitchen."

I turned and walked back to the kitchen, Ike followed.

Ike walked in front of me and stood in my face, and said, "I'm not lying for you."

Gina said, "Lie about what?"

He said, "About the window!"

I put up my hands in front of me, and said, "I'm not asking anybody to lie to mom and dad. I would never do that, and that's wrong."

Ike said, "So what do you want from us?"

I folded my arms, smiled, and said, "Forget it ever happened, (pause), the window looks good as new. No one would ever know the difference."

Ike took a few steps back with his eyes wide open, "Have you lost your fucking mind? There is no way I'm going to be part of this!"

Gina was listening intently as my brother started to panic. I sat down at the kitchen table next my sister, and put my arm around her shoulder.

I looked up at Ike calmly, and said, "You're already involved, you are the reason the window got broken in the first place, right, Gina?"

Gina looked at me, and said, "Yep, you hit Dickie, and he threw the football, because you wouldn't clean the dishes."

Ike ran up to me, pointed his finger in my face, and said, "That's not what happened."

I looked up at him, and said, "That's how she saw it, and if you look at the list mom left us, you would supposed to wash the lunch dishes."
I picked up the list off the table, and handed it to my brother. He snatched the list from my hand, and looked at it.

He took a step back, and said, "It doesn't say if Ike doesn't do the dishes, to slap me in the head, and spike me with a football."

I smiled, and said, "No, but mom did say to listen to me, and do the things on the list. So, that means you're guilty, too. And you're also the reason why the window got broken, and you are going to get blamed, too."
Ike stood there, realizing that he was going to be in trouble too.

He said, "This is bull shit, and I'm not lying!"

I said, "I'm not asking you to lie, I'm asking you to forget."

Then I put my arm around Gina shoulder, and said, "Gina forgets all the time, right, Gina?"

Gina turned to me, confused, and said," Forget what?"

I looked at Gina, and said with a smile, "Exactly!"
My brother rested his back against the counter, crossed his arms, and looked at me for a moment. Knowing that Ike was a hard sell, and time was running short, I knew that I had to sweeten the deal. I got up and pushed the chair in toward the table.

I said, "Okay, mom and dad come home, they ask how things went, you both don't say a word, I say everything went fine, end of the conversation."

I continued, "Nobody lied, everybody just forgot about the window. If they ever find out, I will take 100% of all the blame, that's a good deal for everyone. Okay?"

My brother looked at me with skepticism, and said, "You're going to take 100% of the blame? Yeah, right!"

I said, "I cross my heart and hope to die. Gina can be a witness."

Ike said, "If mom or dad asked me what happened to the window, I'm telling them you did it."

I said, "Only if they ask. Okay?"

He said, "Okay, but I don't think you're going to get away with it."

Then he walked back to the living room.

Gina got up, and said, "I won't say a thing, Dickie, alright?"

I said, "Okay, thanks Gina." Then she walked back into the nursery with her doll.

About an hour later, my parents came home from a long day at the wedding. I made sure I met them in the kitchen first, and stood waiting for the door to open.

My mom walked in, and said, "How did everything go?" She looked around the kitchen.

I said, "Everything went fine, the babies are changed, and we gave them a bottle around 2 PM."

She said, "They need to be fed again."

Then she walked into the nursery, I followed.

Mom said, looking at Gina, "How are the twins, honey?"

Gina looked at her, and said, "They're fine, mommy, Pam pooped and Pattie only peed."

Then mom picked up Pam, and said, "She's wet again." Then she began to change the baby.

I heard my father come in through the side door, and I walked into the kitchen to meet him.

Dad said, as he took off his sport jacket, "How did it go?"

I looked at him, and said, "Okay, how was the wedding?"

He said, "It went okay, where's your brother?"

I said, "In the living room."

Then he walked into the living room, and I followed.

My father said, "Ike."

My brother looked up, waiting nervously for the question. Dad said, "Didn't I tell you to put your bike in the garage before I left?"

Ike said, "Yeah, I'll do it now," then my brother walked out of the room.

My father walked through the dining room and down the short hallway into the bathroom. As I stood in the living room, I realized that I had pulled off a major deception by getting my siblings to be my co-conspirators, and of course, my quick wit and ingenuity. I was basking in the thought that I could pull off anything with proper planning, and influence. I was patting myself on the back, and thinking that I was a pure genus.

When we went to bed that night before Ike and I went to sleep, Ike turned to me, and said, "You'll never get away with it!"

I turned to him, and said, "I'll get away with it, if you don't rat."

He turned away from me, and said, "Yeah, we'll see." As I lay there, I thought about the old man in the truck that gave me a lift. I thought about how lonely it must be not to have anyone left in the world, and how he blamed himself for his only son's death. I thought that if anyone needed a prayer that night, it should be that old man. His son was in heaven with his friends, and so were the old man's buddies from WWII. They were all together and could not be lonely with God. I pray for the old man not to be lonely anymore, to find someone that would fulfill the rest of his short life, and not to blame himself for his son's death.

A few weeks have gone by after the Great Window Breaking Cover-Up of the fall of 1970. It was that time of the year to install the storm windows of the house. This would be the ultimate test to see if my broken window deception would be discovered. The changing of the exterior storm windows happens twice a year, once in the fall, removing the wooden framed screens, and replacing them with wooden framed storm windows, and once in the spring, when we would reverse the process. This bi-annual home maintenance project was a Kraemer family team effort, and took the entire day to complete. My dad was the leader of the project, and everyone worked under his direction. My father would start swapping out the screens for windows in the bottom front of the house, and work counter clockwise around the house, and then we would move to the second floor. Dad would get on the ladder, remove the screen, hand it to one of his sons, and clean the outside of the window with window cleaner and paper towel. Ike and I would bring the storm windows out of the garage, clean each window, and then hand it to my father to be installed. In addition, mom would be keeping up with the installation process from the inside of the house, cleaning each interior window, as we went along. This was a fine-tuned assembly line process, and you do not want to full behind, because everyone gets pissed off at you. This was going to be the real test to see if my dad would notice that the nursery window had been broken. As the window installing team reached the back of the house, where the window had been broken, I noticed that the window in question was halfway open. I did not want to draw attention to myself by running into the house, and closing the window. Therefore, I waited nonchalantly at my assigned assembly line position, which was in front of the garage. My dad went to the nursery window, climbed up the ladder a couple of steps, and removed the screen.

Dad said, "Ike, take this."

My brother grabbed the screen, walked to the garage, making eye contact with me the whole time, and placed the screen into the garage. Then he walked back towards his position between dad and me. Then my father grabbed the nursery window frame, and closed it. Suddenly, as the window frame hit the sill, the whole pane of glass fell out and crashed on the ground. My father, still standing on ladder, was stunned about what just happened.

He said, "Holy Shit!" He looked on the ground at the broken glass, and then he looked at the window frame. My dad then raised his head, and had an"Ah-Hah!" moment. Then he turned around and looked at my brother.

Ike immediately raised his arm and pointed at me, and yelled, "He did it!"
My father looked at me, silently for a moment, waiting for me to say something. However, I did not say a word, looking back at him, and by not saying anything, it was the admission of guilt.　　　Dad got off the ladder, and said, "Dick, get the garbage can, pick up all this glass, and be careful not to cut yourself. I don't want to take you to the hospital, too." Then he walked into the house.

I picked up all the glass, and then I realized that I was alone in the back yard. I figured Ike was inside the house spilling his guts out about the Great Broken Window Deception. I walked into the house, and everyone was having lunch. Mom had made me a sandwich at my place at the table. I sat down and started to eat. My dad finished his lunch, and said, "Now that we have heard your brother's story about the window, we would like to hear your side. I stopped eating, and explained the whole story, leaving me 100% accountable for the broken window, as promised, and my actions. My parents were both surprised by the story, and had explained to me the great risk I took by leaving all the children alone in the house. They had given me an example, that if there was a fire, what would happen, which was a very sobering thought. I had not thought of that before. Overall, it was a civil discussion about responsibility, that I should think about the chances I took and how they could affect others. In addition, my parents expressed their disappointment in the choices I made, and said that they would think long and hard before leaving me with the children again. I think that losing my parents trust at that time hurt more than any other punishment they could ever dish out. I had learned from my mistakes, and had earned my parents trust back just a few short weeks later, when I would again be left to tend to the little darlings once more. However, from that day forward, just before my parents would go out, they would say to me, "Stay in the house," just for reinforcement.

Chapter 15 - Turning Sixteen

In May 1972, I turned 16 years old, and one of the first things I did was get my driver's learning permit. I passed the written test with flying colors, because I studied hard for the exam. This was a big milestone for me, and it scared the shit out of my parents that I would soon be on the open highways of America. I truly was a pain in the ass about getting my driver's learning permit. I would not let up on my constant badgering until my mother drove me to the DMV to take the test. My parents were always trying to stall the inevitable, because they knew what would come next, teaching me to drive. Once I had my learner's permit, I was always asking to drive. I was like a broken record, if anyone was going somewhere, I would ask to drive. It got to the point that when my parents would say they were going somewhere, before I would ask, they would say, "No, you can't drive." One of the reasons was because my parents had recently bought a 1968 Oldsmobile Cutlass Cruiser station wagon, a nice car without any scratches or dents. Another reason was that once I got my driver's license, I would be looking to buy my own car. However, once my parents rationalized that I only had about $150 in the bank, and I was a part-time dishwasher making $2.25 an hour, they thought I would be about 21 years old before I could buy my own car. Funny thing, I never did the math on how long it would take to buy my own car, back then, stupid me. But after much procrastination, my parents gave in on teaching me how to drive. However, there were some limitations to teaching me to drive, they were:

My mother would be the teacher. My father was not a patient man. He could not stand for anyone driving but himself when he was in the car, except for when he was drunk.

There would be no one else but mom and I in the car, while I was driving. This is because they were afraid that I could wipeout the entire family in an accident.

If I damaged the car, I would pay for it.

Mom would pick the day and time to teach me to drive. This would mean that Ike would look after the rest of the Kraemer flock during my lesson.

My mother was supportive of me learning how to drive, after the rules were laid out. As I had mentioned before, my mom was a very high-strung person with a lot of energy, due to her personality, diet pills, and a dozen cups of tea a day. So teaching me how to drive was going to be an adventure for her, and she was up to any challenge that parenthood would have to offer. She would do almost anything for her kids, within reason.

On the first day of my driving lesson, it was a bright, sunny day in June. She first instructed me to go through my checklist, fasten my seatbelt, check the rear and side view mirrors to insure that there is no one behind you, check to make sure the car was in park, and then finally turn the key. It took us a few tries to back out of the driveway, due to over steering, but I did finally get into the street. We drove around the neighborhood streets just to get the hang of things, but anytime in that area, there were kids, dogs, cats, people, and other cars in the streets. Anytime that I would get remotely close to something, my mother would slam her foot on the floorboard as if she had a brake pedal. In addition, mom had a certain passenger posture when she would try to teach me to drive. She would buckle her seat belt so tight that it would cut off the circulation to her legs, and would hold the door armrest with both hands. Occasionally, I would glance at her while I was driving, and she looked like she was watching a horror film at a drive-in. One time, she had an idea that I would get a better hang of things on an expressway on westbound route 17, which were two lanes. Driving at 55 miles an hour on the expressway, mom was yelling, "Stay to the right, stay to the left, slow down, speed up." I could hear mom's foot thumping on the floorboard. I would look over at her in the passenger seat clutching the door armrest. I was thinking that she might bailout on me at any minute, and jump out of the car. At the end of one of my lessons, I pulled in the driveway, as I did, Mom said, "Look out for the tree, look out for the tree." I was very careful, pulled into the driveway, and did not hit the tree. However, I hit the porch instead with a big bang, and suddenly brought the car to a complete halt.

Mom yelled, "Holy Shit!"
Ike ran of out of the house because he heard the bang.

Mom yelled, "Put it in park!" I did. She yelled, "Turn off the car!" I did. Mom said, in a low growl, "Give me the keys." I pulled the keys out of the ignition, and she snatched them out of my hand.

Mom jumped out of the car, and slammed the door. I got out to assess the damage, but it was hard to tell because there was a big bush between the car and the porch.

I said, to mom, "It doesn't look like there's any damage, should I pull the car back to get a better look?"

She looked at me and flinched as if she was going to smack me, and mumbled, "I'm gonna move it."

Then she got in and backed the car away from the house. I looked at the car, it was fine, just a little porch paint on the chrome bumper that easily would come out with some steel wool. The porch had a 3-inch gouge in the 8-inch post, a little painting, and you would never know the difference. The only real damage to the car was the front passenger armrest that had puncture holes in it, from my mother's fingernails.

But after that day, my mother's nerves were shot, and plowing the family Cruiser into the house was a good reason for discontinuing mom's driving lessons. After a couple of days, I realized that my mother was not going to teach me to drive anymore, so I hired a driving instructor with my own money. When the driving instructor showed up at the house, mom was a little put off, that I hadn't told her. After she found out that the driving instructor was getting paid $10 an hour, she almost fell on the floor. Mom wrestled with her conscience for a week, and offered to pay half the fee, once a week. After a few weeks of lessons, I went for my driving test, and failed the first time, but passed on my second test.

Once I got my driver's license, I was only allowed to drive the station wagon while my mom rode with me. I was never allowed to drive the family car by myself. They were afraid that if I wrecked their car, my mom would not have a car to drive. So one milestone completed, the next would be buying my own car.

After the summer of 1972, I was working for the Hot Shoppes on the New York State Thruway, for about two years, when I decided to make a job change. During the summer, I worked full-time there, but when school was in session, I could only work there on the weekends, because of the distance to and from my job. During my last year there, I learned to be a dishwasher, which paid more money. But it was harder work, and sometimes I would be scrubbing pots and pans for the entire eight hours. The cooks there were not the gourmet chefs of five star restaurants, who graduated with a culinary degree. These cooks learned their trade in the military, or in prison, so they burned the food on every pot and pan they could get their hands on. This was a tough buck to earn, at $2.25 an hour. But, I did not complain, I sucked it up, and collected my paycheck. The problem was that I needed to work after school, and continue to save more money. The reason I needed to increase my savings is that I wanted to buy my first car. My parents told me to save my money, so I could buy a car, because they were not going to buy me one. They didn't have any money to blow on a car for their 16-year-old son, end of story. Because they were living on one income, supporting five kids, and had a mortgage to pay. I accepted that fact, I didn't say things like, "But Joe Blow up the street got his parents to buy him a car." I knew, because of my upbringing, that I had to work for things I wanted. So I was faced with the task of earning enough money to buy and maintain my first car. Not a small challenge, when you're making $2.25 an hour part-time.

Therefore, I applied for a dishwasher job in the newspaper. I showed up, afterschool the next day, at the Monroe Diner, which was a red and silver trailer from the 1940s in a dirt parking lot on 17 M. This was the only diner in Monroe, at the time, it was humble looking, and that is being kind. But it was clean, the food was good, and local people liked it. I interviewed with the owner, he was a retired Navy cook from World War II, and I would call him "Boss". He went through my duties as a dishwasher, showed me the dishwashing machine, and showed me around. He introduced me to a waitress, his daughter, Nellie, a very attractive college girl with big breasts; I would fantasize about her often. The other waitress was his wife, Bess, a nice lady. Tom, the daytime dishwasher//back up short order cook/assistant cook, was a college drop out about 25 years old. Boss laid out the ground rules of employment, be on time, do your job right, otherwise your fired, do not date his daughter, no dope smoking or drinking on the job, and be courteous to customers. I accepted the terms, at $3.00 an hour, 4 hours after school, Monday through Friday, and 8 hours on Saturday. I was hired on the spot and started work the next day. As a perk, I ate anything on the menu for free.

I was a little concerned because Boss came across as a hard ass when I first met him, and he had a very deep voice, looked like a weathered old man, and he was very cranky. Therefore, I did not give notice to my previous employer for a couple of days, just to see how this job would shake out. But it turned out that my perceptions could be deceiving, he and his staff were very helpful in getting me acclimated to my new job. In fact, they turned out to be pretty friendly people, and I felt like one of the family, well, maybe a stepson. But Boss and the rest of the family made it pretty clear that I was the lowest man on the totem pole, and I would get all the shit jobs nobody else wanted to do. The next one in-line for shit jobs was Tom, but he did not care, he was mostly stoned all the time. He was 4-F with the draft board, dropped out of college, and was working this job to survive. Tom was a very likable guy, who always had a smile on his face, and enjoyed joking around. But he did work hard, too, Boss would never have a goof off work for him, and Tom knew it. When I worked at that diner, I was constantly working, from the time I got there until I left. During lunch and dinner hours, it got crazy busy. Sometimes, I had to bus tables, because the waitresses would fall behind, on top of all my other duties. Boss would burn, bake-in, and scorch a lot of pots and pans that I would have to scrub clean. Sometimes, I would assist Boss while he was cooking, opening cans, peeling potatoes, washing vegetables, and anything else he needed. During non-peak busy hours, Boss, would give me side projects like cleaning the storage room, stocking shelves, cleaning bathrooms, and anything else he could dream up. Yes, Boss was a taskmaster, and I worked hard without complaint, because I was being paid for the work I did. Boss would open the diner at 5:30 AM and close at 9:00 PM, six days a week. For an old man like that, this was a tough buck to earn. The diner was closed on Sundays. The daughter, Nellie, was a spoiled bitch, and would always come into the kitchen yelling and screaming about anything or everything. She would be cursing at Boss, Tom, her mother, the short order cook, and me; and they all would let her get away with it. I would be looking at Boss, while his daughter would be screaming and yelling at him, he would stand there calmly, and answer in a normal tone of voice, as she dressed him down. Then she would storm out of the kitchen, and he would resume working, or maybe bang some things around. Tom and I sometimes would be caught witnessing this event, and, Boss would yell, "What the fuck are you looking at?" or "She's on the rag." Boss's wife would pull the same scene, but not as often.

Tom and I thought the Monroe family diner was one big comedy scene, and the dysfunctional family was a bunch of nuts, living together. However, in a funny kind of way, they were likable, too. Almost everyday, Boss would stand behind his steam table, I would be standing at the dishwashing machine, and Tom would be standing in the middle of the kitchen after his shift was over, and we would have a bullshit session. It was those moments that Boss would show the human side of himself, and I got to know him as a person. Boss had a good sense of humor, and he would joke around with the both of us. He would make fun of his wife and daughter, when they, too, would join in on the conversation. Nevertheless, Boss always made sure that, even though we would laugh, joke and kid around, we knew that he was The Boss. I thought it a little funny that he liked being addressed and called Boss by Tom and me. I'm sure I could've called him Mr. So and So, but I could never pronounce his long Italian last name correctly.

Once I started high school in the fall of 1972, I was reading at a fifth grade level, was failing in English, and all my other school subjects I struggled to maintain a C minus grade average. I could read, write, and perform simple math equations, add, subtract, multiply, and divide. All my schooling was a mainstream education, and I did not attend special education classes. The only special education classes that were available, at the time, in the Monroe Woodbury public school district, had been designed for the mentally disabled. The typical mentally disabled student was a person that was severely retarded, and their education at the high school level was geared toward life skills like personal hygiene, cooking, sewing, ironing, and basic house keeping. In addition, the mentally disabled education goals were basic math and reading. Therefore, if the mentally disabled were able to care for themselves, count money, and read a cooking recipe, they were educated by the state's education standards, and ready to be released into the world.

There was only a two-tier education system, students of mainstream and the mentally disabled. So even though a psychologist diagnosed me with dyslexia a few years prior, and my parents and the school district knew it, there were no educational accommodations offered for my disability. The theory was-do not tell me about my disability, mainstream my education, and let the chips fall where they may. Given these choices at the time, they made the right decision.

Therefore, it was apparent that I was not going to Harvard after high school. In fact, it would be a great accomplishment by my parent's standards, if I could just graduate from high school. However, reaching for that high school diploma would be a long haul up a very steep mountain for me. I had trouble envisioning what the future held for me, and what I would do after graduating high school. I questioned myself, "After breaking my ass getting a high school diploma, what will I do for a living?" I knew that I didn't want to be a newspaper boy, a bus boy, or a dishwasher, the jobs that I had experienced. I needed the motivation and a vision of what I would become as an adult, in order for me to move forward in my education.

The Orange County education system had vocational programs called B.O.C.E.S., for kids that were not college bound. This half day, five days a week, two-year programs were geared towards teaching children a trade. They had programs that would teach nursing, auto mechanics, culinary arts, beautician, and construction. Once you complete this program, you would receive a certificate of completion, school credits that went towards your high school diploma, and a chance to get a job in the field you were trained for. I was very excited about the program, and talked to my parents about it. This program would get me out of the classroom setting that I had longed to get out of. This program was something that I could be trained in, and that I could be good at without relying solely on reading and writing. My parents were not enthusiastic about the B.O.C.E.S program, which surprised me. Their reasons were, if I were to complete the certificate program in the first two years of high school, what would happen during my junior and senior years in school?

Would I struggle academically to graduate in the last two years? The second reason was that I had chosen construction as a trade, and my father did not want me to become a plumber. I had this vision of becoming a plumber like my dad. But my father did not want me to become one, because of what he went through every day. He was a Master Plumber, one of the best in Rockland County, and now was a working Foreman of a large company. He was a very successful tradesman. But given the physical demands of a working plumber Foreman, he still preformed all the normal duties as a plumber, which meant carrying cast iron tubs up flights of stairs, contorting his body in many angles to solder pipes, and work in sub-below zero weather or sweltering heat all day. In addition, being responsible for several plumbing crews, had added more stress. Dad started to feel the physical effects weight on him at 38 years old. My dad did not want any of his sons in construction, and wanted them to excel in better careers. My mother was on the same page as dad, she wanted something better for their children, too. However, after much debate, the school had convinced my parents that this program would benefit my education, and eased their concerns about me graduating high school.

I would have regular classroom instruction in the mornings and, after lunch; I would board the B.O.C.E.S bus, which would take us on a 20 min. ride to Goshen, New York. Most of the kids, like me, were not college material, and, for the most part, were friendly. In my high school, about 90% of the B.O.C.E.S programs were boys, and the girls were training to be nurses or beauticians.

Once we got to our respective training sessions, our instructor, Mr. Piazza, would take roll call, and get right to work. Mr. Piazza was an accomplished tradesman and a builder; he was a tough guy that did not put up with any bullshit. The B.O.C.E.S. students came from all over the county; some would travel almost an hour to get to the program. About half of the students admitted to the program were the school district's more undesirable students. These students were the troublemakers, the class cutters, the dopers, the drinkers, bullies, and the stupid. Therefore, the first thing Mr. Piazza did was weed out all the bad apples. He would start to weed them out in the first two weeks. He systematically evaluated students to see if they wanted to learn a trade. He would give everyone a task to do, if you did it wrong, he would instruct you on how to do it right, and give a little sarcasm to test your tolerance level. If you did it wrong again, he'd get irritated, and he either would give you additional instruction with an extra dose of criticism, or if he thought you were jerking him around, he would lean into you, and see if you would revolt. This was an exercise to weed out the knuckleheads, everyone did it wrong the first and the second time around. The student was evaluated by whether they were listening to the instruction, and if they could tolerate sarcasm and criticism. If they were not listening to the instruction, that meant the student did not care about doing the task right, and in the construction trade, it's all about 100% quality, zero tolerance for anything less. In addition, if the student could not take the sarcasm, and criticism, the construction trade was not the place for him. In the adult world, there will be sarcasm and criticism, and if you cannot take it, there was no place for you in his classroom.

Once the undesirable students were encouraged to leave or dropped from the program, the real training would begin for the rest of the students that wanted to learn a trade. But, remember, there were still students that were the troublemakers, the class cutters, the dopers, the drinkers, bullies, and, yes, the stupid that remained, too.

In the first year, we covered general construction subjects like masonry, carpentry, electricity, plumbing, and heating. In masonry, we learned to mix concrete, and cut and lay brick and cinder block. In carpentry, we learned to read a tape measure, use hand and power tools, how to drive a nail, building floors and walls, and building codes. In electricity, we learned about how to wire an outlet, stringing BX and Roam-X electric cables through walls, floors, ceilings, and basic electric building code, and theory. In plumbing, we learned how to solder copper joints, joining cast iron pipe by pouring hot lead into joints, cut and measure copper and cast iron pipe, running pipe through floors, ceilings, and walls. In heating, we learned how to service an oil and gas furnaces, and heating building codes, and fundamentals.

The first year course was designed to determine what specialty in construction you're going to pursue, whether it was masonry, carpentry, electricity, plumbing, or heating. This course gave the exposure of all the construction trades to the student, to find out what their strengths and weaknesses were. These mini courses were pass or fail, so if you had 100% performance, you passed, if you did not, you failed. Just like in the real world of construction. I passed all but electricity the bookwork on an electric theory confused me at the time, and I fell behind. So, I knew enough about electricity to become a plumber, but did not have the knowledge to become an electrician.

Chapter 16 - The Quest for the Opposite Sex

My first year in high school in the fall of 1972, I was 16 years old. I was a year older then most freshmen, but I didn't look like it. I had blended in as an average looking student to my peers. Now that I had already established a new name in junior high, I started slowly to work on my looks.

The first thing I did was I would only wear my glasses when I was reading or studying. I had bought myself a pair of round wire-rimmed glasses, like the rock stars wore. Those glasses cost me $75, which was a boatload of money for me. I lost those glasses in school about two months after I bought them, my parents refused to buy me another pair, and I was not about to blow any more money on glasses. Therefore, I just didn't wear glasses from that point forward. It seemed that my eyesight had gotten stronger over the years, and I didn't need them at the time.

The second thing I did to improve my image was that I started to pay for my own haircuts. I stopped going to Tulli, the Italian barber, and started to go to a hair stylist. There were still limitations on how long my hair could be, and my dad was the enforcer, the Hair Police, and the Fuzz. He was always on my back about getting a haircut. I would respond by telling him that he was jealous because of his baldness. My mother would talk to dad about giving me a little leeway about the hair, and he would, to a point. But once that point was reached, he would continue to break my balls until I would get it cut again.

The third thing I did to improve my looks was that I invested some money in clothes. My parents would not allow me to wear jeans or sneakers to school, even though they were in style. In addition, my parents didn't allow us to dress even remotely like the counter culture hippy or doper type, although that was a popular style, too. But they did allow us, when I reached high school, to wear bellbottoms, and some stylish shirts, on my own dime.

So, there I was, finally in high school, the big leagues, and the final stretch of my education. I was excited, and hoped that things would get better for my future. I had a very short list of friends; in fact, Billy R. was the only real friend that I hung around with, and he had moved to the mid-west to live with his dad, last summer. The rest of the people I knew were casual acquaintances. These casual acquaintances were classmates that were in one or two of my classes. We would talk and joke around during class, the lunchroom, or study hall, but they really didn't see me afterschool or call me on the phone. They really didn't know me, and I really did not know them. During school, I'd be more like the loner/drifter, going from one group of kids to another, with them never really knowing me, nor I them. I was that guy, people knew Rich Kraemer by name, but they really did not know me as a person. I became comfortable with this identity as the loner type, and kept everyone guessing what I was all about, even if they never cared to ask.

There was one thing that I was missing in my young life, more than other friends, which I seemed to cope without, and that was a girl friend. I needed someone intimate that I could trust and share my innermost feelings with. A girl that I could love and have her love me in return. I was looking for a girl that would have faith in me, and liked me for who I am. A girl that would be a happy person, laugh at my jokes, and we could laugh together. This girl would have to be attracted to me, and I to her.

Searching for a girl friend that fit the right criteria was the key to my success. I seemed to have the female rejection part of the process, down packed. In fact, sometimes when I would come on to a girl, I could tell by her reaction what the answer was going to be, and I would finish the sentence for her, smile, and walk away. There were other times when I would start my observation process, found out what the girl was like, or who her friends were, and would move on to my next target. One thing during this process I would not stand for, and that was being made a fool of.

One day, much to my surprise, a girl named Diane said yes to a meeting afterschool, so we could get to know each other a little better. She was an attractive, popular blond girl, and was always smiling. I had agreed to meet her behind her school bus at the end of the school day. About 30 school buses were all parked facing the front of the school in this huge parking lot. My bus was one of the first in line; Diane's was one of the last. After school, I eagerly rushed to the rear of Diane's bus and waited for her to arrive. I stood there for about 10 minutes, and began to get worried, because the school buses started up their engines. Just then, I heard a knocking sound on the back window of her bus. I looked up and saw Diane knocking on the window, and waving at me along with a bunch of her friends in the back of the bus. Diane then flipped me the bird, and said, "Fuck you, Moron." Then I could hear all of her friends laugh, and they all followed up by giving me the finger. I stood there like an idiot for a moment, in amazement at what this bitch did to me. Then I shot them the bird back and ran for my bus. I didn't get too far before my bus and the rest of the buses started to leave the parking lot. I stopped in the middle of this huge parking lot, and watched all the buses leave. I thought to myself," Now, that's what I call the ultimate female rejection, with an extra helping of public humiliation for me to swallow. I did not deserve that, and the only way for me to feel better about what had just happened, is to get even." As I hitchhiked home that day, I thought of a way to get even with Diane, but I didn't want to rush it, I wanted her to think that she got away with humiliating me.

After my grandstand female rejection, I felt that maybe I was trying too hard, and would put the girl friend pursuit on hold for a while. I had a new project called the Revenge. During those long two weeks leading up to me getting even, I would have to see her everyday in my English class. Diane would walk into the beginning of class, give me a look as if I was a dork, and sit right in front of me in class. In addition, she would whisper some snide comments during class to her girl friends, and they, too, would occasionally glance back at me, giggle, and looked at me as if I was a drip. I would sit there trying to ignore Diane's taunting and would make believe that I didn't care about her or the silly game she was playing. However, it did bother me, and it only made me more pissed off about the whole situation. If she was a guy, I would have punched her lights out, but I couldn't do that. In addition, my revenge would have a public humiliation and an ego deflation component. Because that little stunt she pulled really put a big dent into my fragile ego, the humiliation was public and on going. I thought to myself for the next couple of weeks on how to get even with this bitch.

Then it dawned on me like a bolt of lightning in the lunchroom one day. I was eating my lunch, and for dessert, I bought a sugar raspberry jelly doughnut. The doughnut had so much raspberry jelly pumped into it that it bled through the entire top of it. Yes, the lunch ladies made this one big, sloppy jelly doughnut. Then I had a Eureka moment, took a bunch of napkins, and wrapped the big jelly up to go. I ran upstairs to my locker, put it in an old lunch bag, and stored it away for later.

The plan was set, but the circumstances and the timing would have to be perfect. After the plan was hatched, I would have to observe Diane during homeroom period at the beginning of the day, to decide that this would be the day. So that doughnut stayed in my locker for a few days.

Finally, the day had arrived, when all the conditions and circumstances were right. I went to my locker, grabbed the lunch bag with the doughnut in it, and went to my homeroom. After the teacher took attendance, the bell sounded to go to my first period English class. I quickly walked to my class, and sat in my seat. I was in the classroom so early that no one else was there. I took the jelly doughnut out of the bag, and began to remove the napkins. As I did, the napkins had been stuck to the doughnut, so I had to peel little pieces of paper off it, and put them in the bag. I finally removed most of the napkin off the big jelly, and shoved the paper bag with most of the napkins, under the heater unit. Then students started to arrive and they were taking their seats. I had the big sloppy doughnut in my right hand with one napkin underneath it, concealed under the desk. I opened my English Lit book on the desk and held it open with my left hand. My heart started to beat like a snare drum, as the moment of my vindication grew near. I looked up at the clock and realized that the class would begin in 1 min., when the teacher, Mrs. English, arrived. The teacher was a very short, young woman in her late 20s, and yes, her name was really Mrs. English. I was beginning to think that Diane was going to cut this class, and this was just a drill. Then the bell rang for the beginning of class, and I sat up straight in my seat, looking for a place to ditch this sticky thing in my right hand. Just then, Diane popped through the door, and as she walked by the teacher, she said, with a smile, "Sorry I'm late." As she walked toward me, she gave me that look for the last time. Diane, then placed her books on her desk, turned facing the front of the classroom, and began to sit down. As she did, I quickly shoved the Big Jelly Bomb on her seat. When she sat down, she suddenly let out a shrill scream that scared me; her knees banged under the desk, and she quickly got up. I stuffed the napkin in the frame of the desk. As she got up, I saw a huge raspberry jelly blotch that was centered in the middle of her ass, and it had encompassed half the backside of her white pants. The whole class started to stand up and look at her. When she got up, and turned to look at the seat, her eyes then lifted to burn right into mine.

Diane yelled, "You did this!" Then she reached around with her right hand and felt her butt. When she brought her hand back around and looked at it, her hand was full of jelly. I stood up from my desk.

Mrs. English made her way through the crowd, and said, "What's going on here?"

I said, "I think she needs to go to the nurse's office, you know, that woman thing."

Diane stomped her feet, started to cry, and yelled, "You son of a bitch!"

Mrs. English move between the both of us, looked at me, and said, "Did you do this?"

I lifted both of my hands up with palms open, and said innocently, "I didn't do this. Honestly, I don't know what happened."

Just then, Diane lunged at me with both hands open. As she did, Diane's right jelly filled hand swiped Mrs. English's left side of her face, sending jelly flying over one of the lens of her glasses, and landing on my left shoulder. The crowd of students let out a loud sigh, "EEEEEEEWWWWWWW!"

Mrs. English, shorter then the both of us extended both of her arms and pushed the two of us apart. As she did, Diane violently kept swinging her arms, flinging the jelly all over everyone around her. The crowd let out a loud, "AAAAAHHHHH," as they backed away.

Diane yelled, "You're going to pay for this, you mother fucker!"

Mrs. English, still holding us apart, blew some jelly from the side of her mouth, and said, "Now, young lady, there is no reason to use that language. Now go to the girl's room and clean yourself up." Mrs. English then turned to me, and said, "As for you, Richard, go to the principal's office, and wait for me there."

Diane backed away, with tears coming down her face, and yelled, "You're gonna get it!" Then she turned and stomped out of the classroom.

Mrs. English turned to me, and said, "I'm very disappointed in you, Richard. Now go to the office."

I picked up my books, walked through the crowd of kids, as they stared at me, out of the classroom. I walked down the hallways, and went into the boy's bathroom to clean up. I looked in the mirror and saw that I had a big glob of jelly on my left shoulder of my shirt. I took my shirt off, and ran water on it, scrubbing the jelly out. Then I heard Mrs. English's voice through the air vent of the girl's room next door. I turned off the water, and moved closer to the air vent. Mrs. English was talking to Diane, I could hear her as clear as a bell.

Mrs. English said, "Oh, my, that's a big stain."

Diane said, "My pants are ruined, I can't walk around like this."

Mrs. English said, "I'll see if I can get something to cover you up. Why would Richard do something like this anyway?"

Diane said, "Because he wanted to go out with me, and I wouldn't."

Mrs. English said, "That doesn't sound right, a boy like Richard, doing something like this. Are you sure?"

Diane shouted, "He's a dork, and all my friends know it, just ask them. Someone must have seen him do it, just ask them!"

Mrs. English said, "Okay, now, calm down. I'll ask the class and get something to wrap around you."

Then I heard the door open in the girl's bathroom, and footsteps walking away down the hallway. I returned quietly back to the sink, and resumed washing my shirt. I washed off my neck, my face, and hands, and put my half-soaked shirt back on. Then I walked to the main office that was connected to the assistant principal's office. The assistant principal, Mr. Baumgarten, was waiting for me behind the counter of the main office. Mr. Baumgarten said, "Are you Richard Kraemer?"

I said, nervously, "Yeah."

He pointed to the chairs lined up behind me, and said, "Have a seat. We are waiting for Mrs. English to arrive."

Then he turned around, and said, "Millie, pull Richard Kraemer's file and bring it to my office." Then he walked away out of sight. I sat down, among the 10 empty seats against the pane glass window that separated the office and the hallway outside. This was the first time that I had gotten in trouble in high school, but that was because I had only been there for about four weeks. This assistant principal didn't know me yet, but now that he had my rap sheet from junior high, I had a feeling he was going to get the full picture. As I sat there, I began to think through what my plea would be. It is a funny thing that I had not thought through this part of my plot. I knew that I would be in this position, but I did not quite plan out this part of the scheme. I thought to myself, "Maybe I'll just come clean, tell my story, everyone would understand, give me a good scolding, and then I'd be on my merry way." No, that would be a fantasy, more likely, I would be suspended and get a lot of shit from my parents. I know, I could plead insanity. I didn't know what I was doing, and did not know it was wrong to leave a week old, green molded, big jelly doughnut on that bitch's seat. In addition, I did not know the consequences of my actions. In fact, I do not know where I am right now. I could start drooling, ask for my teddy bear, and cock my head to the side. Then I thought that would be too extreme, and it would ruin my cool image. The last alternative was the best choice, plead my innocence. Have them prove that I planted the Big Jelly Bomb with the intent of causing public humiliation to sweet Diane, the victim.

The bell rang for the students to change classes and the hallway quickly filled with kids walking by. Then, the hallway door opened, Diane and Mrs. English walked up to the counter. Diane had a white towel wrapped around her waist, which had a huge wet spot where her ass was located. This was great to see my work in action, because hundreds of kids walk by the office, and everyone instinctively looks inside the office to see what's going on. Diane and Mrs. English, standing at the office counter, unknowingly have their backs fully exposed to the building crowd of students peering through the pane glass windows in the hallway. Suddenly, Diane turns around, and sees a crowd of kids staring back at her.

Diane yelled, "Oh, no, they're staring at me!" She started to adjust her towel, and put her backside against the counter. Mrs. English pulled Diane by the arm, and said, "Come with me." Then I looked behind me and saw a huge crowd of kids looking at her, laughing and banging on the window.

As Mrs. English pulled her behind the counter, Diane was walking backwards trying not to expose her wet ass.

Once they were behind the counter, Diane yelled at me, "You bastard, I'll get you for this!"

I stood up, and yelled, "I didn't do it, you Bitch!"

Mr. Baumgarten came running from his office, and said, "Young man, sit down. You two, get in my office quickly." The three of them went into the assistant principal's office, and closed the door. I looked back through the window and the crowd began to disburse. I sat back down in my seat and awaited my fate. The bell for the beginning of class sounded. I waited for about 10 minutes, until the assistant principal's office door opened. Diane came out, and shot me a look that could kill an elephant. Mrs. English followed behind her and they both walked out of the office, into the hallway.

Then, Mr. Baumgarten stood in the doorway of his office, and said, "Richard," snapped his finger, and pointed inside his office. I got up and walked past him into his office. He closed the door, walked behind his desk, and sat down.

Mr. Baumgarten said, "Have a seat, Mr. Kraemer." I moved in front of his desk, there were two black vinyl seats, one was wet and one was not. I scuffled passed the wet one, then sat on the dry one.

Mr. Baumgarten said, "I'm the assistant principal of this high school. My name is Mr. Baumgarten, I have many jobs, and one of them is that I am the disciplinarian. So, before we get started, are there any questions about what I do here?"

I leaned forward in my seat, and said, "No, sir."

He leaned back in his seat, and said, "Good, I'm a fair person and I believe that there are two sides to every story. So, before I make any judgment, I would like to hear your side of the story." Then he picked up his pen, and began clicking it.

I said," The girl sat on a jelly doughnut, and she blames me for it, and I didn't do it." Then I rose my palms up, shrugged my shoulders, and put my best innocent face on.

Mr. Baumgarten, stopped clicking his pen, smiled, and sat up in his seat.

He said, "That's it, well, that explains everything, Richard. You're free to go." With a surprised look on my face, I got up, and turned slightly to the left.

He barked, "Sit down." I dropped back down to my seat. Mr. Baumgarten snarled, "You don't expect me to buy that crap, do you?"

I said, in a soft voice, "Mr. Baumgarten, it's the truth. I had nothing to do with this; otherwise, someone would have seen me do it."

He said, "Oh, a witness to the crime. Is that what we need? Someone that had actually seen you place the doughnut on that girl's seat, right?"

I said, "Yeah, that would prove it."

Mr. Baumgarten leaned forward in his chair, and said, "Did you ask this girl out? Didn't she reject your advances? And when she did, you got mad? Wouldn't that motivate you to seek revenge and get even with her?"

I sat up straight in the chair, and said, "Is that what this is about? I have asked other girls and been rejected. If I got mad at every girl that rejected me, and smashed a doughnut on each one of their butts, you would have a big line out into the hallway."

Mr. Baumgarten stood up, and leaned over his desk, "We're going nowhere with this." Then the phone rang on his desk. He said, "Hold that thought," then he picked up the phone. He said, "Yes, (long pause) he's in my office right now. I see, (pause) where are you now? Okay, I'll be right there."

Then he hung up the phone. Mr. Baumgarten said, "I'll be right back, Richard." Then he walked out of the office. I thought to myself, "I guess there were some new developments in the Big Jelly Attack. Maybe they have some witnesses that saw me slip the doughnut under Diane's ass, and now they're going to sweat me for a confession. If that is the situation, I'll just come clean and take my punishment." After all, there is a price to be paid, and it was worth every penny.

Mr. Baumgarten walked back into his office, closed the door, and sat back down in his chair.

He said, "Well, Mr. Kraemer, I just talked to Mrs. English, and she found two witnesses, they were sitting behind you in class."

I jumped up, and said, "Mr. Baumgarten, I can't sit here any longer.........." Mr. Baumgarten interrupted, and said, "Son, do not interrupt me when I'm speaking. Now, sit down." My face got beet red, I started to perspire all over my body, and I slowly sat back down. He sat straight up in his chair, and said, "Now, as I was saying, Mrs. English had found two witnesses that sit behind you in class. After Mrs. English and I had talked to the students, they are absolutely certain that you did not slip that jelly doughnut on that girl's seat. The reason that they were so certain is because they were seated at their desks before you arrived into the classroom. They observed you from behind until this incident happened. In addition, Mrs. English remembered that Diane was late for class, and that the girl was in a hurry to sit down, and didn't notice the doughnut on her seat, and thus, an accident occurred. It seems pretty apparent that someone in the preceding class had left it behind. Therefore, Richard, I apologize for this misunderstanding. Do you have any questions?"

I sat there, for a moment, with my mouth open, and said, " Ah, no."

Mr. Baumgarten slapped his hand on the desk, and said, "Good, you're free to go."

I closed my mouth, paused for a moment, and than I got up looking at him.

He said, looking up at me, "You see, Richard, I told you I was fair. Didn't I?"

I said, "Yeah, you are." Then I turned, walked to the door, and opened it. Mr. Baumgarten said, "Leave the door open."

I walked out of the office and into the hallway. As I walked to my locker, I was dumbfounded by the chain of events that got me off Scott Free. I was very puzzled by the mystery witnesses that were sitting behind me. I cannot even remember what they looked like. In addition, I was the first one in that class today, of that, I was certain. I also knew that if it were not for Mrs. English asking for witnesses and supporting a bogus theory, I would be hanging from the gallows.

The next day, I went to my English class early, waiting to talk to these witnesses. Then a blond girl, named Susan, and a tall guy, named Chris, walked in together, with huge smiles on their faces. They walked right down the same row of desks where I was sitting, and Chris sat right behind me. Susan sat in the next row of desks beside Chris. I turned around in my seat, and whispered, "You two are the witnesses to what happened?"

Chris smiled from ear to year, and whispered, "Yeah, you got that bitch Diane good."

Susan leaned over, and whispered, "She got what was coming to her."

I was confused, and whispered, "Yeah, but why did you lie for me?"

Susan whispered, "Because it's even more humiliating when you get away with it."

I said, in a low voice, "What has she done to you guys, to make you hate her so much?"

Chris whispered, "Because Diane and her girl friends stole Susan's pants and underwear while she was in the shower, after gym class."

Susan said, "Yeah, and I had to wait for an hour and a half for my father to bring me more clothes. You don't know how embarrassed I was."

I told them my story also. I also said that we should not look too friendly during class, because Mrs. English would catch on to the conspiracy. A couple of moments later, Mrs. English walked into the classroom, and called me to her desk. She apologized for doubting my innocence, and realized that this was all an accident. Then she sent me back to my desk. Then Diane walked into the classroom. She stopped in front of Mrs. English's desk, and stared right at me, with her mouth open. I smiled and waved at her.

Diane turned to Mrs. English, and said, "What is he doing here?"

Mrs. English stood up, and said, "Let's go into the hallway and talk." Diane stomped out of the classroom, and Mrs. English followed. I turned to look at Chris and Susan; they were both trying to suppress their laughter by hiding their faces in their hands. Suddenly, I heard a lot of Diane's shouting as follows:

"An accident, that's Bull Shit!"

"Don't tell me to calm down!"

"I'm not going to apologize to the Fucking Dork!"

"My language!"

Then Diane appeared in the doorway, she looked right at me, and yelled, "My brother is going to kick your fucking ass!"

Mrs. English grabbed Diane by the arm, and said, "You're going to Mr. Baumgarten's office."

As they both walked down the hallway, you could hear Diane's yelling fade away. Chris tapped me on the shoulder, and said, "I wouldn't worry about Diane's brother. He's a fat, fucking draft dodger, and he can't leave Canada."

I laughed, and said, "Well, that's a relief; I wouldn't want him to sit on me."

As for Diane, when she reached Mr. Baumgarten's office, she couldn't compose herself from cursing. This caused her to be suspended for three days.

After that day, Mrs. English took a real interest in teaching English to me. I think she might have seen my folder, and found out that I was dyslexic. There would be times afterschool when we would meet, and work very hard so I could keep up in class. One of a few teachers who took real pride in the work they did.

Chapter 17 - Teenage Wedding

As I had mentioned before, I had quite a few cousins on my father's side of the family. He had a sister named Carol, and she had three sons and one daughter. Of that family, I was closest to Bobby, who was a year older than I was, and Kenny was three years older than I was. They lived about 15 miles away from me, and occasionally we would get together to have some fun. The relationship was a close one, but the distance from one home to another was too far to see each other often. They were like distant big brothers to me.

One day, I had gotten the word in the late summer of 1972 that Kenny had gotten his 15-year-old girlfriend, Fran, pregnant, and they were going to get married ASAP. I felt happy for Kenny and Fran, and thought it was exciting for them to start a new life together, and that it was all part of growing up. Of course, the adults had a different viewpoint of the situation, but they also thought that marriage was the only solution for the teenaged lovers. Therefore, the wedding was set for the following month, for this fast track shot gun marriage.

The ceremony was performed in a cute little church in the middle of the village in Harriman, New York. Kenny had a very nice 1969 Nova SS with a 396 four-barrel engine, with four on the floor, a mighty fine machine. It was a beautiful day for a wedding, the sun was shining, and it was a very warm September day. Fran was a very pretty bride, and to tell you the truth, I was quite jealous of Kenny. At the time, he seemed to have it all, a hot car, beautiful wife, a nice job, and a baby on the way. Of course, I was looking at his situation through the eyes of a 16-year-old boy. Nevertheless, I was happy for them both, and I had a sense of coming of age myself by seeing them get married.

For this event, my parents had gotten one of my aunts to baby sit the twins for the wedding. My dad had bought Ike and me new sport jackets at Julie's, a nice men's shop in

Monroe. My mom bought Gina a new dress, and sent her to the beauty parlor where she got an elaborate hair-do. My parents spent a shit load of money to dress the entire family up for this wedding. I think that they really wanted to look good, and present our family as best as possible. In addition, the wedding reception was going to be held in one of the most extravagant halls in Orange County, The Bells.

As our family drove onto the estate like property of The Bells in New Windsor, New York, my parents gasped in awe. The reception hall looked like a huge plantation mansion at the end of a very long circular driveway. The property had a huge manicured lawn, the trees and bushes meticulously maintained. When we pulled in front of the building, a parking valet had opened my mother's door, my dad reluctantly handed over the car keys to the attendant.

Once inside The Bells, you would think that we were inside a wealthy plantation owner's home, entrance doors were 18 feet high, inside, the foyer had two huge staircases on each side, and there was red wall to wall carpeting everywhere. Looking back on it, I guess my family must have felt like the Clampetts when they took their first look at their mansion in Beverly Hills. The Kraemer's did not get out much as a family. When we got to the huge reception hall, there must have been seating for, at least, 200 people. The waiter seated my family at the edge of a big dance floor. When we took our seats, I could not help but notice that, there were two 6 foot high, 4 feet in circumference, fountains on each side of the dance floor. However, these fountains were not spewing water, but booze, one had Whiskey Sours and the other had Screwdrivers. Well, I must say that I was quite taken back by this sight, and thought that I must have a sample. Bobby had walked over to our table with the rest of his family, before the bride and groom had arrived. My parents, and Aunt Carol and Uncle Lawry, who were the groom's parents, sat down and talked for a while as they had a few drinks. My mother sent me over to the Whiskey Sours fountain to fill her glass, and, on the way, back I got a Screwdriver for myself. When I returned to the table to deliver the drink, my mom protested to the idea of me drinking. My Uncle Lawry interjected, and told her that he was allowing Bobby to drink under supervision, because he, too, was under the drinking age. Uncle Lawry said, "Jeanie, Kenny is getting married today. Bobby and Dickie are about the same age. Let them celebrate my son's marriage with a few drinks. They'll have to learn to drink sometime."

Mom said, "I don't know if that's such a great idea."

Aunt Carol said, "She may be right, Lawry."

Uncle Lawry said, "Well, I'm letting Bobby drink, I'll look after them."

My dad said, "I'll watch them, too."

My dad turned to me, and said, "You can drink, but don't get shit faced. Okay?"

I smiled, and said, "Yeah, okay."

I smiled at Bobby, and we walked off with our drinks.

I could hear mom say, as we walked away, "You better watch those two, Richard."

As I passed the Screwdriver fountain, Bobby and I topped off our drinks, and continued on to the other side of the room where the action was. Once we reached the other side of the room, there was a whole bunch of guys and girls that Bobby and Kenny knew that were from the Washingtonville area, and they were my age or older. Everyone was dressed up in suits and gowns, and the girls were RED HOT. Bobby introduced me to many people that night, and I was truly having a great time. The band was playing some great rock music, I asked a few girls to dance, because I had the alcohol courage to do so. Some accepted, and some rejected. If I was rejected, I still danced in the crowd on the dance floor. After each dance, I would refill at the Screwdriver fountain, and return to the table of teenagers. I could see that many of the teenagers were getting pretty intoxicated, but I felt fine. In fact, I got a little buzz, but was still very thirsty because I was dancing so much, and sweating like a pig.

After about an hour and a half, my father came over to the table to retrieve me, because they were about to serve dinner, and he wanted the family to eat together. When we walked past the Screwdriver fountain, I refilled one more time before sitting down.

My Dad said, "You better slow down on that," then he grabbed me by the arm, "Are you listening to me?"

I looked at him, "Yeah, Dad, I heard you, I'm okay."

When I sat down, mom started making small talk with me, to do her field sobriety test on me. I was talking and walking fine. In fact, I was so talkative during dinner that my father told me to shut up and eat. The dinner was the most gorgeous prime rib, an inch thick, medium well, with mashed potatoes, and green beans. The best we ever had at the Kraemer house was London Broil, but most of the time, Chuck steak. At that very moment, I thought that this would be great to live in a house like this, to have a meal like this every day, to dance until my legs fell off, to have a wife like Fran, a cool car like Kenny, and, most of all, my own Screwdriver fountain. That would be so groovy; it would be like living in heaven with style. Ike didn't seem like he was having a good time, my parents thought that because he was only 14 it was better for him not to be drinking alcohol. Therefore, Ike was served kiddie cocktails with a cherry and a little paper umbrella that made him feel like a little kid. I slipped him a couple of big boy drinks, but it wasn't a lot. Gina was having a great time, and did not need any alcohol. Mom was drinking Whiskey Sours; she was getting a good buzz. Dad was mostly a beer man; he, too, had a half a buzz on. There was a lot of activity; relatives that my parents had not seen for years were there. In addition, my grandma Kraemer, Grandpa Dick, all my aunts, uncles, and all the cousins were moving from table to table socializing. The band was playing loud rock music, people were dancing, laughing, shouting, and everyone was having a great time. Therefore, with all that was going on at this wedding reception, it would be hard to keep track of an alcohol fueled 16-year-old boy. I did take full advantage of the situation.

My mom asked me to get her another Whiskey Sour, and dad, a beer. I walked across the crowded dance floor. As I did, I started to wobble a little, and felt a little light headed. On my return trip on the dance floor, I danced through the crowd holding the two drinks. When I reached my parents' table, I gave my parents their drinks and sat down in my seat. I sat there grooving to the music and drinking my drink, after that great meal. Then the music changed to something slow and old, while they prepared to cut the wedding cake.

My glass was empty, so I got up from the table, and started to walk to the Screwdriver fountain, that was about 20 feet inside the dance floor. There wasn't a soul on the dance floor, as I walked I began to stagger, and became very light headed. When I reached the Screwdriver fountain, I put my glass under the streaming Sunshine Drink. Suddenly, without warning, I got very dizzy and started to fall to my right. I dropped my glass into the fountain, and grabbed the edges of it, to keep me from falling. The fountain snapped apart from my weight, sending the Screwdriver fountain and me to the floor. When I landed on my back on the floor, about 20 gallons of the Screwdriver drink dumped on top of me, and the rest of the broken fiberglass fountain parts surrounded me. My legs and arms flopped around like a trout out of water, reacting to the coldness of the beverage. I then rolled on my stomach, and lifted myself to my knees. Just then, I felt someone grab me from under my right armpit, and I was thrusted to my feet. I looked to see who had saved me from drowning, and it was my Dad. Then, uncle Lawry grabbed me under my other arm, and they began to walk me out of the Screwdriver Pond. As they did, we all slipped and slided off the dance floor, as everyone stared at us. At that point, my legs felt like rubber, I could not walk without assistance, and everything was very blurry.

Dad said, "Lawry, I got him, I'm going to put him in the car."

Uncle Lawry said, "Are you sure, Dick?"

Dad said, "Yeah, I got him."

I do not remember anything until we got to the car, but I am pretty sure it was not easy getting into the parking lot. My father rested me on the side of our 1968 Oldsmobile Cutlass Cruiser station wagon, and opened the tailgate. As he did, I fell on the blacktop parking lot. He picked me up by grabbing my shirt at the chest, and rested me back on the side of the car. Dad then sat me on the tailgate.

Dad said, "Get in."

I slurred, "I don't want to sit back here."

He said, "I don't care what you want, I want you to lie back there, and sleep it off!"

I crawled, like a dog, into the back of the station wagon, and laid down curled up into a ball. Then dad slammed the tailgate shut, and rolled down the back window.

Dad poked his head in the opened tailgate window, and said, in a low voice, "If you need to puke, do it out of the window, if you puke in the car, you're really going to piss me off. Second, if you need to take a piss, do it in the parking lot. Do not, I repeat, do not come back inside. You have embarrassed your mother and me, I told you not to get shit faced."

I slurred, "I'm sorry, Dad."

He said, "Yeah, me too. Just remember what I said."

Then dad walked back into the building. I laid there drunk, soaking wet, stinking like a Big Screwdriver Flounder, thrashing around in the back of the station wagon for a couple of hours, puking my guts out the back window. I finally fell asleep. The next thing I remember was dad throwing me on my bed that evening.

When I awoke the next morning, the first thing that I felt was a great pain in my eyeballs, when opening them to the sun-filled bedroom. My head hurt so bad, that I had thought someone hit me in the forehead with a baseball bat. As I started to get up, the clothes that I was wearing had stuck to the sheets like glue, from the Screwdrivers I took a bath in, and sweating out the alcohol from every pore of my body. I peeled the sheets off me, and rose to my feet, I still felt dizzy. I looked at the clock, and it was 12:45 PM. I walked into the bathroom, took a piss, then knelt down to the Porcelain Princess, and engaged in a few rounds of dry heaves, and asked for God's forgiveness. I peeled off my clothes, drew a hot bath in the big claw foot tub, and soaked in it for about 40 minutes.

I had gotten dressed, walked downstairs, took some aspirin in my parents' bathroom, and sat down at the kitchen table. One thing I did not want to do was to face my parents, after what had happened. Especially with my very first mega hangover, not to mention the fool I had made of myself, and embarrassed the entire family. I felt very bad about the whole thing. I folded my arms on the kitchen table, and rested my head on them.

Mom walked in, and said, "How do you feel?"

I raised my head, looked at her, and said, "I feel like crap."

Mom said, "You look like crap. Do you have a headache?" Then she smiled.

I looked at her, and said, "Yeah, I took some aspirin." She walked out of the room, came back into the kitchen, poured a glass of water, and dropped two Alka-Seltzer tablets into it. She waited for the tablets to dissolve, handed me the glass, and said, "Drink this."

I looked at her, and said, "I can't, it will make me sick."

Mom forced my hand around the glass, and said, "It'll settle your stomach, now drink the whole thing in one shot, down it." Then she forced the glass to my mouth, and I drank the whole thing in one shot. My mother then grabbed the glass from me, and put it into the sink.

I started to brace myself for another run to the bathroom. She stood there, smiling with her arms crossed, leaning against the counter, observing me. It seemed that she was getting pleasure from my suffering.

Then my father walked into the room. Dad slapped me on the back, and said, "How you feeling, boy?" Then he put his face about 5 inches from mine, and smiled. Dad said, "Hey, Jeanie, he doesn't look so good. Hey, Dick, are you thirsty? Do you want some orange juice? I'll pour you a big glass."

I said, "No that will make me sick."
Both my parents broke out in loud hysterical laughter. Then I held my head in my hands, as my elbows rested on the table, and I thought to myself, "This is what I need, both my parents fuck 'n with me while I suffer my first hangover." I think I will beg for mercy.

I waited for the laughter to die down, lifted my head from my hands, and looked at the both of them smiling. I said, "I'm really sorry about what happened last night, and I'm sorry that I embarrassed you. I don't know what happened; the Screwdrivers hit me like a ton of bricks, all at once."

Dad wiped the grin off his face, and said, "Vodka will do that to you. When you get older, you'll learn to hold your liquor. But, I told you to take it easy, and you didn't listen. As for embarrassing the entire family, we'll get over it. But, do you know the good part?"

I looked at my father, confused for a moment, because I couldn't figure out anything good that came from this. I said, "No, what?"

He said, "The only one that looked more stupid then your family, was you."
Then both my parents laughed loudly. After the laughter died down, my dad informed me that I would have to shampoo the carpets and clean the entire inside of the car, because it smelled like booze.

After that day, my parents never brought up the public display of the drunken teenager's dive into the Screwdriver

Fountain. I'm not sure if any of my relatives had captured this Kodak moment, and have it in their family album, I certainly hope not.

I hope that all of those parents out there, who had pondered about letting their under aged children drink alcohol with adult supervision, will remember this story. Imagine my parents sitting there at the edge of an empty dance floor with only their son on it, with that Screwdriver Fountain, surrounded by a couple of hundred people. If an event like this doesn't make any parent want to crawl under a rock, I don't know what will.

This is a photo of me after the wedding at the groom's house. On the back of the snapshot my mother wrote, "After Kenny's and Fran's Wedding – Dick was a Mess". Yeah, that was an understatement; I don't even remember leaving the car.

Chapter 18 - The Girl Friend

After my grandstand female rejection, I felt that maybe I was trying too hard, and would put the girl friend pursuit on hold for a while.

Until one day, I spotted a girl that looked interesting in the lunchroom. I had not noticed her before, but she was sitting with a girl I knew in one of my classes. I was sitting a couple of tables away from where girls were sitting, and was trying to get a better look at this girl.

I asked Andrew, one of my classmates, "Who is that girl sitting with Inez?"

He turned, looked, and said, "Which one?"

I said, "The one with the long, brown hair."

He said, "They all have long brown hair, except for Inez."

I said, "The one with the green top."

Andrew said, "I don't know her, but the one in the red top is Kathy."

I looked at him seriously, and said, "I need to get her name."

Andrew smiled, and said, "Oh, Rich, I think you like that one," and he hit me in the shoulder.

I smiled, and said, "Yeah, but how am I going to meet her?"

Andrew said, "Why don't you ask Inez, she's in our class, Dummy."

I said, surprised, "Yeah, I'll ask her tomorrow in class."

I looked at my watch, and realized that I had to catch the B.O.C.E.S bus.

I said, "I've got to split, I'll see you tomorrow."

He said, with a smile, "See ya, lover boy."

The following day, I saw Inez in class and asked her for her friend's name. At first, she looked at me strangely, and asked me why I needed to know her name. I said that I just wanted to know her name, that it was no big deal. Then it dawned on her that I might be interested in her friend, she smiled and said, "Judy." Then she asked if I would like to meet her, in which I immediately accepted the invitation. I figured that if one of her friends introduced me, it would make for a smooth transition. So Inez said that she and Judy would be in the lunchroom after the next class, which was my lunchtime.

After my next class, I rushed to the lunchroom. Then I nonchalantly walked into the lunch line, and casually looked around the lunchroom for Judy and I Inez. I spotted Inez and she was sitting at a table with a whole bunch of girls. I turned and faced the lunch counter, and made as if I was interested in the slop they were serving today. I turned again and saw Inez standing up, waving at me with Judy sitting next to her, and a dozen other girls at the table waving at me. I waved at them, smiled, and turned around. I thought to myself, "I didn't know this was going to be a public event," and I hoped this was not another set up. I had reached the end of the lunch line, I looked at the lunch lady cashier, and she smiled back at me, as though she knew what was up. I pay for my sloppy Joe, Apple crisp and chocolate milk, and moved slowly to my intended target. I reached the table and about six girls were standing around Judy, who was the only one sitting and looking down at the tabletop.

Inez said, "Hi," and put her arm over Judy's shoulder.

I said, "Hi, Inez," then I put my lunch directly across from where Judy was sitting.

Inez said, "I would like you to meet my friend, Judy." I looked at Judy as she raised her head from the table, and the first thing I noticed was that she had big, beautiful dark brown eyes, then she smiled a great big smile.

I smiled, and said, "Hi, I'm Rich." All the girls around her started to giggle loudly, and she quickly put her head down.

I said, "Can I sit down here?" I waited for a moment for a response and looked at Inez.

Inez said, "Yeah, sit down, Rich; she's just a little shy."

I looked back at Judy, and she made a hand gesture for me to sit down, still looking down at the table. As I sat down, the girls around her, still giggling loudly, took their seats.

I opened my chocolate milk, and took a drink. I said, looking at Judy, "Are you okay?"

She looked up at me, and said, "I'm not comfortable with all this," and motioned her hand around the table. Then she looked back down at the table.

I knew that she meant this public scene with all of these cackling girls around her.

I said, "You know, I feel uncomfortable, too."

Then she lifted her head, looked at me, and smiled.

I smiled, and said, "Maybe they'll get bored and go away." Then I lifted my sloppy Joe, and took a big bite. As I chewed my first bite, I noticed that she had parted her hair in the middle, and that she braided each side with about 1/2 inch thick braid that wrapped over the rest of her hair to the back of her head. I thought that looked nice.

After I finished chewing, I said, "I like what you did to your hair, it looks nice."

She looked back at me, shyly, smiled, and said," Thank you."

Kathy, the girl sitting on the other side of Judy, put her arm around her shoulder and smiled. Kathy said, "Do you like her?"

I was surprised by the question, and sat back in my chair, as they all looked at me.

I said, "Yeah, I like her."

Then all the girls started giggling, and smiling at Judy and me.

Judy smiled back at me, and said," All this is embarrassing for me."

I said, "Maybe we could meet somewhere, and talk?"

Kathy said, "I know, you can meet at my house tomorrow after school, my mom works during the day."

Inez jumped in, and said, "That's perfect, is that okay with you, Judy?

I looked at Judy, she looked apprehensive at first, and she looked at me.

Judy said, "Would that be alright with you, Rich?"

I smiled, and said, "Yeah, sure, where do you live, Kathy?"

Kathy said, "Right in the village of Monroe, Inez will tell you how to get there."   Inez said, "I'll write down the directions, and give them to you in class tomorrow."

Kathy said, "We have to go to class now." Then the three of them got up from the table.

I looked at Judy, and said, "Okay, I'll see you tomorrow."

Judy then smiled at me, and lifted her hand slightly to say good-bye.

Then Kathy leaned over the table, and whispered, "Bring some pot, we like pot."   I said, surprised, "Ah, yeah, I'll try."

Kathy said, "No, really, bring some pot."

I said, "Okay."

Then the three of them turned and walked away, giggling on the way out of the lunchroom.

I finished my lunch, and got on the B.O.C.E.S bus for my construction program. As I rode to the program, I began to reflect on my first meeting with Judy. I thought that she was attractive, had a nice smile, but she was very shy. I needed to get to know her better, and see if she would be the one. This next meeting, I thought, was not going to be the perfect situation with Inez and Kathy hanging around, protecting her from my clutches. However, I guess Judy needed to feel comfortable around me, with her friends being chaperones. My biggest hurdle, at the moment, was to score some pot. At this point in my life, I had only smoked dope a couple of times, and I never got high. In fact, I thought the whole pot-smoking thing was a sham, and the high was all psychosomatic. Now I had to score some pot for Judy and her friends, to make this meeting go right. I was a little put off about this requirement, but if I didn't come through with the goods, I would come off as some dork. I knew some guys in school that would be willing to sell some dope to me, because I drifted in and out of groups all the time.

I scored some pot from a student at B.O.C.E.S, and the following day, I met Inez in class. She gave me the directions to Kathy's house, and asked if I had the pot. I said that I had scored, and asked if Judy would be in the lunchroom, Inez said that Judy had a class during my lunch period today, but the three of them would see me after school at Kathy's house. So the meeting was set.

Later that day, the B.O.C.E.S bus dropped me off after school at the high school. I ran up to the main road, and hitched a ride with another student to the village of Monroe. I stopped at the Collage, bought some Zig Zag rolling papers, and walked across Crane Park to Kathy's house. I walked up on the porch of the brown house with white trim, and rang the doorbell. No one came to the door, I thought for a moment that maybe I had the wrong house. I rang the doorbell again, waited a few moments, and then I knocked on the door hard. Then I could see some one inside coming towards the door and it opened.

Kathy opened the door, with a big smile, and said, "Hi, Rich, come on in."
I followed her into the living room where Inez and Judy were standing.

Judy smiled, and said, "Hi, Rich, did you find the place alright?"

I said, "Yeah, I know this area pretty well."

Kathy said, "Do you want something to drink? I have some Tang."

I said, "Yeah, Tang is cool."

Then I walked over to Judy. I smiled, and said, "I really wanted to talk to you again."

She looked up at me, shyly, and said softly, "Me, too."

Judy was much shorter than I was. She was a little chunky, but that didn't turn me off, because she also had a set of large breasts, that I had a real interest in exploring at a later time. If fact, she had bigger breasts than most of the girls in the freshman class. However, that was only one of many reasons that I liked her at first sight. She was attractive with pretty eyes, long brown hair, and she had a nice smile. Now I needed to know the person behind all those superficial things. One thing I was not looking for was an unhappy, nasty, bitchy, wiseass, or an asshole, for a girl friend. If that would be the case, I would rather be alone. Kathy came back into the living room with glasses of Tang.

Inez said, "Let's play some music."

Kathy said, "Yeah, let's all go to my bedroom, I have music up there."

Kathy, holding her Tang, walked up stairs and we all followed. She opened the door to her bedroom and it was very small, it barely fit two dressers and a bed. Now we had four teenagers in this tiny space. Judy and I sat next to each other on the end of the bed Inez sat at the head, and Kathy stood up. She went to the top of her dresser and opened up her record player. She stacked some 45's and the music began to play.

Kathy said, "Do you like BJ Thomas, "Hooked on a Feeling"?" Then she lit up a cigarette.

I said, "Yeah, that's cool." Judy looked at me and smiled.

Kathy said, "Where's the pot?"

Inez said, "Yeah, let's get high." Then Inez took the cigarette from Kathy, and took a drag.

I reached into my jacket pocket and pulled out a nickel bag, and said, "You have a pipe?"

The girls looked each other, and said in unison, "No."

I said," I got papers."

I had never rolled a joint in my life, but I had seen it done a few times. I figured there has to be a first time for everyone, now happened to be that time. I opened up the baggie, and the pack of rolling papers. I got a teen magazine off the bed and put it on my lap. Then I took a rolling paper from the package, and folded it in half. The girls were watching me intently, as if I was performing brain surgery. Then I took a pinch of dope, placed it inside the paper, and then repeated the process. I evened out the dope into the paper, and began to roll the paper. As I tried to roll the joint, the dope fell out of both ends, and the paper ripped in the middle.

The girls all sighed together, "OOOOOHHHHH!!! I took another rolling paper out of the pack and began the process once more. Again, the paper ripped in the middle with the dope falling on the magazine.

Kathy said, "Don't you know how to roll a joint?"

I said, "Not really, I use a pipe, but I lost it. Do you know how to roll?"

Kathy said, "Not me, how about you guys," looking at Judy and Inez.

They both shook their heads no. At that point, I realized that I was surrounded by amateurs, including myself. But, being a male, I had to find a solution to this problem. Otherwise, I could come off looking like a dork.

I said, "I need a pencil."

Kathy ran out of the room, and came back with a yellow number two. I took the pencil and wrapped the rolling paper around it. Then I licked the gum part of the paper. I moved the eraser part of the pencil to almost the very end of the rolling paper. I took a very small pinch of pot and fed it into the opened end of the joint. I repeated the pain staking process several times, until the joint was filled with pot. Then I twisted the excess paper at one end, and then held it horizontally, removed the pencil, and twisted the excess paper on the other end. Suddenly, the girls jumped up and down, clapping and cheering as if the operation was a success and the patient lived. I pulled out a pack of matches, lit the joint, and passed it to Judy, as I coughed. The joint made popping and crackling noises as she took her first drag. Judy also coughed and gagged, and passed it to Kathy. As the joint made its rounds, it went out a few times. The bedroom had filled with pot smoke as the music played. I looked out Kathy's bedroom window and noticed how beautiful the late fall day was. After the joint took about four or five rounds, it got too small to smoke, and I put it out.

Suddenly, without warning, I became very light headed. I turned to Judy, who was still sitting next to me, and she had a huge smile on her face.

I said, "Did you get a buzz?" Then she nodded her head yes, and let out a little laugh. I looked at Kathy and Inez, and they were dancing together with big grins on their faces. I started to groove with the music, and smiled so hard that my face began to hurt. At that moment, I was scared, because for the first time, I had finally gotten high on pot, and it was nothing like alcohol. Alcohol was a gradual high, and you could stop the elevator at any floor you wanted. Marijuana takes you up the elevator, and it picks the floor for you. I was not used to this kind of high. I said to Judy, "Wow, I got stoned on that joint."

She put her hand on my hand, and said, "I'm really glad you came."

I looked into her eyes, smiled, and said, "Me, too."

Kathy yelled, over the music, "Why don't you kiss her?"

I began to laugh, and said, "What?"

Inez yelled, "Go ahead and kiss her!"

Judy covered her face in embarrassment.

I laughed, and said, "Who, Kathy," and I got up off the bed.

Kathy smiled, and said, "I don't want to kiss you, dummy. Judy," then she pointed at her.

Then I smiled, and said, "Oh!" I was just trying to put a little humor into an embarrassing situation for the both of us.

Inez said, "Look at her, she wants you to kiss her."

I looked at Judy, and she looked up at me. I sat on the bed next to her. I put my hand gently on her cheek, and turned her face towards me. I moved my face close to hers and tilted my head slightly. Her eyes were closed before our lips touched. Judy's lips were so soft on mine, as I put my arms around her shoulders. I was in euphoria for a moment or two. I knew that it was a long kiss, but I could not tell you how long. Although the music was loud, and Judy's girl friends were squealing, all that noise was suddenly muted. As we broke our kiss, I moved away slowly from her face, and she opened her eyes and looked deeply into mine. We both smiled at each other. Kathy and Inez started cheering and laughing, and they were just being stoned teenaged girls.

I asked, "Where's the bathroom?"
Kathy opened the door and pointed down the hallway. When I returned from the bathroom, everyone was standing in the bedroom doorway.

Kathy said, "I guess we'll leave you and Judy alone for a while to get to know each other." Then Inez and Kathy went downstairs and left us alone.

I closed the bedroom door behind me, walked over, and sat next to Judy. I smiled, and said, "Finally we get to talk alone."

She said, "Yeah, I know they can be a pain in the ass sometimes."

I said, "Where do you live?"

Judy smiled, and said, "On the other side of Monroe, on Cunningham Drive."

I said, "Yeah, I think I know where that is. I live in Highland Mills."

She said, "Isn't that far from here?"

I said, "Nah, it's about 7 miles from here. I usually hitchhike, that's no problem."
I then lit a cigarette and offered her one. We both moved to the floor by the opened window and talked for a while about our families, and our likes and dislikes. Judy was a shy girl. However, she became to know me a little better, and started to open up to me a little more. I asked her if I could kiss her

again, and she said yes. In fact, we sat on that hard floor for a while and kissed a few more times. The song that was playing during those moments turned out to be our song as a couple.

THE JOKER-by The Steve Miller Band

After a while, Kathy and Inez emerged again into the bedroom, and told me that her mother was due home in about half an hour, and that there were no boys allowed in the house, so I had to leave. I had arranged with Judy that I would see her at lunch the next day, and needed no further chaperones or proxies for our relationship.

I had finally found a girlfriend that I could confide in, and who would be my only closest friend.

In between going to school, working at the Monroe Diner part-time and seeing Judy every chance I could, I had very little idle time. I was always on the move, I did not hang around the house much, and I always had something going on. Most of the time, to get from one place to another, I was hitchhiking in rain, sleet, or snow, weather did not stop me from going somewhere. The only limitation was that, even at the age of 16, my parents were afraid of me hitchhiking at night. In those days, it was not so much that a serial killer would pick me up, although I had my share of being picked up sometimes by fagots and weirdoes. My parents were afraid that on the dark country roads, where I was traveling with no streetlights, I would be mowed down and left as Road Kill in the middle of the highway. Therefore, my parents would pick me up when it was dark, after work or if I had a date. Sometimes, they would even drive me to my destination, if they could fit it into their schedule. But that was only if they could catch up with me, before I left the house. I understood that they had four other kids to look after, and their own schedules to keep. I did not pester them to drive me all over the planet, and would only ask for a ride at night a few days in advance, if it were outside their regular schedule.

Occasionally, I would get Tom to work my shift for me at the diner, so I could see Judy afterschool, and he didn't mind making a few extra bucks. I would hitchhike to Monroe, and meet her either at her home or in the village. We would get together, maybe get something to eat, hang out with some of her friends, but, most of all, we liked being together alone. When I went to her house, we would mostly hang around in her bedroom. Judy's mother was a nice woman who always had a smile, and was always happy. Judy's mom used to make these mini chocolate pudding pies in little graham cracker pie shells, they were great after smoking some pot, and we would get the munchies. Judy used to close the bedroom door and lock it. We would listen to some music, talk, and, most of all make out. I was always very nervous about making out with Judy in that bedroom, with her mother in the house. There was some heavy-duty petting going on behind that door, sometimes we would be almost totally undressed, enthralled in the heat of passion and lust. Then, suddenly, Judy's mother would yell some question to her from 10 feet away. My body would jolt as if 1000 volts of electricity went through me, and my heart would be beating so fast, I thought it was going to jump out of my chest. Judy, with an annoyed look on her face, would yell back the answer to her mother, but never was nervous about it. I knew most times that if we were in that bedroom making out, and if her mother ever did walk in on us, it would be impossible to make it look like anything other than biology homework for extra credit. But Judy was fearless, it never bothered her, maybe she knew that her mother would never walk in on us. I would tell her that I was worried about her mother walking in on us, and planting a butcher knife in my chest for touching her daughter. Nevertheless, she would always ease my concerns, I have to admit, I did have a few nightmares of Judy's mother walking in on us, and they did not end well. Yet, those late afternoon heavy petting sessions in Judy's bedroom, with the fear of her mother walking in on us, made it even more exciting.

As for Judy's father, he did not get home from work until 7:30 PM at night, and I rarely saw very much of him. A few times, Judy would come to my house, but I would have to arrange transportation for her. My mom and Judy's mom used to share in the pickup and delivery. Judy was not allowed to hitchhike. My mom and Judy got along fine and they liked each other. In fact, Judy got along with everyone in my family, with the exception of Ike. The two of them just did not get along. Judy would sometimes come over on a Sunday, and we would have dinner with the family. One thing that was forbidden was for me to bring Judy into my bedroom alone, it was just not going to happen. My parents did not want to attend another shotgun wedding, where the groom was their own teenaged son. Therefore, my mother kept a close eye on me when she could. Judy really fit in well with my family, and they had grown to like her.

Once in a while, Judy and I would go to the movies at the Old Monroe Theater. The theater was owned and run by an elderly couple. At the time, the old couple must have been in their late 60s, and they moved very slowly. We would purchase a couple of tickets from the old woman in the window outside the theater. Then we would walk inside, and the same woman would come out of the ticket booth, walk over very slowly, and rip the ticket in half. Then the old lady would give us the stubs, unhook the rope to let us into the lobby, and then she would return to the ticket booth. Yes, the movie business was booming in Monroe. Once in the lobby, we would go to the snack counter. The old man would be behind the counter, and say, "Yes, may I help you," every time, it never failed. Your snack choices were very limited. Popcorn, one size only, Milk Duds, M&Ms, Hershey Bar, Peppermint Patties, Coca-Cola, and Orange Crush. The pricing was also very simple for the mathematically impaired everything was one dollar. After we ordered up the eats, the old feller would hammer out the sale on an antique cash register, sometimes the keys would stick, and he would have to bang on it to free up the jammed machine. Once we made our purchase, we would walk to the roped off theater entrance, and wait for the old man to check our ticket stubs. Security was very tight at the Old Monroe Theater. These old folks were not happy people and I had never seen them crack a smile. In fact, they were cranky, old farts, and would throw you out in a minute, after they got your money, if you did not follow the rules. Sometimes, Judy and I would go to the theater stoned, bust out in hysterical laughter, and have Mr. and Mrs. Geriatric threaten to toss us out if we didn't stop laughing. But Judy and I enjoyed going to the movies together, just to be alone with one another. I could tell you the titles of the movies we went to, but we were not there to watch the movie, we were there to be together alone, we were lovers.

Chapter 19 - Why do they call it High School

    The B.O.C.E.S. program had purchased property around the school, so they could build new homes as part of their construction program. Some of our training began inside the school, in a shop like setting, and then we would walk down the road to our construction site, and work on a new home project.

    I had become friendly with most of the other boys in the program. They were not college bound or book smart, but they were kids who were street smart and had common sense for the most part. We would go down to the construction site and would smoke cigarettes and some times a joint. Sometimes the instructor would work with students on a one on one basis, and would assign the rest of us to do something else like clean up the construction site, pull bent nails out of wood that could be reused, and more of the less glamorous work that construction has to offer. So, if you were not working one on one with the instructor, and not doing something that could cut your leg off, we would smoke some pot and have a few laughs. One thing was certain, if you were caught smoking dope on the job site, you were going to be dropped from the program. Mr. Piazza was pretty good at pinning somebody out that was smoking dope. Therefore, we would be very careful about concealing the fact that we were stoned. If you were working one on one with him, he would definitely pin you out, and make you empty out your pockets. We lost some good guys because they were busted. A few times, he would gather a group of boys, and make them all empty out their pockets. He felt that smoking dope on a job site was very dangerous for everyone around you, not to mention that you cannot learn anything when you're stoned.

    But, as the old saying goes," Boys will be boys." I say, "If there is a rule, it must be broken. Otherwise, what's the sense of having rules"? To prove the rule's validity, it must be broken, and prove the desired outcome. Thus, we must incur an injury on the construction job site while being stoned on illegal drugs, and prove that the instructor was right on his hypothesis." This made perfect sense to most of the students in the program. We were sure that by proving the instructor was right, it would make him very happy.

This brings back a fond memory of teenaged pot smoking, and the dangers of a construction job site. On one cold January afternoon, the temperature was about 5°, and most of the students were hanging out at the basement level of a bi-level shell that we were working on. Mr. Piazza was working with a couple of students up on the main level of the building. We all had a hard hat, coveralls, work boots, gloves, knitted hats, and coats on. The bi-level shell had no windows, doors, or insulation, the wind was blowing at about 20 MPH, and it began to snow. Most of the guys were in the basement area to shield us from the wind. We would stamp our feet and move around just to keep from freezing to death. The conversation would keep on coming back to the same subject, about how cold it was. A guy named Chip C., a big Italian guy with a full goatee, pulled out a fat joint and lit it up. There were about six of us in the basement, and we figured that it was better to be stoned cold rather than cold straight. Soon afterwards, we forgot how cold we were, and started joking around. A big guy with an Afro, Chuck, piled some scrap wood in the back of the building, and poured some gasoline on it. He set the gas can about 5 feet from the pile.

Then the instructor came down to the basement, and assigned work projects for all of us. We would all work in pairs, Billy, a longhaired blond guy, and I was assigned to cut a vent opening in the roof, we would be in the attic. Chip C. and Tommy B., a little bucktooth kid who looked like he was 10 years old, but was 15 would be on a scaffold below us in the kitchen. They would cut the vent opening into the ceiling and feed the copper vent pipe through the new opening. Chuck and Mike T. would be below the scaffold on the floor; they would cut a 3 inch in circumference copper vent pipe, feed the vent through the new openings and solder the first coupling.

Before we took to our respective workstations, all of us were waiting around for Chip and Tommy to finish their task first, because Billy and I needed the same saw to complete our task. Chip and Tommy moved the scaffold next to the ceiling area where they were going to cut through. Then Tommy pulled the reciprocating saw out of the tin box and pretended he was shooting a machine gun with it, as Chip climbed up to the top of the scaffold. Then Tommy climbed halfway up, carrying the saw, and handed it to Chip. Chip put the saw on the scaffold foot plank, and Tommy climbed the rest of the way up to the top. They needed electric, so Mike took the electric cord down stares and outside to the generator. The generator was not running, so Mike plugged the cord into the electrical outlet, and pulled on the recoil cord handle to start it. I heard the electric generator start. Suddenly, the reciprocating saw started on its own, because the trigger lock was on, and it started moving quickly towards Tommy. As Tommy moved out of the way of the saw, he lost his balance and fell off the scaffold. Chip, then stepped on the handle of reciprocating saw and pulled the electric cord out of the saw. Everyone ran to Tommy, you could see that he was in a lot of pain, holding his left leg, and crying. Mr. Piazza made his way through the group of kids, and told everyone to stand back. The instructor knelt down beside Tommy, and said, "Lie still, and tell me where it hurts."

Tommy said, in a sobbing voice, "It's my leg, I think it's broken."

Mr. Piazza said, "Okay, son. Do you think you can stand up, and put some weight on it?"

Tommy nodded his head, and said in a weeping voice, "I'll try," as he sat up.

The instructor said, "Billy, get him under one arm, Mike, you'll get him under the other." Then they both lifted Tommy to his feet, but resting most of the weight on his right leg. Tommy then put a little weight on his left leg, and he let out a loud sigh in pain.

Mr. Piazza said, "Do you think if these boys help you to the nurse's office at the school, you'll be able to make it, son?"

Tommy was a small, skinny kid, they could have piggy- backed him back.

Tommy said, "Yeah, I'm sure I can make it."

Then the instructor turned to rest of us, and said, "Don't do anything until I get back."

Tommy put his arms over Billy's and Mike's shoulders, and they all walked out the front doorway, Mr. Piazza trailed behind them.The rest of us went back downstairs into the basement. I went out the basement doorway, walked over to the electric generator, and turned it off.

Chuck walked out the doorway, and said, "Chip, who set the trigger lock on that saw?"

Chip stood in the doorway, and said, "I don't know, man, it wasn't me. Tommy gave it to me that way."

I said, "I saw Tommy take it out of the box, pointing it like a gun, and playing with it, making machine gun noises before he climbed up the scaffold."

Then Chuck and Chip looked at each other, surprised, and busted out in laughter. The laughter was so loud and contagious that I, too, broke out in hysterics.

Chip was laughing so hard that he was bent over, and he said, "That beaver tooth mother fucker did it to himself."

Chuck was laughing so hard as he staggered over to me, he put his hands on my shoulders, and said, "You should have seen Chip's face, trying to stop that saw before it cut his feet off."

I said, still laughing, "Chip, you're a lucky man!"

We stood there for a few moments, trying to laugh off the irony of the situation. The cold wind whipped around the back of the house, and it began to snow harder.

I said, "Holy shit, it's cold out here," then I walked back into the basement.

Chuck grabbed the gas can, and dumped a lot of gas on the woodpile.

Chip said, "Do you have enough gas?"

Chuck took out a pack of matches, and said, "Yeah, I think so."

Chuck bent down at the edge of the woodpile, struck a match, and it blew out. He tried to light the matches, but they kept blowing out because of the wind.

I said, "Hey, I saw a rag upstairs, let's light that to get the fire started."

I ran upstairs, grabbed the rag off the floor, went back into the basement, and handed the rag to Chip. Chip grabbed the gas can, and poured a little on the rag. Chuck ran over, and took the rag from Chip.

Chuck said, "You got your lighter?"

Chip reached in his pocket, and whipped out his Zippo. Chip struck the flint wheel several times, but it couldn't light in the wind.

Chuck said, "Let's light it in the basement, come on."

We all walked back into the basement. Chuck, holding the rag, stood close to Chip, trying to shield the wind.

Chuck said, "Okay, let's light this baby up."

Chip lit the rag. Chuck shielded the burning rag with his other hand, and started walking towards the woodpile. Suddenly, the rag burst into a fireball, and Chuck dropped the rag to the ground. Then Chuck put his right foot on the rag to put it out, and his leg busted out in flames. Chuck then threw both arms in the air, lifted his burning leg, and screamed. Chip and I ran over to Chuck. But Chuck turned and ran over the woodpile, setting it ablaze with a big whoosh. Chip and I stopped, in front of the blazing woodpile, as Chuck dropped and rolled in the snow. We both ran to Chuck as he got up, with his pant leg still smoking.

Chip yelled, "You're burning!" Then he scooped some snow from the ground, and threw it on Chuck's leg. Chuck then started slapping his leg, trying to put out the smoldering leg.

I said, "Are you okay? Are you burnt?"

Chuck said, "I think I'm okay," he then lifted his pant
leg.

We all looked at his leg, and it looked a little red, but nothing
that serious. Chucks white coveralls were scorched brown, but
his jeans underneath were okay.

Chip said, "You look okay, but the coveralls are shot."

I said, "You've got to hide that from Mr. Piazza, he is
going to freak out if he finds out that you set yourself on fire."

Chip said, "Yeah, first Tommy, now you, he is going to
have a shit fit when he has to write another accident report."

I said, "Try to hide that one side of your coveralls, until
we get back to the shop."

Chuck said, "Yeah, you're right."

We walked over to the blazing woodpile, to get warm; the
flames were 4 feet high.

Chip turned to Chuck, and said, "You'd better not get
too close, knucklehead!"

I said, with a smile, "Where did you learn to build a
fire, the circus?"

Chip laughed, and said," Yeah, now appearing, Chuck
the Human Torch!"

I laughed, and said" Chuck, the Human Torch, and
Beaver Boy should join the circus."

Chuck smiled, shoved me towards the fire, and said,
"Fuck you, man."

I gained my balance before I fell onto the fire, and moved
farther away from it.

Just then, Mr. Piazza quickly walked out the basement
doorway, came up behind the three of us, and said, "Who
started the fire?"

We turned around, startled, and started mumbling.

Mr. Piazza said, in an angry voice, "Didn't I say don't
do anything until I got back?"

Chip said," We were just getting rid of some scrap wood."

Mr. Piazza fired back, "Are you kidding? Now, put out that fire, and make sure it's out. Then gather up all the tools, it's getting late, we're going back to the school."
Chuck and Chip grabbed a couple of shovels, and began throwing snow on the fire. I went into the house with the instructor behind me. Mr. Piazza went into the other part of the house, spreading the word that we were leaving, as I gathered the tools in the middle of the floor.

After I was done, Billy and Mike walked in, and said, "Nice fire."

I said, "Yeah, Mr. Piazza said put it out, we're leaving. How's Tommy?"

Mike said, "The nurse thinks his leg is broken, an ambulance came and took him to the hospital for x-rays."
Chip and Chuck walked in.

Chuck said, "Beaver Boy wasn't crying for his mommy, when they loaded him in the meat wagon, was he?"

Mike said, "No, but he did ask for his sister."

Chip laughed, and said, "Same thing, he's an inbreed from Circleville."

We all laughed, and began to pick up the tools. Chip picked up the reciprocating saw out of the tin box and pulled the trigger to make sure the trigger lock was off. Then he placed the saw back in the box, and closed and locked it. Mr. Piazza came into the room and looked out the back window to insure that the fire was out. Then he gave the order to move out. Chuck quickly moved in front of us to conceal the charred leg of his coveralls.

After we got back to the school, Mr. Piazza called Chuck, Chip, and I over to his desk while the others changed.

Mr. Piazza said," What in the hell were you boys thinking when you started that fire?"
The three of us started to stammer, trying not to piss him off.

Mr. Piazza said, "Okay, do not start any fires; otherwise I'll drop you from the program." Then he asked," Do you numbskulls get that?"

Then, the three of us, in unison, said, "Yes, Mr. Piazza."

Mr. Piazza yelled," That goes for the rest of you, do not start any fires, like these morons; otherwise I will drop you from the program!" Then he said to the three of us, "Go get changed."

As we scurried to the back of the room, the instructor said," Chuck, come here, son." Chip and I stopped in our tracks, turned and watched Chuck return to the desk.

I whispered, "Oh, shit!"

Chip said, "This is it."

Chuck reached the desk, and Mr. Piazza said," What happened to your leg?"

Chuck acted as though he knew nothing about his leg, and said, "What leg?"

Mr. Piazza got up, and pointed at Chuck's burnt pant leg, "That one."

Chuck said," Oh, that, it just caught on fire a little bit, I'm fine."

The instructor said, "It caught on fire a little bit? It looks like your whole leg was on fire. Pull up your pant leg, son." Mr. Piazza looked at his leg for a few moments, and he pulled the pant leg up to his thigh. Then he sat down at his desk, took his hard hat off, and he looked up at Chuck.

He said, "You know, son, you're lucky, now go get changed, and take your knucklehead buddies with you."

Mr. Piazza was a great instructor and really took an interest in his students. He wanted to teach only to the ones that wanted to learn, and toss out anyone that did not want to learn a trade, or waste his time. Mr. Piazza stayed with the B.O.C.E.S vocational program for years. You could drive down Gibson Rd., Goshen, NY, today and see all the homes that the program had built over the last 40 years. The school still stands there today and trains many young men and women in learning a trade. Occasionally, I run into an old B.O.C.E.S. classmate, most of them are in the trade they trained for so many years ago. After all of the teachers I have had over the years, I feel that Mr. Piazza had the most impact on so many students lives, and gave them the gift of knowledge and a trade that would feed them and their families for the rest of their lives. This man had been blest to have such a positive impact on so many lives.

Chapter 20 - The First Father and Son Drink

One of the more memorable endings from my date with Judy was after we went to the movies, late January 1973. Judy's mom picked us up and drove us to her house. While I waited for my father to pick me up, I had a rare meeting with Judy's father. He was a very short man, and he was an accountant in New York City. He had a bar in his family room, and he asked me to have a drink with him, I had accepted. Judy was worried that her father had a few too many scotches, but I eased her concerns. When he poured both of us a Scotch, I could see that he had a few drinks in him already. I thought Judy's father looked like Peter Lorre, the actor.

Judy's father said, in a heavy Jewish accent, "So, Rich, what does your father do?"

I said, "He's a plumbing foreman for a big company in Rockland County."

He said, "Oh, what's the name of the company, maybe I heard of it?"

I said, "Hans and Boslam Plumbing and Heating."

He said, "Oh, it's a German company, are you German?"

I said, "Yeah, could I have some ice for my drink?"

He said, "Sure, so you like my daughter, Judy?"

Judy said, "Dad, you're embarrassing me."

I said, "Yes, Mr. B, I do like Judy, she is a very nice girl."

He said, "I want her to stay a nice girl, you respect her, don't you?"

Judy said, "Dad, you're an asshole, come on, Rich."

I said, nervously, as Judy was pulling on my arm, "Wait a minute, of course I respect her, is there a reason why you wouldn't think so?"

He smiled, took a drink, and said, "No, just making sure. Because I don't know what I would do, if you didn't respect her." Then he laughed.

Suddenly, I heard a horn outside.

Judy said, "It's your father, he's outside, he's waiting."

Mr. B said, "Ask your father to come in and have a drink."

I said as I put my coat on, "He can't tonight, he's meeting some people tonight, and he is going to be late." One thing I did not want was for those two to meet.

Mr. B said, with a smile, "Maybe another time?"

I said, "Yeah, another time, nice to see you again, Mr. B."

Judy walked me to the door, and said, "I'm sorry about my dad, he's drunk."

I said, "Don't worry about it, he doesn't bother me. I will call you tomorrow, okay?"
We kissed and I walked over to my father's car in the driveway.

I got into the car, and dad said, "How was the movie?"

I said, as we pulled out of the driveway, "It was okay, thanks for picking me up."
As we drove, I thought about my conversation with Mr. B., I really didn't think he liked me very much. Maybe it was because I was German, and maybe he had an ax to grind that dates back from World War II. Of course, the other possibility would be that I was dating his daughter, and molesting her every time I had the chance. I could have confessed to the crime, when Mr. B was grilling me. But, then I thought better of it, because I had envisioned him sticking an ice pick in my skull, and sending Judy to Siberia. The reason I didn't want my father to meet Mr. B was, my father hated Jews, and they are both drinkers. I really didn't want my relationship with Judy to end because these two did not like the country their families originated from. My father was okay with me dating Judy, go figure.

As we drove home, dad said, "So, what was the name of the movie?"

I said, "Ah," then I paused for moment, thinking, "The Poseidon Adventure".

Dad said, "What was it about?"

I said, "It's about this ocean liner that gets hit by a tidal wave, flips over, almost everyone dies, and about five people survive, it was pretty cool."

He said, "So, the boat sank?"

I looked at him, as if I was being quizzed, "Nope, not in the movie."

He smiled, and said, "All those people die and the ship doesn't sink? Are you sure?"

I looked at him, annoyed, "Of course I'm sure, see the movie yourself."

He laughed aloud, "You think I don't know what goes on in movie theaters? You know, I was once your age, too."

I looked at him half-smiling and half embarrassed at what he was implying. I said, "No, really, the boat doesn't sink."

Dad said, "Yeah, okay," as if he didn't believe me. He said, "Hey, let's stop at Murphy's, I'll buy you a couple of beers."

I said, with a surprised voice, "Ah, okay."

At this point, at 16 1/2 years old, my father never took me to a bar, and I was excited to have a few drinks at the only watering hole in town. It was a Friday night, the end of the workweek for my dad, and he would usually go straight from work to the bar on that night. Therefore, he figured that night, rather than cutting his night short by taking me home; he would treat his oldest son to a few beers. When we got into the parking lot, and got out of the car, I could see that he was not drunk. But, considering that he most likely started drinking at 5:30 PM, and picked me up at 10:00 PM, he may have had a half a load on. Nevertheless, he didn't show it, he was straight as an arrow.

We walked in to Murphy's Bar. I noticed that there was a pool table on my left, and nobody playing.

As we approached the bar, Mr. Murphy said, loudly, "Hey, Dick Kraemer."

A couple of men sitting at the bar turned around, and greeted my dad with handshakes and pats on the back.

Dad said, "Hey, Murphy, I would like you to meet my eldest son, Dick."

Mr. Murphy held out his right hand, I shook his hand, and he said, "So, you're Dick's son, pleased to meet you."

I said, "Good to meet you, too, Mr. Murphy."

Mr. Murphy looked at dad, and said, "He's a good looking lad, Dick."

My dad laughed, and said, "Yep runs in the family, Big Dick Kraemer, lady's favorite."

The bar laughed at my father's old motto that I had heard 1000 times before.

Mr. Murphy said to dad, "A couple of beers for you and your son?"

Dad said, "Sounds good."

As I sat at the bar drinking my beer, my dad started talking to the other men at the bar. My father was an extrovert, and he was not shy at all. He was a very likable person and he had a great sense of humor. As he networked around the bar, you would think he was running for mayor. It seemed that everyone knew my father. The bar was filled with working class men, there wasn't an empty bar stool in the joint. This was a very small bar for so many men. I finished my first beer, and Murphy refilled my glass. I noticed that the pool table was still empty, so I walked over, put a quarter in it, and racked up the balls. I was hoping that I could pull my dad away for a game.

Then I heard my father yell to me, "Dick, come here, there's someone I want you to meet." I put the pool stick on the table, and started to walk towards him.

Dad said, "Jim, I want you to meet my oldest son, Dick."

Jim was a big man, about 6 inches taller and at least 75 pounds heavier than my father was.

Jim said, "That's your son? I thought he was a girl at the end of the bar. I was looking to get a blow job."

Suddenly, my father punched the big man on the left side of his head, sending the man sideways into a crowd of men. Then dad delivered a body blow to the big man's rib cage. Big Jim punched dad on the right side of his head, sending his glasses flying. The crowd of men started to pull Jim and my father apart. As they did, I had been pushed backwards in the pool table area. After a couple of more punches were thrown, about three men had restrained dad by holding his arms with his back against the bar. A couple of men had tried to hold back Jim, but he punched a few of them for holding him back. Jim was a man that was too big to restrain, but a couple of men put themselves in between Jim and my father to try to keep them separated. Unexpectedly, Jim barreled through the two men, and landed a solid right cross against my dad's head, while the other men still restrained my father. I turned and picked up the pool stick off the table, and held it like a baseball bat, fat end of the cue up. A couple of men grabbed Jim from behind, pulling him backwards, and they struggled for a few moments. As they did, the crowd in the bar was yelling for Jim to stop and calm down. The big man was like a bull in a China shop, as my father tried to break free from restraint, and go after this big man. Jim broke free of the two men on his back, one falling on the floor, the other falling on a table. Jim stood alone in the middle of the bar floor with his shirt half ripped off his body, standing about 6 feet in front of my father, facing him. I held the pool stick high, ready to knock this big baboon's head off, if he made a move towards my father while these drunken fucking dummies were holding him.

Big Jim yelled, "You know, Kraemer, you're a fucking big mouth. Bringing your fucking son in here...... Where is that little fucker?"

He looked around the bar and then he turned around. I was about 6 feet behind him, ready to knock one out of the park.

Jim yelled, "What the fuck is this?"

Then he quickly ran over to me, and I swung as hard as I could.

Jim caught the pool cue with his open left hand, and yelled in pain, "Ah, Mother Fucker!"

Then he bitch slapped me, with the back of his right hand, sending me to the side of the pool table. Then the Jim turned and walked over to my dad with the pool cue in his hand. I then looked at my father, and he looked directly at me, our eyes met for the first time since this brawl had started, as he still struggled to get free from his restraints from his so-called buddies.

Big Jim yelled, "Is this what you're teaching your fucking kid," then he waved the pool stick around.

Mr. Murphy jumped from behind the bar, with a baseball bat, "Okay, Jim, this ends now, get the fuck out."

Jim threw the pool stick on the table, and yelled, "I'm not leaving, Kraemer hit me first. Have him leave and take his fucking kid with him."

Then Mr. Murphy walked towards Jim. Jim turned his back and went to the far side of the bar.

Mr. Murphy turned to dad, and said, "Dick, I think its best that you and your boy leave; I'll take care of this."

A man handed dad his glasses, as the men released him from their grip. My dad put his glasses on, walked to the middle of the floor, stopped, and turned to stare at Big Jim. I turned and walked out of the bar.

Jim yelled, "Go home, Kraemer, get the fuck out of here."

My father, without saying a word, walked out of the bar behind me. Dad and I got into the car, and drove out of the parking lot. We made our first right turn on Elm Street, drove almost all the way down the street, and pulled into our driveway. He turned off the car, and looked at me.

Dad said, "You shouldn't have picked up that pool cue!"

I looked at him, surprised, "Hey, Dad, those guys were holding you back, and that big ape kept on coming."

He said, "Yeah, but you just don't do that."

He turned on the dome light in the car and said, "Let me see your face."

I turned and showed him my right side of my face.

Dad said, "It's a little red, how does your face feel?"

I said, "It hurts a little, I'll be okay."

Then he looked in the rearview mirror to check his face, he had a couple of red marks on his face, and his lip was bleeding. He took a tissue out of the glove box, spit on it, and wiped away the blood off his mouth.

Dad said, "Do not tell your mother about this. In fact, do not say anything to anyone about this. I'll take care of that Cocksucker."

Then we both walked into the house, I went straight to my room, and dad quickly ditched his ripped shirt in the basement before he got into the kitchen. My mother was sitting in the living room, watching TV.

When these men were restraining my father against the bar, while that goon was loose in the bar because they could not hold him back, it was just wrong. My perception in the heat of the moment was, they held my dad back, and Big Jim laid a good one on the side of his head. In addition, these men continued to hold onto my dad even after he took the crack to the head. At the time, I seriously doubted that these guys really were my father's friends at all. How could my father defend himself against that kind of cowardly attack? Of course, this part of the incident took only a few quick moments. In short, I perceived everyone as an adversary in the bar in those few moments, and I felt that I would be the only one to stop this Big Dope from hurting my Dad.

After the first father and son bar brawl, my father never spoke of the incident again. He did not intend our first drink together in a bar to end in a brawl to show how tough he was, it was not like my father. He was a type of man who was happy, comedic and friendly, he had few enemies. If you met him on the street, you might assume that he would be harmless and nonthreatening. However, you would be dead wrong; he was a tough guy through and through. My father liked the image he portrayed to people, he was comfortable with it, and he felt it gave him an edge. In addition, he was not a man that would suddenly flip out, and start beating people up, at the drop of a hat. He had a great deal of self control, normally if he had a beef with someone, he would ask them to step outside, and dish out his beatings in a non-public form like a gentleman. He did not like public spectators witnessing his street fights. He felt that a fight was between two people, felt by two, resolved by two, and it was nobody else's business. But, this incident was different, a public disrespect of his son, in front of his oldest boy a room full of people he knew, and he was half in the bag. All of the elements you need to set my father off, in a blind rage in an instant. I did not know it at the time, but my dad and Big Jim hated each other. Big Jim was always bad talking America, the government, and he was a liberal. All the things my father respected, Big Jim disrespected. Therefore, they hated each other, and this fight was a long time coming.

About two weeks later, a friend of mine had an older brother that used to go to Murphy's, about once or twice a week. He heard that Big Jim had been drinking in Murphy's one night, and he had left the bar a little after midnight. Mr. Murphy discovered Big Jim laying along side his car pretty beaten up, and they took him to the hospital in an ambulance. Big Jim had a skull fracture, a broken leg, and a couple of broken ribs. The guys in the bar think my dad did it. But, when the men asked my father if he did it, he would neither claim responsibility nor deny the allegations.

I had to know for myself, so when we were alone, I had asked about the Big Jim beating. Dad looked at me for a couple of seconds, with a straight face, and looking straight into my eyes, he said, "Yeah, Jim, he must have slipped in the parking lot, and fell. It must have been an accident."

I said, smiling, "Come on, Dad, what really happened?"

Dad said, "Bad things happen to bad people, the guy got what he deserved. Now, do not bring it up again."

From that day forward, we never spoke of this first beer in the bar incident again. I think that he felt ashamed of himself for not setting the right example as a parent that night. He did not want to raise a bar brawler. As for him admitting to me that he put the Big Monkey in the hospital, he knew and I knew he did. As for admitting it to his friends in the bar that he did it, he did not want to admit it because he could have been charged with assault, and get sent to jail. He did not need that, he had a wife and five kids to support, and a mortgage to pay.

As for Big Jim, he used to own a black 1970 Chevy Chevelle with four on the floor and a 396 engine. I never saw that car parked in Murphy's after his hospital visit.

Chapter 21 - The Move

One day in February 1973, my parents had a big announcement to make to all the Kraemer children. The setting would be after our evening meal on a Saturday night. My brother and I speculated of what great news they had to deliver. Ike and I thought that the only good news my parents could possibly deliver was that mom was pregnant again. The prospect of having more kids in the house did not excite either one of us.

As we sat with anticipation of the great announcement, mom had made a cherry pie, and bought a half gallon of vanilla ice cream to put on top. Mom served up the dessert and poured coffee and tea. I remember thinking, "Gee, this has got to be good; we hardly ever get dessert after dinner."

As the kids dug into the cherry pie a la mode, my father banged his spoon on his coffee cup. We all looked at him, and stopped eating for a moment.

Dad said, with a smile, "Your mother and I had talked it over, and we have decided that I'm going into business with Helmut. The company will be called Kraroe Plumbing and Heating."

I said, with excitement, "Hey, Dad, that's great, congratulations!"

As the other kids started to get excited, they were asking questions all at once. I looked at my mother across the table, and as my father answered some short questions, I noticed that she did not seem as enthusiastic, and she was only half smiling.

After a few moments, my mother looked at dad, and said, "Tell them the rest of it."

Dad cleared his voice, "Ah, yeah, there's more good news."

Ike and I looked at each other, and thought," More good news, he's on a roll."

Dad said, with a straight face, "Your mother and I also decided," then he looked at mom as she crossed her arms, "that we are going to sell the house, so I could go into business."

I said, surprised, "Sell the house, where are we going to move?"

He said, "We found a nice house to rent that is almost identical to this one."

Then all the kids started asking questions about who was going to get their own bedrooms, etc.

I said, "Where is this house?"

He said, "Greenwood Lake, it's a nice village about 18 miles from here, and nobody has to change schools. You will still go to the same school."

I looked at him angrily, "You're kidding, right, Greenwood Lake?" Then I looked at my mother.

He said, "No, I'm not kidding. It will be a better commute for me, too."

I said, "Yeah, but you doubled the distance to my job and to Judy's house."

He said, "Maybe you could get a new job there, and a new girl friend."

I jumped out of my chair, and said, "It seems like it doesn't matter how it affects me."

Dad looked at me, and said, "You're right; everyone will have to make sacrifices."

I said, "It looks like I'll have to change my whole life. When are we moving?"

Mom looked at me, straight faced, and said," April 30." Then she looked at dad.

I yelled, "Two months? That's just great!" I threw the napkin on the table, and walked out of the kitchen.

My parents had discussed this, apparently, in great length, months prior to dropping this bomb on the kids. Since my parents had purchased this house in Highland Mills, it had appreciated quite a bit by 1973. My father's life long goal was to have his own plumbing business some day. While working as a plumbing foreman for a big company in Rockland County, he learned the inner workings of running the company. He was not college educated, so at the age of 38, he had peaked at his pay scale, and career position. If he had not gone into business for himself, he would have to be satisfied with his current pay scale and position for the rest of his life. However, he saw opportunity in those days to make far more money, and to achieve a better life for himself and his family. Therefore, mom and dad put the house on the market, and did not tell the kids about their plan. There wasn't even a sign in front of the house, and they would only show the house to potential buyers on weekdays when the kids were in school.

Knowing my mother, it must have taken months of convincing her to make such a decision, to sell the dream house she always admired, take all the equity from it and risk it on a business venture. My mother did hammer out a deal with him, in order for him to go into business. First, Pat and Pam were about to start school, and she demanded that they go to a Catholic school. Second, mom demanded some new furniture when we moved. She would pick it out, and there would be no squabbles over how much it cost. As for her sacrifices, she, too, would have to travel great distances to see her girl friends, and carting the kids around. In addition, the house we were moving into was similar in the floor plan, but was not the same quality or as nice, a neighborhood compared to the house in Highland Mills. I would've loved to have seen my father squirm in his chair over my mother's demands, so he could go into business. Those eagles were screaming when they flew out of my dad's pockets. You should have seen my fathers face when they delivered the furniture from the high-end store, and they handed him the invoice. I thought he was going to have a stroke.

As for the rest of the kids' sacrifices, Gina didn't really have any neighborhood friends, but had a couple in school, no real change for her. Pat and Pam were really too young to have built a meaningful friendship, besides they were each other's best friend. But Ike was also affected. Most of his friends came from the neighborhood, so there would be a big adjustment for him also.

One thing my parents did not know was that within the school districts, there were two adversary groups of student's, Monroe-Woodbury and Greenwood Lake. Some of the students would even refer to them as real gangs. They would have gang fights all the time between these two groups of kids. It was not well publicized by the newspapers or the school district, but it was a reality. Ike and I knew of the threat even though we had never engaged in this type of gang activity. We knew of the problem, but were unaware of what kind of reception we would receive. This gang part of it did concern us.

The move To Oak St., Greenwood Lake, New York, went smoothly with some help from relatives that weekend. Ike and I started taking the long bus rides back and forth to school everyday. We both had our run-ins with other Greasers, as they were called back then. However, we would try to blend in with the other kids. To me, this exercise seemed all too familiar from the last time we moved, and I was really pissed off that I had to go through this process one more time. I do not make friends easily, and I did not intend to make new friends because I did not need any. So trying to make friends, just so I did not get my ass kicked, did not make any sense to me. I decided that if I kept a low profile, and stood up for myself as a loner, I would be okay. The lighter side of things was I really had no old friends to lose, and all I had was Judy.

The travel back and forth to work or to Judy's house was twice as long, and hitchhiking on Lakes Road was more difficult because it had a lot less traffic. This, too, in turn, made me even more pissed off. My mother had to travel these extra distances, and she would bitch all the time, and would refuse to drive me. This resulted in me hitchhiking more often.

Once I moved to Greenwood Lake, and got a good dose of how my life would be from here on, I stopped talking to my parents. I stopped asking for rides anywhere, and made my own schedule.

My father rolled into the driveway with his new fire engine red GMC ¾ Ton Custom 30 pick up truck, with custom made tool boxes and pipe racks. This truck was truly a very nice work truck for that time. Dad was excited about it and told the whole family to come out to take a look. I was the last one out the door, and I watched my family, as they looked it over. I just stood there in front of the house, and I realized that we were all sucked in on my father's dream. After the rest of the family went back into the house, dad started wiping the fingerprints and dust off the paint. Dad noticed that I was still standing outside in front of the truck.

Dad said, "So, what do you think?"

I walked over to the driver's door, and opened it. I said," I like the color, but brown interior seems odd to me."

He said, "The interior only came in black or brown. I ordered it that way because black gets too hot in the summer, and I got the custom interior, see, with the designs, it looks like leather."

I said, "It looks off to me with the red, oh, you have A/C, nice."

Dad said, "Yep, it's fully loaded, the only thing I didn't order was power windows"

I looked at him, "No power windows?"

Dad said, "Yeah, I knew a couple of guys that had them and they had problems."

I turned, looked him right in his eyes, and said, "When am I going to get to drive it?"

He looked right back at me, and said, "You're not!"

I smiled and him, and said, "Why doesn't that surprise me?" I slammed the door and smirked at him.

He moved towards me, and said, "Don't slam the door!"

I turned my back on him, and walked back into the house.

A couple of days went by, and I started to feel sorry for stealing my father's first new vehicle moment, because he never owned a new car or truck in his whole life. So, I gave him a couple of quotes like, "Gee, that truck looks good in the shade." Alternatively, "Maybe nobody will notice the brown interior, at night." Just to make him feel better about his purchase.

In late May 1973, my birthday rolled around, and after school, I went to Judy's house for a few hours, then I hitchhiked home. At this point in my life, celebrating a birthday at 17 was pretty much a routine thing, my mom would bake a cake, and I would get a couple of shirts and a pair of pants, we would sing happy birthday, and that would be the end of it. There was nothing to look forward to but being another year older. I was walking towards my house, and I noticed that my dad was home, because his truck was backed into the driveway. I thought that maybe he was home because he was going to meet a builder for dinner. There was a white car parked in front of the house, and I thought it was one of dad's friends or Helmut, my father's business partner. I walked into the house around suppertime, and, as usual, my mother was all bubbly about it being my birthday.

I said, "Hey, Mom, who's car is outside?"

She looked outside through the hallway from the kitchen, and said, "I don't know, maybe it's someone's car from across the street."

Then she resumed icing the birthday cake. I went upstairs to wash up for dinner, and returned downstairs. I walked back into the kitchen, and poured a glass of iced tea. I sat down at the kitchen table.

My father walked in, and said, "Hey, Dick, where were you?"

I said, "I was at Judy's house, and it took a long time hitching a ride home."

Dad looked at me and smiled for a moment or two. I thought the next thing he was going to say would be some wise crack about me catching a freight train with the rest of the hobo's.

Dad said, "Well, you don't have to worry about that anymore."

I thought to myself, for a moment, "Okay, another riddle for me to solve."

I said, "Oh, yeah, why is that?"

He said, "Did you see that car out there in front of the house?"

I said, "Yeah."

Then my mother walked into view.

He said, with a straight face, "Well, it's yours."

I looked at him in shock with my mouth open for a moment, and I remained in my seat and looked outside at the partial view of the car. I said, "You bought me a car?"

He leaned against the counter, and said, "Yeah. Sort of."

I looked at him, confused, "What do you mean, sort of?"

He said, "I bought the car for cash, and you'll pay me back."

I looked at him, stunned, and said, "You bought me a car that I'll pay you back for, and I didn't even pick it out?"

Mom said, angrily, "You see, Richard, he doesn't appreciate it, take the fucking car back, he's an ungrateful fucker!"

I looked at my mother, she was about to self-destruct any moment, and dad crossed his arms and started grinding his teeth.

I jumped out of the chair, and said, "It isn't that I don't appreciate this, it's that you took me by total surprise."

My fathers face got red, and he placed his hand on the kitchen counter.

He said, "Well, you certainly don't act like you appreciate it, I'll take the car back right now."

My mother said, angrily, "Do it, do it, take the fucking car back!"

I yelled, "Wait a minute, you're hitting me with all this, and I haven't even really looked at the car, yet."

My father said, "You saw it outside, didn't you?"

I said, "Yeah, I glanced at it, and thought it was someone else's car."

He looked at me, and quickly slammed the keys down on the counter.

He said, "Go look at it, but don't take it anywhere."

I picked up the keys, and walked out the front door. As I did, I could hear my mom say, "You're taking that car back."

I approached the car for the first time and really looked at it. The car was a white 1968 Plymouth Fury II Sport, with black vinyl interior, the front bench seat had a fold down armrest, the speedometer went to 120 MPH, and the odometer clocked 42,000 miles. The car was spotless without a scratch or a dent anywhere. My father came out of the house and looked at me from the porch. I tried to open the hood, but could not figure out how to do it.

Dad then walked over, and said, "The latch is right here." Then he opened it for me.

I said, "What kind of engine is it?"

Dad said, "It's a V-8, with a 318 cubic inch, two barrel carburetor."

I said, "Great, a V-8! Where's the dip stick?"

He bent over, and pointed, "This is for the oil, and this is for the transmission."

I said, "Ah."

Dad closed the hood, walked over to the driver side, and said, "It has all new Michelin 4 ply radial tires with a warranty. The car itself has a six month or 3000 mile warranty."

He opened the door, and pointed at the dash and said, "It has A/C, and a three speed automatic transmission."

He closed the door, and said, "Let me have the keys." I handed the keys to him, and we walked to the back of the car. Dad opened the trunk, which was as clean as a hound's tooth, and flipped over the trunk liner.

He said, "A new spare, and the jack is under the tire." He closed the trunk, leaned against the back of the car, and folded his arms, looking at me.

I said, looking at the car, "Wow, it's a nice car, dad."

Dad said, looking at me straight faced, "It's a really nice car, your mother's girl friend, Mrs. Todd, gave us a very good deal on it."

I said, " Oh, yeah, how much?"

Then Dad stood straight up, and said, "Let's go in the house and talk about it."

Dad walked back into the house, and returned to the kitchen, I followed. I began to cry, because Mom and Dad had misread my reaction to the greatest present I had ever received from them. In addition, I broke down in sobbing tears of joy. Because, after all of these years of hitchhiking in all types of shitty weather, and begging for rides, those days were finally over. Dad opened the folder with all the car information in it.

I said, in a sobbing voice, "Dad I wanted to say thank you to you and mom. That I really do appreciate it, and all of this just took me by total surprise."

He looked at me, and said, "You certainly didn't show it."

Then he looked down at the folder, and said, "The car cost $900, and you'll pay me every month, 50 bucks a month, no excuses that you can't pay me."

I grabbed a tissue off the counter, and blew my nose, and said, "Nine hundred dollars?"

He said, "Yeah, $50 a month to me every month."

I said, "Wow that is a lot of money. Nine hundred dollars."

My dad looked straight my eyes, and said, annoyed, "Hey, Dick, if you don't like it, I'll take it back."

I looked at him with eyes filled with tears, and said, "No, no, I like the car, I can handle it."

He said, "Are you sure, because I could still bring it back."

I stepped back, and looked at him, "I told you, I like the car, and I can handle it."

At that point, because my parents had been misreading my reactions, and taking my questions as some type of an attack, I decided to not ask any more questions, and to go along with anything they said.

He said, angrily, "Good, how much do you have in the bank?"

As I wiped away the last of my tears, with a new tissue, I said, "Three hundred and fifty."

Dad said, "Good, I'll need two hundred for insurance, and I'll tack on the taxes, tags, and plates on your balance of the bill."

I said, "Yeah, okay."

Then he resumed going through the rest of the paperwork. After he finished, he closed the folder and handed me the car keys.

I said, "I want to thank you very much for the car, dad." Then I hugged him, but he didn't respond by hugging me back.

After I released him, he said, "I hope you like it."

I said, "I do, I really do."

Dad said, "You better thank your mother."

I walked into the living room, and she was sitting in her chair overhearing the conversation in the kitchen.

I stood in front of her, and I said, "Mom, I want to thank you and dad for the car, and I really like it and appreciate it."

I leaned over her to kiss her, but she turned her head away from me. I kissed her anyway, and stood up straight.

She looked up at me with those glaring blue eyes, and said, "I hope you do appreciate it." Then she folded her arms, and started tapping her feet.

I took a step back, held my arms open, and said, "I really do."

She just stared at me. I realized that I could not convince either one of my parents that I was grateful for the gift. I just walked out of the house and sat in the car.

As I sat in my car, I thought about what just happened with my parents. I always envisioned my first car experience to be much different, and I am sure my parents did, too. I had imagined myself jumping up and down in excitement, with tears of joy rolling down my cheeks. I would have acted that way if the car were a gift. Instead, my birthday gift was a debt of over $900, at $50 a month, for a car that was selected by my parents. The gift was a loan from the Bank of Kraemer, with no interest. As I said before, I never expected my parents to give me a car, and it never entered my spectrum of thinking, because of my upbringing. The concept of credit or monthly payments was foreign to me. Therefore, when my parents bought a car that they picked out, using their money, they then tagged me for the bill by offering payments for the next year and a half, and it caught me totally off guard. After working my ass off in shitty jobs, hitchhiking all over the planet, and saving my money, I would occasionally walk on car lots and look at cars. I always imagined myself in a hot car like a Mustang, Camaro, GTO, or some other muscle car. But that wasn't really that important to me. I think what was important to me was being part of the purchase process. I would have liked to have looked at a few cars with my dad, and make a decision with my parents' approval. Even if they found a car for me and showed it to me before they bought it that would have been okay. But that's not the way it went down. Looking back on it, I guess my mistake was asking the big question, "You bought me a car?" Alternatively, maybe before I walked into the house, I should have really looked over the strange car parked in front of my house, and should have fallen in love with it, before I knew it was mine. Another scenario, maybe my parents could have walked me outside, and then sprang the good news while I was looking at it, then give me the details later. I guess all of the scenarios would have had a better out come, if I could turn back time. However, instead I came off as a spoiled and ungrateful fucking brat. I guess time would heal all wounds, because I could not talk to my parents about it anymore, they were too pissed off. After dinner, I drove over to Judy's house, and took her for a quick ride before it got dark I was not used to driving at night. Judy liked the car, and she was very happy for me.

Having my own car had a completely new prospective in my life. The first was that I had the freedom to come and go as I pleased without hitchhiking, or asking for rides. Second, I didn't have to deal with any of the local kids or gangs in the neighborhood, because I did not have to ride the school bus anymore. Thirdly, I could take Judy anywhere we wanted, and making out became more relaxing in the car. Life was good having my own car. I believe that I had never been happier, and it just seemed that everything was going my way.

My mother also benefited from me having my own car, because now she had an errand boy on wheels. I would run to the store, the dry cleaners, or run the other kids to some of the functions they were supposed to attend.

Two months after I had my car, I had to drive Gina to a bake sale for Girl Scouts. Even though we moved to Greenwood Lake months ago, Gina was still a member of her Girl Scout troop in Highland Mills. So one Sunday morning, I was drafted to drive Gina, with cakes and cookies that my mother had baked the night before, to St. Patrick's Church for a bake sale in Highland Mills. In addition, I would later have to pick her up and bring her back home. I was pissed off because Sunday was my only day off, and I had been working full time at the diner, since the summer started. It was just another family flunky job that my mother pushed on me. So I loaded the cakes and cookies in the back seat of my car, and yelled for Gina to get into the car. Gina came out of the house with her Girl Scout uniform on and jumped in the front seat. She had the green beret pulled down on top of her head, and she really looked goofy. There was nothing cool about driving through town with your little sister riding shotgun in a Girl Scout uniform, and her hat pulled down over her ears. I just stared at her for a moment sitting in the front seat.

I said, "Buckle your seatbelt."

She did, and then I said, "Pull it tight." Then she struggled with the seatbelt.

Then I unbuckled, adjusted the strap, and said, "Now buckle it."

She struggled to do it, but she finally buckled it, and she said, "Dickie, it's too tight."

I said, "It's fine, leave it," then I started the engine and turned the radio on full blast.

I pulled out slowly from the front of the house, and took a right at the end of the road to a side street that led to the main drag through town. I rode out of town on to the main highway called Lakes Road; a 9 mile County Highway where the speed limit was mostly 55 mph, which would lead me to my destination. As soon as I got out of the village limits, I put the gas pedal to the floor. The Fury had plenty of horsepower for me. I had grown to love my first car, even though the body style was conservative looking. Lakes Road was a series of long straightaway's, many curves, and a few that were blind curves. After a few months of hitchhiking, and then driving on this road, I felt like I knew every inch of it. I felt that I had fine-tuned my driving skills to the point that I should be in the Indianapolis 500, with no problem. As I drove down this county highway, I would whip through curves at least at 55 mph, and then when I anticipated a straightaway, I would accelerate coming out of the curve, even the blind ones. When I came to the first straight away, I targeted two cars I had to pass, so I floored the car and blew right past them like they were standing still.

As I did, Gina yelled, "Slow down."

After I passed the cars, I looked at Gina. She had both hands gripping the dashboard, and she was leaning forward with her mouth wide open. In an evil kind of way, I was getting some pleasure seeing Gina scared shitless sitting next to me. I did slow down, thinking that if I scared her too much, she would tell my mother, and mom would try to take the car away from me. Therefore, I decided to drive normally and safely. As I went through a blind curve with a small downhill slope, I knew that there was a straightaway beyond it, and I coasted through it at about 50 mph. Unexpectedly, I saw a 1966 Mustang turned over on it's roof along the side of the road. Then I realized that a yellow sports car was parked on my side of the highway, along side the Mustang. In addition, there was oncoming traffic in the opposite lane, so I could not get around the parked car in my lane. I slammed on the brakes, as Gina screamed, and we skidded straight into the back of the sports car. On impact, the big rear fastback window broke into a million pieces, and the gasoline tank ruptured, which sent shards of glass and gasoline raining all over my car. I was stunned for a moment or two, looking straight ahead into the sports car. I then snapped out of my trance and looked at Gina, who was hysterically crying.

I yelled, "Get out of the car!"

Then I unbuckled her seatbelt and mine, and pulled her by her arm out of the driver side of the car. I then ran over to the driver side of the sports car, a man in his 30s was sitting inside stunned.

I said, "You have to get out, there's gasoline everywhere." The man looked at me with a blank face, tried to open the door, but it would not open. The woman sitting next to him, crying, opened her door and got out, the man climbed out of the passenger side. I turned around and saw Gina, still crying, wandering in the middle of the road, dazed by the crash. I walked up to her, pulled her over to the side of the road, and put my arms around her to comfort her. An elderly man walked over and helped me calm down my sister.

There was a group of people that gathered in the middle of the road. Some were the people involved with the crash of the Mustang, the rest of the people were Good Samaritans just trying to help. I finally spotted the two in the sports car; they were pacing about 30 feet from the road in the woods to insure that another car would not mow them down.

I yelled to them, from the road, "Are you okay?"

The man looked at me, as he held the woman around her shoulders, and said, "She is pregnant."

I thought to myself, "My God, please do not let anything happen to this baby."

Just then, the state troopers, the ambulance, and the fire trucks arrived in quick succession. As the troopers assessed the accident scene, making sure that the most injured got medical attention first, Gina and I stood by the guardrail. After they loaded the people from the Mustang accident into the ambulance, they loaded the couple from the sports car, too. The troopers then interviewed me on my account of the accident, and then measured off the skid marks of my car. The fire department hosed off the gasoline and glass off the cars and the roadway. Then the tow trucks came, and they asked me to back my car away from the yellow sports car. I started and backed my car up with no problems. Then I put the car into park, to assess the damage. The yellow sports car was all fiberglass, and was smashed from the rear bumper to the back of the bucket seats; that car was totaled. I turned to look at my car, there was a one-inch dent filled with yellow paint in the front hood, and the front grille had a small three-inch piece missing out of it. I could not believe the amount of damage that I had inflicted on this sports car, and my car ended up with a tiny little dent.

My car was certainly drivable, so when the troopers got down all my information, they let me drive the car home. After I drove the car home, and informed my parents that I was in an accident, they were both very upset. Later that afternoon, my father went to the trooper barracks in Monroe, picked up the accident report, and looked at the sports car. Then dad handled reporting the accident to the insurance company when he got home. My parents had gotten scared about the accident, had taken the car keys, and forbade me from driving. The next couple of days, all I did was pray for that unborn baby and it's parents. At that time, I really did not care about driving after that accident. A few days after the accident, Dad had convinced my mother that I should begin driving again, because he knew that if I didn't drive soon after an accident, that I could develop a fear of driving, and maybe never drive again. I never did find out whether the couple in the sports car had their baby, I surely prayed for a healthy baby.

Ever since that accident, I always expect the unexpected going into a blind curve, because you never know what is at the end of it.

Regina "Gina" M. Kraemer

Chapter 22 - Good Time Summer of 1973

In the summer of 1973, it seemed to me to be one of the greatest summers I'd ever had. Certainly, I had some rough patches along the way, moving to Greenwood Lake, and having my first car accident were some of my low points. However, there was a lot more good that came from that summer. Primarily, I had my own set of wheels that had opened a completely new world for me. The freedom to go anywhere, at any given time was priceless. Of course, I had responsibilities. I worked full time at the Monroe Diner, and had various tasks and chores around the house. However, after my work was done, I had a lot more free time because I wasn't attending school during the summer. So, after work, I would go out with Judy, to the drive-in, of which there were many at the time, or hiking in the woods, and sometimes even going on some of my family outings.

One time, my mother had an idea that Judy and I, and the rest of the Kraemer children would go to Jungle Habitat in West Milford, New Jersey. At the time, Jungle Habitat was one of the first natural habitat zoos in the country, where you could drive through most of the park in your car, and view the animals in an open environment. Best of all, it was only about 9 miles from my house. Therefore, Mom had organized that we would pack the kids in the station wagon, and make a day of adventure out of it. Ike, for some reason, did not go that day, I believe that he would've had to ride in the cargo area of the station wagon, and that would've made him feel like a little kid. So, I picked up Judy early one morning, and drove her to our house, and from there, we were on our way by 10 AM to Jungle Habitat.

My mom decided that I would drive, so it was Mom, Judy, and I in the front seat, Pat, Pam, and Gina in the backseat. As we drove on Jersey Avenue, which runs along side the entire 7-mile length of Greenwood Lake, we enjoyed the beautiful view of the crystal blue waters shimmering in the summer sunlight. When we arrived at the front gate, a man dressed up in a safari outfit took our money and told us to roll up our windows. Thank God, we had A/C in the car that day; it was already 80° at 10:30 in the morning. At the time, the twins were five years old, and would not stop talking, and screaming with excitement. First, we drove through an African village, and they had some black people dressed up in tribal costumes. We traveled by a large pond area where there were some exotic birds, and further on, there was a huge flock of ostriches that blocked the road. The ostriches would come up to the windows and peck on the glass, looking for food. These big birds had learned that some visitors would feed them through the opened window. I looked at the car behind me. A man had opened his window, and begun to feed an ostrich a sandwich. I looked away for just a second, looked in the mirror again to see the ostrich violently pecking at the man's head, as the man tried to fight him off. I turned and looked out the rear window. The wife and the children in the car were screaming, and crying, as the man began to crank his window up. He finally rolled the window all the way up, and the bird slowly walked away. I could see that the man was bleeding from his forehead from the attack. I didn't want to scare the twins by saying anything about the attack of the big birds. They both thought the ostriches were so cute. The family behind **us** couldn't do anything but move along this narrow road in traffic to seek medical attention for the next hour and a half. As we moved along in a long caravan of cars through the habitat, we saw lions, rhinoceroses, buffalo, elephants and giraffes. Then we stopped in the middle of the park, where they had rides, food concessions, walk by exhibits, and a petting zoo. We had lunch, and the twins really got excited when they saw Bugs Bunny, Daffy Duck, and the rest of the Looney Tune characters. Then the twins rode on this small kiddie train, I guess my mother forgot about the Great Train Tragedy at the Nyack Drive-In, when I was a kid. Gina and Judy also became friends, joking and kidding around most of the day. There was one part of the walk by exhibits where there was a herd of zebras when Judy and I were walking alone. Then we both spotted, from about 20 feet away, a zebra with a hard-on that must have been 3 feet long, trying to mount a female zebra from behind.

I said, with excitement, "Holy shit, look at the size of that pecker!"

Judy looked with her eyes popping out of her head, and her mouth open, and yelled, "Oh, my God," then she covered her face.

Some little kids standing a few feet away asked their mother why the zebra was acting funny. The mother quickly covered her children's eyes and rushed them away from the sex act. The male zebra was really hammering it home, and the female was making these donkey squealing noises.

I said to Judy, "Come here, take a look at this, it's educational!" Then I wrapped my arm around her shoulder and turned her in that direction. A crowd of people moved quickly away from the zebra bonking, as I pried Judy's hands away from her face.

She whispered, "He is so huge!"

I said, excited, "Yeah, ha?"

I turned around to see Mom, Gina, and the twins approaching from about 50 feet away. I said," Time to go!" We both turned around and walked towards my family. Just then, a fat dude in a Safari outfit 3 sizes too small for him, turned a hose on the passionate zebras to break it up.

Pam yelled, "Zebras, let's go see the zebras."

I said, "Maybe we should wait a couple of minutes." I turned around again, and the over heated zebras took off for the other side of the park.

I said, "It's okay now."

Then we walked over and looked at the other zebras. As we did, I realized that I had a rock solid hard-on from the Zebra Sexual Voyeur Experience, and I was walking funny. I was walking as if I had a peg leg; nature is a funny thing, isn't it? My mother asked what was wrong with my leg, and I said that I had a leg cramp and needed to walk it off. Judy laughed and that killed it pretty quick.

We walked over to the elephant and camel rides, and Gina and I took the twins on those after waiting in a long line. Then we jumped back into the car, and continued the Kraemer safari through the rest of the park. We had seen black bears, water buffalo, tigers, moose, deer, llamas, alpacas, and gazelles. When we got to the baboons, they stormed our car and crawled all over it. It was a little scary at first, but then they climbed down, and became very cute. As they departed to another car, one baboon squatted, took a big shit on the middle of the hood of our car, and smeared some of it on the windshield. As it smashed more shit on the passenger side of the windshield, Mom banged on the windshield, and yelled, "Go away, you dirty little bastard!" Then the baboon got mad, went to the dung pile in the middle of the hood, and started throwing the crap at my Mom's face through the windshield.

My mother yelled, "Let's go, he'll get off the hood." I moved the car slowly forward, and the baboon ran to the passenger side of the windshield, again smashing more of his dumper on the glass, Mom glared at him.

Mom yelled, "Turn on the windshield wipers with the wash." I put the windshield wipers on as fast as they could go, and held the windshield wash button down. The baboon jumped back on the hood, as he smeared shit all over the windshield. Swiftly, the baboon ran to the windshield, grabbed the wiper arm, ripped it off the car, and began beating it against the glass. The twins started crying loudly and everyone was yelling hysterically. I threw the car into drive; put the gas pedal to the floor, the rear tires squealed, and then the baboon bounced off the windshield, and over the roof of the car. With everyone still screaming and crying, I looked in the rearview mirror, and saw that little fucker run for about a quarter mile after the car, with the wiper arm in his hand. I turned off the wiper on the driver side of the window after it was sparkling clean, but mom's side of the windshield was caked with baboon fertilizer. The traffic was backed up to the next attraction, the squirrel monkeys.

Mom said, in a sighing voice, "Not more of these filthy fucking animals?"

I said, "Come on, Mom, they're cute."
I could see the little monkeys crawling on a couple of cars in front of us. Gradually, the cars moved ahead and we moved where the squirrel monkeys were. Unexpectedly, the monkeys scattered into the trees and onto the rocks, avoiding our car. The monkeys would not go near the car because the baboon shit was all over it, and that meant that the baboon had marked his territory. The Squirrel monkeys looked scared to get close to the car.

Mom said, "Let's go, let's get out of here, this has got to end soon."
She was right, and we ended up at the front gate again. I parked the car and ran over to an African shack to report the incident. I walked into the grass hut, and there was a guy in uniform with Manchu mustache and mutton chop sideburns sitting behind a desk.

He said, "Greetings, young customer dude, can I be of assistance, man?"

I said, "I would like to report a crazy baboon that ripped off my windshield wiper arm."

The guy stood up, and said, "Wait a minute, man, did this baboon take a dump on the hood, and smear it on the windshield?"

I said, "Yeah, how did you know?"

The guy smiled, showing his gold front tooth and slapped his hands on the desk. He yelled, " Oh, wow, man, it's Marvin, he is such a freaky animal, dude. He is like a little King Kong, man. My boss, you know, he's a nark, and he's been trying to catch Marvin for three weeks now. Wait until he hears about this, man, he is going to wig out!"

I looked at him, as if he was tripping, and said, "Yeah, what about the wiper arm, Jungle Dude?"

He raised his hands up, and said, "Yeah, da Habitat is not responsible, man. I know it's a bummer and all that. Hey, if it were me, man, I'd pay, because you look like a cool brother. Hey, man, you know big corporations, always fucking the people."

I said, "Yeah, it's a bummer, Jungle Dude. So, that's it?"

The hippy dude jumped from around the desk, and said, "Hey, man, I could hose that Marvin dung off your car. Would that be cool?"

I said, with a smile, "Yeah, that's cool."

So we walked outside, and he hosed the shit off the car. I thanked Jungle Dude, as we drove off, he raised his right fist up, and said, "Power to the People, man!" I raised my fist up in return and yelled, "Right on, Jungle Dude!"

Mom said, "One of your friends?"

I laughed, and said, "No, he is one of my brothers, Jungle Dude."

Judy laughed, and said I was crazy. Mom said he was a weirdo and he shouldn't be around children. Perhaps that's why he was hosing shit off the cars at the gate. That is a good point.

This was one of a couple of day trips that we took that summer, with Judy and the family. Growing up, our family never really went on vacations, we mostly had done day trips, and you could count those on your hands once. My family simply could not afford vacations, because they were mostly trying to make ends meet. As for the day trips, I could count on one hand when my father went on those trips. Dad was the breadwinner, and for the most part, he was too busy making a living. I could not fault him for that, because he knew that he had a responsibility to his family, and he took it very seriously.

One thing that my father did carve out for himself, in his life, was deer hunting, where he would go away for about five days a year. He would save a few bucks every week, and squirrel it away in a secret place in the house. Then on that faithful night before the first day of deer hunting season, he would pack his hunting gear up and take off. Dad would meet his hunting buddies, sometimes his brother, and some of his brother-in-laws, and they would rent a cabin for a few days. This was a real man's outing, in which they would drink and play poker all night, get up before sunrise the next morning, and hunt all day, hung over. This is what my father worked for all year, five days of hunting deer. One might suspect that he must have bagged quite a few deer, after going away every year since I was a baby, but you would be wrong. In fact, he never shot and killed a deer his entire life, but he did hit and kill one with the car once. After years of my father coming home empty handed, his friends and family called him the Great White Hunter. Every year, dad would talk about getting a big buck that year, but he never did. His real motive for going hunting was really getting close to nature by himself, and, of course, drinking, playing poker, and being with his buddies. It wasn't too much to ask, for a man who worked his ass off all his life, five days of hunting. He would go hunting every year, no matter what the circumstances were. My dad never bought flashy cars or clothes. All he wanted was five days of hunting, and going into business for himself, not much to ask for in life.

The summer was ending and school would begin the following week. The Monroe Diner had been hit with a lot of Department of Health violations. If Boss didn't get these violations fixed, the Department of Health was going to shut him down on Monday. Therefore, Boss had asked me to perform a major clean up in the kitchen, which would take the entire night to finish, after my regular shift on Saturday night. On Sunday morning, Boss and the rest of the diner crew would finish the major cleaning, because they were always closed on that day. It was good for me because I could make overtime for the entire time.

So it was set that I would work all night, and Boss would meet me in the morning to inspect my work. Boss wrote a big list of things for me to complete, and he reviewed each item with me. Then he locked the front door and left me there with only the kitchen light on.

I began taking everything off the shelves, so I could start cleaning from the top down. Then I called Judy and told her that I would pick her up in 15 minutes. I moved some stainless steel tables to the center of the kitchen, and went to pick up Judy. I brought Judy back to the diner, and showed her the kitchen for the first time. She looked at it in horror, and couldn't believe that I worked in such a dump. After she brought it to my attention, I realized that I indeed did work in a real greasy spoon diner, and if any of the other customers saw the kitchen, they probably would never eat there again. The kitchen and bathroom part of the diner were not part of the original 1940s trailer diner, and were made of wood. The walls and ceilings had not been painted since Ike Eisenhower was president. I knew that because, when I removed his picture from the wall, the original paint was there. There was a very sharp contrast of the light green paint behind the photo and the dark brown grease that covered the rest of the walls and ceilings. In addition, the wooden plank floor with at least a quarter inch gap between each one was caked with black crud all over it. If someone dropped anything on the floor here, the 10-second rule would not apply. Yes, indeed, it was a filthy diner, and it was my job to clean 30 years of dirt in one night. After Judy vowed never to eat there again, we smoked a joint. Then we got the munchies, so I dished out some ice cream and made sundaes with chocolate syrup, whipped cream, and maraschino cherries. We ate our sundaes in a booth of the darkened diner, with the only light coming through the windows was one streetlight by the road. It was a special moment alone for the two of us, we talked, laughed, and we looked into each other's eyes. We started to make out in the booth, and then we moved to the stools, and finally ended up on the kitchen floor after spreading about 10 clean white aprons on it. This moment was one of the most bonding, exciting, and loving moments we shared together.

After about two hours, I dropped Judy off at her home and returned to the diner. I wiped down all the walls and the shelves. Then I cleaned everything that was on the shelves. After that, I completely scrubbed down all the stainless steel tables, rewashed all of the utensils, and placed them back in the respective racks. Then, I spent the remainder of the night scrubbing the kitchen floor with a hard bristle broom and cleaning solvent. At sunrise, I was totally exhausted from trying to complete every item on Boss's list. The walls were clean enough for Tom to paint in the morning, and the floors in the kitchen were so clean you could see the wood color. I worked extra hard that night without any breaks, to make up for the two hours I spent with Judy the night before. When Boss rolled into the parking lot, with his green 1970 Dodge Duster, I was standing on the back steps having a cigarette. He climbed out of the car, and walked towards the steps. He didn't look happy, but then again, he was not a happy man to begin with.

Boss said, "How did it go last night?"

I said, with a smile, "You're not going to recognize the place, it's real clean."

Boss said, with a growling deep voice, "Oh, yeah, we'll see about that."

Boss walked through the back door of the kitchen, and I followed. He walked over to the grill area and looked at the floors.

I said, "Did you ever see this floor so clean?"

He didn't say a word, walked over to the other side of the kitchen, and looked at the walls and shelves. Then he rubbed his hand over the walls and shook his head.

I said, "What's wrong?"

Boss said, in a deep nasty voice, "I can't paint over that."

Then he walked over to the storage room, I said as I followed, "I didn't get to that."

He turned around, looked me in the eyes, and said, "You're kidding me, right?"

I said, "No, I didn't have time, I was too busy doing all this other stuff."

Boss growled, "You're fucking kidding, what were you doing all night, sleeping?"

I looked at him, shocked, and said, "I worked my ass off all night, cleaning."

He yelled, "Oh, yeah, well it certainly doesn't look like it!"

I raised my voice, and said, "You could look around and you can see all the work I did."

Boss said, "It looks like shit. Are you going to clean the storage room?"

I held up my hands, "I'm really beat, Boss, from working all night."

Boss growled, "I have to do that, too?"

I said, "If you want me to, I'll do it, if you're paying me time and a half."

Boss yelled, "Pay you time and a half? I'm not paying you anything for this shit!"

I stood there, stunned for a moment in disbelief about what he just said, as Boss stared at me. I said, "You're not going to pay me for this work?"

He said, "Fuck no, I'm not a sucker."

I looked at him, and yelled, "Oh, yeah, you're not going to fuck me over again! I fucking quit!"

Boss said, "Go ahead, I'll get someone else."

I untied my dirty apron, threw it on the floor, and yelled, "Yeah, another sucker!"

Then I walked out the back door and jumped in my car. I started the engine, put it into drive, and peeled out of the dirt parking lot, leaving a huge plume of air born dirt that covered the diner.

As I drove home, I was so pissed off that I was beating my fist into the armrest. I thought of all the other times Boss had fucked me out of money I had earned. Tom told me when I first started there, to keep track of the hours that I worked, and what Boss was paying me. Boss was good at clipping me for an hour or two off my paycheck. I would catch the so-called errors and match my hours worked to what he paid me. I would confront him about it, and he would always win the argument that he paid me the right amount, by using the hours that he wrote down. It got to the point that I would check with him every day about the hours I worked, to make sure we both agreed, and he would still fuck me over. I would always complain, but would let it ride, until the next time. I finally had enough, stood up for what was right, and I was determined not to be fucked over anymore.

When I got home Sunday morning, Mom and Dad were eating breakfast. Normally I never discussed my dealings with employment to my parents; they had enough problems to deal with. Nevertheless, I was so pissed off I had to tell them about Boss fucking me over. Dad would never be involved with my dealings with the outside world if he knew I could settle it myself. He felt that solving my own problems was part of learning to become an adult. However, this time, he felt he needed to intervene, and set things right. Later that day, my father paid a visit to the Monroe Diner, and had a conversation with Boss. I do not know what my father said, but by the end of their meeting, Boss agreed to pay me for everything, and dad would pick the check up the following day. Dad came home with my check on Monday evening. When I asked dad what he said to Boss to get him to pay, he declined to answer the question, and said that Boss just needed a little coaxing.

Chapter 23 - The Extortion

After about a week or two, school had started, and I landed another dishwashing job a few blocks away from the diner, The Goose Pond Inn. I would work after school, three times a week, and eight hours on Saturday, and for four dollars an hour. I would work fewer hours for more money, much better than the diner. The Goose Pond Inn was a nice restaurant and had real chefs from culinary schools, a real top shelf place. I made a friend there, he was an assistant chef, his name was Ollie, and he was black. Sometimes after work, we used to go to his apartment next-door, get high, and have a couple of drinks. Ollie was in his early 30s, and he was a really cool black guy. We would sit in his apartment, smoke a doobie, listen to some Motown music, and have a drink and just bullshit for a while. Ollie's outlook in life was peace and happiness, and as far as race was concerned, everyone was his brother. On Friday nights, he would go into New York City and stay the weekend, and then come back on Monday mornings.

In September of that year, school started, and when I drove to school, Ike would ride with me because he was a freshman in high school at the time. In fact, Ike would ride shotgun most days when I drove to school, but on his ride back home, he would have to ride the bus because I would go right to my job afterschool.

Everything was right in my life, I had a new job, my own car, and a nice girl friend, and school had just begun. Just like the previous year, I would go to B.O.C.E.S half the day, and have regular classes the other half. Like I said before, I got along with most kids by casual acquaintance as classmates, but for the most part, I was a loner. Sometimes being a loner, could be a problem when it came to the gang elements in school.

After gym class, I took a shower, and went to the locker room to get dressed. When I got my pants on, this guy, Rick V.

came up to me and got into my face.

Rick V. said, "Hey, Kraemer, were you in my locker?"

I took a step back, and said, "No, what would I do that for?"

He said, "Someone told me that you were in my locker, and you ripped me off."

I said, "Who said that? They're a fucking liar."
Then Rick V. pointed to a gang of about seven guys standing at the end of a row of lockers, staring at us.

One of the little guys yelled, "Yeah, I'm a fucking liar?"

A big guy said, "No, he called me a liar?"

Rick then turned back to me, and said, "I want my $15 back, you thief."

I said, "I didn't steal your money, and I'm not giving you anything."

Then Rick turned as if he was walking away, he suddenly turned around again, and sucker punched me in the gut. Because he knocked the wind out of me, I was gasping for air. As I did, the gang of guys surrounded me. Rick then grabbed me by the throat and held me against the locker as I was still gasping for air.

Rick gritted his teeth, and said, "I want my money tomorrow, or we're going to kick the shit out of you."

As Rick and the rest of the gang started to walk away, one of them said, "Tomorrow."

I knew Rick and his gang of buddies, they came from Greenwood Lake, and some of them used to ride on the same bus that I did. I had a run-in with Rick before, but I pretty much had stared him down then. But now this was different, he had some back up, and these guys were a gang. These geniuses had dreamed up this scam to accuse me of sealing money out of a gym locker, and then make me pay them cash. However, the reality is they had targeted me because I always had money, and I was a loner. This would be extortion or robbery, with an alibi if they were caught, saying that they were only trying to recover the stolen goods. My problem was what was I going to do about this. I would have definitely beaten the shit out of Rick if it were just him and me. I could maybe catch him alone, but it would not end there. I decided that I would just avoid the situation, so I cut gym class.

After I cut gym class a couple of times, Rick and his merry gang of assholes caught up with me in the lunchroom. I was sitting on the windowsill, talking to Judy. When Rick walked up to me, with his crowd behind him, he grabbed me by my shirt.

He said, "You got my money, Kraemer?"

I said, nervously, "I told you, I didn't steal your money!"

Rick then punched me in the gut, and the gang of goons surrounded me. Then I stood up straight, pulled a $10 and a$5 bill from my pocket, and handed them to Rick. He snatched the money from my hand and smiled. He pushed me with both hands into one of his big buddies.

Rick said, "I forgot to tell you, I'm missing $30, you still owe me $15. Have it for me tomorrow."

Then he and his crew walked out of the lunchroom. Judy was crying, and I looked at about 100 kids staring at me. I walked out of the school with Judy and we sat in the car and talked. We talked for a while and I tried to stop her from crying, she was really upset. We both talked about a logical way to solve this problem, but nothing made very much sense to me. My biggest mistake was paying this fucking guy off, because now he had a patsy. If I go to the vice principal with this, Rick would say I stole from him and his gang will back him up. Nobody was going to back me up I am a loner. I was quite troubled with this problem, and the only way out of this was to fight my way through it. I would have to catch Rick alone, and beat the crap out of him. Then, later on, I would have to face the gang, one at a time, or all at once. There was no other way to settle this.

When I got home that evening after work, my mother and father were sitting at the kitchen table.

My father said, "I hear you had some trouble in school today."

I said, surprised, "Yeah, who told you?"

Mom said, "Judy's mother called, Judy's really upset and she is afraid you're going to get hurt."

I said, "Don't worry about it; I'll take care of it."

Dad said, "I want you to sit down and tell me the whole story."

I sat there with my parents, and explained the whole story, even the part that I punked out and paid the thug. Then my father asked how I was going to resolve the problem, and I told him.

He said, "Hey, Dick, Judy and your brother said that these guys do not fight fair. Some of these kids have knives, chains, and baseball bats. What are you goanna do when they pull their tools out?"

I said, "I have my old bat in the basement, I'll put it in my trunk."

Dad said, "Let me handle it, what's this punk's last name and spell it."

Then he grabbed the phone book, and found his number. I looked at him, and thought that dad was really going to fuck this up for me now. Dad dialed the number and walked into the other room.

After about 5 minutes, he came back to the kitchen and hung the phone up. Dad said, "Okay, it's all set. That fucking kid and his father are coming here at 5:30 tomorrow, and we'll settle things once and for all."

I said, in disbelief, "They're coming here?"

He said, "Yeah, you're not going to school until we settle this, okay?"

I stood up, and said, "Yeah, okay."

I called Judy up and told her about my father's plan, and she was sorry that her mother had called my parents about this. I was not quite sure how this was going to shake out, but when my dad was involved, anything was possible.

My father came home from work, took a quick shower, and changed his clothes. My mother was told to get out of the house and take the kids with her for about an hour. The doorbell rang at 5:30 sharp, dad answered the door, and let Rick and Mr. V. into the house. They all walked into the kitchen, and I was sitting at the table.

Dad said, as he waved his arm towards him, "Mr. V., this is my son, Dick."

Mr. V. nodded his head, and said, "Hello, Dick, Mr. Kraemer, this is my son, Rick."

Dad said, "Hello, Rick, now that the introductions are out of the way, let's talk about what I called you about."

Mr. V. said, "Okay, let's talk about it."

Dad said, "Good, your son claims that my son stole money from him. My son works after school and weekends to make money, he doesn't need to steal and he didn't do it."

Mr. V. said, "How much money was it?"

I said, "Thirty dollars."

Mr. V. looked at Rick, "Where would you get $30 from? You don't work."

Rick looked down at the floor, and said, "I don't know."

Dad said, "Oh that means there was no $30, and you used your friends to help you extort money from my son, is that right?"

Mr. V. looked at Rick by tilting his head sideways, and said, "Is that the way it is, Rick?"

Rick looked at his dad, and said, "Yeah, sort of."

Just then, Mr. V. slapped the back of Rick's head, making him jolt forward.

Mr. V. growled in anger, as he grabbed his arm, "Yeah sort of? So, what's not right?"

Rick said, "I only got $15, and I didn't need any help."

Dad said, loudly, "Well, that's different; you only got $15 and no help."

Mr. V. pulled Rick by the arm, in a low angry voice, he said, "You're fucking kidding me."

Dad crossed his arms, and said loudly, "And that's why we're here, because you don't need help extorting money from my son. You could do it all by yourself, that's why you're here."

Mr. V. looked at my father, not sure what would come next.

Unfolding his arms, and standing up straight, Dad said, "Mr. V., in order to settle this, we should have Dick and Rick here, duke it out in the back yard. What do you think?"

I looked at dad, and then I looked at Rick.

Mr. V. looked at dad, and said, "Sounds good to me. Ready, Rick?"

Rick looked at his father, and whispered, "Dad, I don't want to fight him, I don't have a beef with him."

Dad said, "Well, I didn't think so."

Mr. V. pulled Rick close to him by his arm, and said, "You're a fucking punk and a disgrace. Now apologize to Mr. Kraemer and his son."

Rick said, softly crying, "Mr. Kraemer, I'm sorry," then he turned to me, and said, "I'm sorry."

Dad said, "I want this to be over now, so if any of your little friends bother my son again, I'm going to call the police and the school. Okay?"

Mr. V. said, "Mr. Kraemer, I'll make sure this is the end of it. I'm so embarrassed. I don't know where he gets it from; we come from a good family. Maybe it's the streets of Brooklyn where we moved from."

Dad said, as he patted Mr. V. on the shoulder, "Okay, if anything else happens, I'll call you."

Mr. V. said, "It won't, but thank you."

As dad walked them out the door, dad said, " Oh, what about the 15 bucks?"

Mr. V. stopped, and said, "Rick?"

Rick stood in the hallway, held out his arms, and said, "I don't have it."

Mr. V. took out his wallet, handed dad $15, and said, "He'll pay me back."

Then dad walked the both of them out the door. When dad came back in the house, he walked into the kitchen and placed the money on the table.

He said, "This should be the end of it, if you have any trouble with these kids, you let me know."

I stood up, and said, "Yeah, okay. I'm sorry I had to drag you into this."

He said, "Hey, Dick, I want you to always stand up for yourself and solve your own problems. But sometimes you can't take it on all by yourself, and you need help, it's all about growing up. It's also knowing when to ask for help."

I said, "Thanks for the help, Dad."

Dad said," That's my job."

I was skeptical of whether or not my father's plan of action would work. However, much to my amazement, it did, and, from that day forward, I did not have any more problems with the clowns from Greenwood Lake again. The school nor the police ever got involved, and my parents never heard of the problem again. I could only speculate that even though my family had only been in the village a short period of time, people in the area became quickly acquainted with my parents. One reason was that it was a very small village of fewer than 2000 people. The other reason was my father joined the American Legion post 1443 in Greenwood Lake, where he became quickly familiar with the other veterans and their families. There were many kids that I went to school with whose parents belonged to the American Legion, and my father was a very social person. Therefore, I am sure that word spread within the parent circles of gang type activity, and it was something they wanted to stop.

Chapter 24 - The Big Mistake

One Friday night in late October 1973, the kitchen at the Goose Pond Inn needed some repairs because of a gas leak, and the staff was let go early that night. So, Ollie and I started partying earlier then usual that night. He bought a new bottle of Seagram's-7 and a big bottle of 7-Up, took a large bucket of ice from the restaurant, and took it to his place. We sat there, listening to Marvin Gaye, Diana Ross and the Supremes, The Temptations, Smokey Robinson, and Stevie Wonder. It was Ollie that really introduced me to the Motown music that I love so much to this day. We would sit there in his apartment, and talk about anything-politics, people, and girls. He talked of a race neutral world, where everyone could look past the color of a person's skin, and take people at face value. He spoke of Martin Luther King and Gandhi as people with great visions of how the world should be. We lost track of time in our conversation, Ollie missed the last bus to New York City that night, and he always goes to the city on Friday night. He was also upset because he was supposed to have gone to someone's birthday party that night, and he was going to miss it.

I said, "Wow, I'm sorry I messed up your plans."

Ollie said, "No, man, it wasn't you. I should have been watching the time more closely."

I said, "Hey, maybe we could catch the bus at another bus stop down the line?"

He said, "No, that won't work, the bus is an express, it only has one other stop in New Jersey. We'll never catch it in time."

I said, "Wow, that's a bummer," taking another drink of my Seven and Seven.

Ollie said, "Hey, man, I got it! Why don't the both of us go to the city? I'll pay for the gas and the tolls. You could go to the party with me, there's some really hot chicks at the party."

I said, "I don't know, man. The city, I don't know how to get there, or my way around the city."

He said, "I know the way there, I lived in the city my whole life, I'll show you the way, man."

I looked out the window into the darkness, and said, "Yeah, I don't know."

Ollie said, "I understand, man, it's a lot to ask, its okay, man."

I said, "How long does it take to get to the city?"

He said, "Less than an hour, we could be at the party."

I looked at my watch, it was 8:00 PM, and I could drive him down, hang out for an hour, and he home by 11 PM.

I said, "Okay, Ollie, pack your stuff, we're going."

Ollie jumped up, and smiled, "Aw, man, that's cool. I owe you one."

He rush around the apartment, gathered his stuff, and put it in his suitcase. I started the car up and pulled it in front of his apartment door. He threw his suitcase in the backseat, and ran back inside.

Ollie came back outside, locked the door, and walked to the car carrying a big paper bag. He jumped into the front passenger seat and opened the bag.

Ollie said, with a smile, "I brought the refreshments for the ride."

Then he pulled out the bottle of Seagram's 7, the bottle of 7-Up, the bucket of ice, and two glasses.

I had already been drinking for about two hours and had four glasses of Seven and Sevens to this point. I smiled and told him he was crazy. As I drove, he mixed the drinks for the both of us. We drove down route 17 South, which is a two-lane highway in to New Jersey. I was going about 55 mph. Ollie turned on the radio; he would hold my drink as I drove, and give me directions. Every once in a while, I would drift into the other lane and would have to correct my steering. I had driven before after having a couple of drinks, but I surpassed my previous drunken experiences.

Occasionally, Ollie would have to say, "Hey, stay in your lane," or "Watch out." We drove all the way to Rutherford, New Jersey, and got on to route 3 east, a four-lane highway that goes to the Lincoln Tunnel. Everything seemed very blurry at this point, and Ollie's bitching about my driving was becoming more frequent. I continued drifting in other people lanes, and they were blowing their horns at me, I even cut a few of them off. As we approached the tollbooth, Ollie dumped the rest of the drinks out of the window, and put the bottle of Seagram's 7 and the glasses in the glove box.

I pulled up to the tollbooth. Ollie handed me the money for the toll, and I handed it to the toll taker. Just then, a police officer appeared on the toll island, and waved for me to stop. The cop bent down to the window, and said, "We had a report of a white car driving erratically. Where are you going?"

Ollie leaned over, looked at the officer, and said, "We're going to Manhattan, officer."

The police officer pointed to a huge stonewall leading to the tunnel, and said, "Pull over there."

I carefully had to pull the car over through several lanes leading to the tunnel, and finally pulled the car against the stonewall. The young police officer walked to my window as another cop walked up behind the car.

The officer said, "Could I see your license, registration, and insurance card?"

I said, "Yeah, sure, officer."

I reached into my rear pocket, pulled out my license and handed it to the cop. I then reached over, opened the glove box, and the bottle of booze and the glasses rolled out on Ollie's lap. The other police officer shined his flashlight on Ollie's lap. I took the registration and insurance card out, and handed them to the officer.

The police officer said, "Greenwood Lake, you're pretty far away from home, aren't you?"

I said, "Yeah, I'm just dropping my friend off in the city."

The young cop said, "Yeah, okay, I would like you to step out of the car."

I said, "Yeah, okay," I opened the door and the officer escorted me to the back of the car.

The young officer said, "Son, have you been drinking tonight?"

I said, "Yeah, I had a couple, but I'm okay."

He said, "Okay, we're going to do a sobriety test, if you pass, you can go. Okay?"

I said, "Yeah, okay, officer."

So then he instructed me to stand straight, hold both arms out, tilt my head back, and touch my nose with my right hand, I failed. Then he told me to walk in a straight line, I failed that, too.

The young officer said to the other officer, "Stan, he's drunk."

Officer Stan, the older officer with sergeant stripes, said, "Okay, let's process him and impound the car."

Then Officer Stan opened the passenger door, and said to Ollie, "Okay, we're impounding the car. Get your stuff and call a cab."

Ollie said, in a pleading voice, "Isn't there another way to handle this, without throwing my friend in jail, and impounding the car?"

Officer Stan looked at the other young officer, shrugged his shoulders, and smiled. Officer Stan said, "Can you drive? Are you drunk?"

Ollie said, "Yes, I can drive, I'm not drunk."

Officer Stan said, with a smile, "Okay, I want you to pull the car away from the wall, and park it over there," he pointed about 30 feet away, "If you do it right, you and your friend can go."

Ollie jumped into the driver seat, and closed the door, as I stood with the young officer. Ollie started the car up, turned the wheels to the left, turned on the directional, and began to pull out. Suddenly, Ollie slammed on the brakes, causing the tires to screech, and the car to rock. Then he began to pull out, and again slammed on the brakes, and he yelled out the window," I'm not used to power brakes."

The younger officer looks at Officer Stan and shakes his head. Just then, Ollie accelerates quickly moving about 5 feet and again he slammed on the brakes, as the tires squealed to a halt.

Officer Stan ran up to the window, and yelled, "Okay, that's enough, put the car in park and turn off the car." Ollie did what the officer told him, and Officer Stan opened the driver's door.

Officer Stan said, "Okay, get out."

Ollie said, pleading, "Let me have another chance, I'll get used to it," as he got out of the car.

The young officer laughed, and said, "Oh, yeah, sure, you'll get better."

Officer Stan quickly spun Ollie around, and said, "Put your hands behind your back, you're under arrest."

Ollie said, "Under arrest, what did I do," as Officer Stan slapped the cuffs on him.

Officer Stan spun him back around, smiled, and said, "Drunk driving."

Ollie said, "I was only trying to help my friend."

Officer Stan said, "Yeah, when we get to the station, we're going to have a long talk about how you're such good friends with a young white kid from upstate New York." Then he grabbed Ollie by the arm, and walked him to the door in the huge stonewall.

The young officer said, "Follow them, kid, and walk in front of me." When we walked inside the door, the young officer said, "Kid, I'm going to put the cuffs on you for now, I'll take them off when we get to the station." I held my hands out front of me, and he placed the cuffs on me gently. Then we continued to walk, in a series of brightly lit stone encased narrow hallways and stairways. I thought for a moment that we were going into a dungeon, and we walked for about 20 minutes. I started to realize the gravity of this situation, and I began to cry. We reached an elevator. We all got in and rode it to the top of this big building. The elevator door opened to the Weehawken Police Department, where they read me the Miranda rights, gave me a breathalyzer test, fingerprinted me, and checked in my watch, wallet, belt, and shoelaces. The young officer was with me the whole time, and led me to the phone to make a call, but the line was busy. All through the processing, I did not see Ollie anywhere. I told the officer that I could not get through. He said the desk sergeant would keep trying to call my parents. The police officers took pity on me because I was young, crying, drunk, and very scared. The desk sergeant thought that if he put me in the drunk tank with the rest of the low lives, they would eat me for a snack. Therefore, he placed me in a single holding cell, away from everyone else. There was a window right outside my jail cell, it was broken, and it got very cold that night. An officer came in and said that they contacted my parents, and they would be here in the morning to bail me out. I asked for a blanket that I received a couple of hours later. Even with a blanket, it was very cold in there, but I did not want to complain, for fear of being locked up with some whack jobs. I did not sleep at all that night, occasionally a police officer would check on me. When the sun came up the next morning, I began to get a headache. An officer gave me a bacon and egg on a hard roll in foil, and a cup of coffee in a paper cup. I thanked him very much, because I knew this was not jail food, and that he bought it at a bodega. I sat in that cell a long time thinking about how badly I fucked up, and what was going to happen to me now. Sitting in that jail cell alone, in silence for hours, reflecting on how stupid I was, and feeling sorry for myself, was a very memorable experience. About 11:30 that morning, a police officer came and said that my father had posted bail. The officer let me out of the cell and walked me to the front desk. My father and Helmut, dad's business partner, were standing on the other side of the divider as the cops processed me out. I was happy to see my dad, even though I knew I was going to get a boatload of shit from him.

Once they released me, my father said, "Are you alright?"

I said, "Yeah, I'm okay."

Dad said, "Good, let's get the car out of the impound lot."

The three of us walked down to the street, got into my dad's truck, and drove a few blocks to the impound lot, without saying a word.

Dad said to me, "I'll be right back, stay here." Then dad and Helmut got the car out of the lot. Helmut would drive my car and would follow dad and me in the truck.

Dad jumped into the truck, and said, "Okay, let's get out of this hell hole."

Dad found his way onto route 3 west, and began our trip home. As we traveled a short distance, it was total silence in the truck. I believe that my father was waiting for me to say something, so I did.

I looked over at him, and said, "Dad, I'm really sorry about all this."

He looked at me as if he wanted to kick me out of the truck while we drove. Then he put his eyes back on the road, and said, "Oh, yeah, I'll bet you're sorry."

I turned my eyes to the road, and said, "I know I really fucked things up this time."

He said, loudly, "Oh, yeah, you really fucked up, that's for sure." Then there was silence for about 5 minutes, as we turned onto route 17 N.

Dad said, "Well, you won't be driving, starting today for about six months or maybe a year."

I said, surprised, "A year? You've got to be kidding."

He said, "Maybe six months, if you're lucky."

I said, "Holy Shit!"

He said, "Don't do the crime, if you can't do the time."

Then dad said, "Dick, what in the hell were you thinking, driving around with a bottle of whiskey, glasses, and even an ice bucket in the car?"

I said, "That was Ollie's idea, big mistake."

He said, "That's another thing. What are you doing hanging around with niggers? Not just any nigger, but one that is 32 years old, and did time in the joint."

I said, surprised," Ollie did time in prison?"

Dad said, "Yeah, no shit. The cops told me."

I said, "Wow, I didn't know that."

He said, "Yeah, let me paint a picture for you. You and your black friend go to the city, and meet some of his other nigger friends. Then they take your car and your money, and then they cut your fucking honky throat."

I looked out the window, and said, "I don't think Ollie would do that."

Dad said, "Yeah, you know him real well. You didn't even know he did time, stupid."

I said, "Yeah, you're right."

He said, "You better start thinking, or you're going to get yourself killed, Dick."

I knew all along that my father was a racist and a bigot. In fact, most of his friends called him an Archie Bunker clone. As I was growing up, I did not share all my father's views about other people's races and religions. However, this was not the time to pull my Meathead routine. Besides the point of not knowing Ollie well enough, did get me thinking about the possibility of getting carjacked, and maybe even killed.

I looked at my dad, and said, "You're right, Dad."

Dad said, "Damn straight I'm right."

When I got home, Mom gave me her verbal beat down, and told me that I would never drive again. I went upstairs, took a bath, and went to sleep. The next morning, Dad woke me up for school, and I walked up the street to catch the school bus. As I rode that bus to school, all I could think about was how badly I fucked up, and how it was going to impact my life.

Because I didn't show up for work at the Goose Pond Inn, they fired me and replaced me with one of my so-called friends. When I went back to the job a week later to pick up my last paycheck, I was told that Ollie was not seen or heard from since we were busted. I felt bad about what happened to him, and hoped he was okay. I never heard from Ollie again.

I had no car and no job, and as far as I could see, no future. I could not, for the life of me, shake the depression, which had encompassed my life, for weeks on end.

After I pled guilty to the drunken driving charges, they suspended my license for six months, along with some fines.

My parents decided to do some checking on me at school, right after I was charged with DWI. They found out that I was flunking all my subjects, except for B.O.C.E.S. The school had informed my parents that I would need to repeat the 10th grade. As I had mentioned before, I had been left back in the second grade, because of my eyesight. Therefore, if I were to repeat the 10th grade, I would be 20 years old when I would graduate high school. Once my parents broke the news to me in the second week of November, that I would have to repeat the 10th grade, I had totally flipped out. The prospect of me graduating high school at 20 years old sent me into a downward spiral of depression, and into a fit of rage.

When I say a fit of rage, I do not mean that I started busting up furniture, which would've gotten me killed in my parent's home. But there would be some heated debates about me graduating high school, even if it took me until I turned 30.

My mother had graduated from high school with honors, and she could have been college bound if she hadn't fallen in love and married my father, and then started hammering out the Kraemer litter.

My father, on the other hand, was not the scholarly type. Dad was a C student and had his share of juvenile misadventures. When the Korean War rolled around, the draft was in full force, but at the time, my father was too young to be drafted. Shortly after the Korean War broke out in June 1950, my dad at the age of 16 forged his father's signature and came up with a phony birth certificate to join the Army. The Army discovered the forgery, and his application was rejected. Nevertheless, that did not deter him from joining the Army a year later on his 17th birthday, with his father's consent. Dad earned his GED high school degree while he was in the service.

In my mind, after my parents read me the riot act about how I was going to finish high school, and they did not care how long it was going to take, I knew that it simply would not happen. Therefore, I decided to just cut all my classes, get high, and be with Judy every chance I could. As far as I was concerned, when I turned 18, I'd drop out of high school legally, move out of the house, and get a job. It was just a question of time until I would have control of my own destiny.

My parents turned down the screws pretty tight on me for the first few weeks after the DWI. My mother was getting weekly reports from the school. Then my parents and I would have our usual weekly screaming and yelling sessions. This argument would always end with dad reciting his "Straighten Out and Fly Right" doctrine, and then threaten to kill me and bury me in the back yard in the cover of darkness. At this point in my life, my parents had given up on corporal punishment because I was too old. However, because of their frustration of dealing with a rebellious teenager, if I did not, "Straighten Out and Fly Right," the death penalty was still an option.

Mr. & Mrs. Kraemer A.K.A. Mom & Dad 1973

Chapter 25 - Straighten Out and Fly Right

My parents had come to the realization that I was just stalling for time, until I would turn 18. Then I would drop out of school and fly the coop.

Then one day in school, I saw an old classmate who had dropped out of school and joined the Army. I knew of other guys who had also dropped out of high school, and joined other branches of the armed services. They all seemed to adjust well to military life. The Vietnam War was ending, and America was already withdrawing troops from the country. The draft had ended on June 30, 1973, six months ago, and the military was changing to an all-volunteer service. Because the Vietnam War was a very unpopular war, especially for young people, it was hard to recruit young souls to volunteer and join the armed services. The military was struggling to fill the void of many exiting draftee veterans with volunteers. Therefore, they would be more than happy to recruit young high school dropouts, even a fuck up like me.

I went to the Army recruiting office, talked to a sergeant, and got some information packets and the application form. I talked to Judy about it, and she thought that I had lost my marbles. She really didn't visualize me in a uniform, and the thought of me going away for a long time started to make her cry. My thought was that I only had two options: join the Army, or wait until I turned 18 and drop out of school. The second option was not very productive or conducive to my future.

I waited for my parents next, "Turn the Screws on Dick" session to get really heated, then I sprung my, "Hey, what if I join the Army?" statement. I put the recruitment folder on the table. Then there was silence in the kitchen, it was so quiet you could hear the mice fart. Both my parents just looked at each other for a moment, as if they did not understand the statement. Swiftly, mom jumps up from the table, and lunges at me from across the room. Dad jumped in between us. Mom, gritting her teeth and arms fully extended, passed my father and she was reaching for me.

She yells, "The Army, fuck that, I'll kill you myself!" I backed up into the hallway, in fear that dad would release her on me.

Dad said, "Jeanie, calm down, the boy doesn't know what he's talking about. He can't join the Army without our signature."

Mom backed up, pointed at me, and yelled, "Well, I'm not signing, forget it, buddy boy." I yelled back, "Fine, so don't sign, I don't care."

Then mom on the other side of the kitchen leaned on the counter and lit a cigarette. Dad sat back down, and opened the recruitment folder.

I walked back to the kitchen doorway, and said, "I don't see why I couldn't join the Army. I'll get my GED in there, and it would be faster, too."

Mom said, "Because it's what you want, not what I want. You're not getting your own way this time!"

Dad turned in his chair, and said, "I'm not signing either."

I said, "Hey, Dad, you dropped out of school, joined the Army, and got your GED."

He said, "That's different, it was a different time. And you're not me."

I said, "How is it different?"

Mom was tapping her foot, still leaning on the counter, and staring at me in silence.

Dad said, "The Army is filled with pinko's, fagots, losers, hippies, and drug addicts. You're not joining the Army."

I said, "OK, I'll join the Navy, they'll take me."

He said, "No, they're just as bad or even worse than the Army."

Then he got up, standing in between mom and me, and handed me the folder. He turned, walked to the center of the kitchen, and looked at my mother.

Then he turned again, looked me in the eyes, and said, "But, if you join the Marines Corps, I'll sign."

I looked at him as if he was crazy, and said, "The Marines?"

Suddenly, my mother started running towards me; dad blocked her from getting to me. She yelled," No fucking way are you going into the Marines. I won't sign and you can forget about it."

Then she backed up, and yelled at dad, "Are you out of your mind, there's a war going on, he'll get himself killed."

Dad then put his hands up, and said, "Calm down, Jeanie, take it easy, let's talk."

I said, "Yeah, I'm not sure about Marines, those guys are crazy."

Dad turned around, and said, "It's the Marines or nothing, no debate."

Mom, standing in the middle of the kitchen, began to cry, and said, "You're crazy if you think I'm signing that paper."

I turned around with the folder in my hand, and walked up to my bedroom. I figured that maybe if I was not within eyesight, things would calm down after a while. After these kinds of fights, everyone was emotionally drained and arguments would just go around in circles. I thought of what my father had said about the Marines being my only option. I knew that he was serious about his proposition, and he wasn't going to back down from it. At first, it was tough for me to get my head around the idea of becoming a Marine. I certainly did not fit the tough guy image of a Marine, at 5'10" tall, 155 pounds, and skinny as a rail. The basic training alone might kill me, because there had been reports of men dying during training, mysterious deaths. I was not at all sold on the idea of becoming a Marine. However, I would investigate the prospect of joining the Marine Corps.

My father had many reasons why he hated the Army and the other branches of the armed services, with the exception of the Marine Corps, during the Vietnam War era. Those reasons would be as follows:

➢ The drug use during the Vietnam War was rampant my father would see on TV and read in the newspapers that Army soldiers were smoking dope and shooting up in massive droves.

➢ The Army soldiers would wear peace signs, love beads, and other hippy garb in the combat zone.

➢ The Army soldiers would grow long sideburns and Manchu mustaches in the bush

➢ Some Army soldiers openly criticized the American government in Vietnam on the six o'clock news.

➢ Many large Vietnam battles were won and held by Marines. Nevertheless, once they turned over the real estate of those held positions to the Army, they could never hold those positions, and would retreat. This would mean leaving the Marines to fight again to regain control of a previously held position. Most of all, sometimes Army soldiers that were dead or wounded were left in the jungle after a skirmish, for the Vietcong.

This last reason deeply troubled and infuriated my father. Because in the Korean War, my dad was a medic in the Army, and he nor his superiors would leave the dead or wounded on the battlefield. In fact, many people died and were wounded in Korea retrieving the injured and the dead, including my father. My father did not hear, see, or read anything about the above atrocities when it came to the US Marine Corps. These Marines were filled with Honor, Loyalty, and Discipline. In addition, I had uncles on my mother's side that were in the Marine Corps. All of them were stand up law-abiding, red-blooded Americans, and they were tough guys. My father loved them like brothers. Therefore, because of the above reasons and many more, he would never give up his eldest son to the likes of the U.S. Army or any other Pinko armed service, with the exception of the Marine Corps.

In November of 1973, the situation of the Vietnam War was ending slowly. In January of that year, The Paris Peace Accord was signed, which called for a cease-fire in North and South Vietnam, and a draw down of 150,000 troops to 250,000 total US service members in Vietnam. The major part of the Paris Peace Accord was a commitment from the US government to leave Vietnam, and gradually withdraw troops from the country. The US military was not deploying new troop replacements to Vietnam. However, there were many bumps in the road with the Viet Cong not adhering to the cease-fire, and the US military running many covert operations that violated the Paris Peace Accord. The US military still were bringing their service members home. Given the current circumstances of the Vietnam War, my father felt that it would be highly improbable that I would be deployed to Vietnam, with the war ending. Of course, peace treaties can be broken, and US plans could change, but my father was okay with that possibility. My mother, on the other hand, was scared to death at the prospect of me going to war, and that was her real opposition of me joining the Marine Corps.

The next day I called the Marine Corps recruiter, Gunnery Sergeant Fox, and set up a meeting later that day. When I met him at his office, much to my surprise, he was a friendly and happy guy. Gunny Fox was in his early 40s, a big man 6 feet about 230 pounds, with a crew cut and chest full of battle ribbons on his dress blue uniform. We talked about what my motivation was in joining the service, the DWI, and school. He seemed to take a real interest in me as a person, and not just another dumb kid to fill his recruiting quota, unlike the Army recruiter. I felt that all the questions he had asked about me meant that he genuinely cared about whether or not it was good for me as a person to join the Marine Corps. Then Gunny Fox reviewed all the details about basic training, the jobs that I might qualify for once I took their aptitude test, the places I could be stationed in life in general as a Marine. He gave me a brochure, and a folder with the paper work. I told him that I would talk it over with my parents, and get back to him.

I told Judy about my father's requirement about joining the Marine Corps instead of the Army. She thought that the idea was insane, and I was out of my head for considering it. I, too, had a problem getting my head around becoming a Marine, but Gunny Fox assured me that after basic training in Paris Island, South Carolina, I would be a Mean, Green Fighting Machine. After giving it great thought, I figured that I should give it a shot. After all, what am I doing right now except wasting my time, hanging around, waiting to become 18, where I could be working on bettering myself, instead of fucking off. Besides, what do I have to lose? However, I did want badly for the Marine Corps to work out for me. As the old saying goes, "Nothing ventured, Nothing gained."

I caught Dad alone one evening, because Mom was still not buying the Marine Corps idea, and I did not want to start another family brawl. I told him that I called Gunny Fox, the Marines recruiter, and that I was interested in joining. My dad said that he already knew that I called Gunny Fox, because the gunny was a member of the American Legion, and lives in Greenwood Lake, too. It turns out that Dad and Gunny Fox knew each other well, and would occasionally get together with the other vets, and knock back a few. My father questioned me to insure that I was serious about joining the Marines, before getting into the next phase of the process. I reassured him that I was serious about joining the Marines. Then Dad said that he would talk to Gunny Fox about how we could convince my mother that joining the Marines would be good for me.

A few days went by and Dad said that Gunny Fox was coming over after dinner tomorrow night. Gunny Fox was also going to bring with him a new Marine from Greenwood

Lake that had just finished basic training, and was home on leave. My father informed Mom about the meeting the following night, she put up a big fuss, and still vowed to never sign the papers. My father said that he just wanted to ask some questions, and explore all of their son's options. Dad also promised that under no circumstances would she be forced or pressured to sign anything, if she did not want to. My mother reluctantly agreed to the meeting.

The next evening after dinner, Gunny Fox and Private First Class, John D came to the house at exactly 7 PM, as agreed. My dad answered the door, and led the two Marines into the kitchen. My mother would have normally offered our guests coffee or tea, and a seat, being a gracious homemaker, but this was different. These Marines were trying to kidnap her oldest son. Therefore, she sat at the opposite end of the kitchen table, and she looked like she was ready for battle

Dad said, "Gunny Sergeant Fox, I'd like you to meet my wife, Jeanie, and you already know my son, Dick."

Gunny Fox, holding his white hat under one arm, said, "Pleased to meet you, Mrs. Kraemer. I would like you to meet Private First Class; John D. John just finished basic training. His family also lives in Greenwood Lake. Perhaps you know Mr. and Mrs. D. from the American Legion?"

Mom looked at my dad, and said, "I know John and Betty D., right, Dick?"

Dad said, "Yeah, they were at the Tip Cup party a couple of weeks ago."

Mom said, "So you're their son, John. So, what are you doing home?"

John D said, "Well, ma'am, I just finished basic training, and after basic, everyone gets 10 days leave before going to their next duty station."

Dad said, "Where are you going to be stationed, John?

John said, "I'm going to be trained in tanks in Camp Lejeune, North Carolina, then I'll maybe get assigned somewhere else."

Mom sat up straight, and said, "You don't know where you're going after that?"

Gunny Fox said, "After Marines are trained, they could remain in North Carolina, or be assigned to many duty stations in the world or an amphibious fleet with NATO in the Atlantic or in the Pacific."

Mom looked at dad and said, "Vietnam is in the Pacific Ocean, Richard."

Dad folded his arms, and said, "Jeanie, they're ending the war, and sending troops home by the tens of thousands."

Gunny Fox said, "He is right, ma'am, the war is ending and we're not sending any new troops to Vietnam."

Mom folded her arms, crossed her legs, looked at Gunny Fox sternly, and said, "Can you guarantee me that my son will never go to war?"

Gunny Fox cracked a grin and said, "Ma'am, I could never make a guaranty like that."

Dad took a step towards mom, and said, "Come on, you know he can't make a promise like that. It's the Marine Corps, not the Boy Scouts."

Mom put both hands on the table, and said, "So, John, how did your mother feel when you told you wanted to join the Marines?"

John started to twist his uniform hat in his hands, and said, "Well, Mrs. Kraemer, she was worried at first, like you, but now she is okay with me joining the Marines. My mom noticed that I changed for the better."

Mom said, "Well, John, you're a very well mannered young man. Your parents must be very proud of you."

John said, "Yes, ma'am."

Mom turned to me, and said," Dick, you haven't said anything. Do you have any questions for John?"

I turned in my seat, looked at John, and said, "How much money do you make?"

John said, "Well, while I was in boot camp, I made $162 twice a month. But now, since I graduated in the top 3% of my platoon, I was promoted to Private First Class and I'll get a raise."

Gunny Fox said, "With his new pay rate, he'll make $185 twice a month."

I said, "Ah," then I scratched my head, and said, "I probably have other questions, but I can't think of any right now."

Gunny Fox said," If you have any questions, call me, or you could call John before he leaves." He then said, "Well, folks, I hope I answered all of your questions, if you have any others, you could always call me at my office. John and I have to leave now."

Mom stood up, and said, "Well, I'm still not signing anything."

Gunny Fox said, "It's your decision, Mrs. Kraemer. It was a pleasure meeting you."

Then Gunny Fox reached over the table and grasped mom's hand. I stood up, and shook hands with both men.

Dad shook Gunny's hand, and said, "Thanks for coming out, Gunny." Then dad shook John's hand. Dad escorted the two Marines to the door, and waited for them to drive away before closing the door.

Dad returned to the kitchen, and said to mom, "That John D was an impressive young man, wasn't he?"

Mom, still standing, said, "Yeah, he is, he comes from a good family, his parents are nice, too."

Dad turned to me, and said, "Did you know him from school?"

I walked to the sink and said, "I'd seen him in school a few times but I really didn't know him. He had hair back then."

Mom said, "His mother must be sick with worry."

Dad said, "Why don't you call and talk to her? Her number must be in the phone book."

Mom looked at my father, as if a light bulb went off in her head, and stood there in silence for a couple of moments.

Dad looked back inquisitively, and said, "What is it? What's wrong?"

She crossed her arms, glared at him, tilted her head to one side, and said, "The fix is on, isn't it, Richard?"

Dad looked surprised, extended his arms to his side, and said, "What are you talking about?"

Mom pointed her finger at dad, and said, "Every single person involved in this thing belongs to the American Legion. Gunny Fox, John D, Betty D, and that kid, they are all connected to the Legion."

Dad waved mom's finger from his face, and said, "So, what does that prove?"

She yelled, "IT PROVES THAT YOU SET THIS WHOLE THING UP WITH YOUR WAR BUDDIES!"

Dad took a step back, and yelled, "OH, YEAH, A BIG CONSPIRACY. ARE YOU CRAZY?"

Mom yelled," YOU SET THIS WHOLE THING UP, BECAUSE YOU WANT DICK TO JOIN THE MARINE CORPS, DIDN'T YOU?"

Dad moved forward as mom moved backwards, and he yelled, "YEAH, I DID IT! BECAUSE I KNOW WHAT'S GOOD FOR MY BOY!"

Mom extended her arms, and pointed at dad, "AH-HAH! SO YOU ADMIT IT!"

Then she turned to me, and yelled, "I'll Never Sign That Fucking Paper, over My Dead Body!"
I picked up the paperwork off the table, shrugged my shoulders, and said, "Okay." Then both my parents looked at me in silence, as I walked out of the kitchen. When I reached the stairs, I heard mom yelled, "Never!" Then the argument continued in the kitchen for a few minutes until the two of them ran out of steam.

I sat in my room that evening, feeling sorry that I had caused all this fighting between my parents. This was all caused by me being popped for DWI and failing in school. Both of these things could have been avoided, if I was not so damn stupid.

I sat in my room and played the what if game in my head. What would've happened if I didn't go with Ollie that night? What would've happened if I didn't quit the Monroe diner job?

What would've happened if I were smarter?

What would've happened if I were not born at all?

The whole what if game was a quite maddening exercise for the human mind where as a person sits for hours, days, weeks, months, and even years of their whole lives playing the game. Only to find the same conclusion repetitively, the answer to your past mistakes is that you cannot go back and fix them. Life does not have a gear for reverse and there has never been a Time Machine. Unless of course the government has a Time Machine in area 51 that nobody knows about.

The last question did intrigue me. What would've happened if I were not born at all? I was in a very deep depression and I did not see the light of day in my mind for weeks. Would the world be a better place if I did not exist? I referred to an old movie "It's A Wonderful Life" with Jimmy Stewart and Donna Reed. When George Bailey wishes that he was not born and he views his friends and families whole lives with out him being there, it was not a pretty sight. However, it was also a psychological illusion and a fantasy. It's too bad that I lived in a reality world because George Bailey's vanishing act could have worked for me. However seeing that I lived in the here and now, I did consider suicide. I thought that maybe suicide could end all my life torments. Of course, I would have to do it right I didn't want to fuck up my own suicide, that could be very embarrassing: "yeah he's so stupid he couldn't even kill himself correctly." I would be lying there in a hospital bed with half my brains blown out with tubes running everywhere and still have enough brains to hear someone say that. While my parents go bankrupt from paying the hospital bills. This vision too was not so pretty.

After giving the suicide option much thought, I decided that it was not an option at all. My family loved me and for that, I was truly blessed. Judy loved me and for that, I was quite grateful. Something like suicide is a crime against the people who love you and care for you. I knew that taking my own life would leave an ever-lasting scar on the people who loved me, for the rest of their lives. In addition, I am a Catholic, by committing suicide my soul would be damned for eternity, which was a long time to wait for god's forgiveness. So I decided to bury the what if scenarios, and to deal only in the here and now. Yes, I was Mr. Reality. The problems that can be fixed could only happen in the present tense, for future results. I referred to it as "the fix it forward effect." What happened to me in the past could only be a learning experience, take corrective action so you do not repeat the mistake and move forward with your life.

After a couple of days of the debate over whether or not my mother would sign the consent form, she finally caved in and signed the paper reluctantly. The moment she signed it, I was not overwhelmed with happiness like getting my first car or my first make out session with Judy. This was something I had to do to get my life back on the right track. I filled out the paperwork with my dad. Dad and I had a debate over how long the active duty commitment should be. The total commitment was for six years for everyone, but there was an option to serve on active duty for two, three, or four years, and the remainder of the commitment would be served as inactive reserves. Inactive reserves would only be called back on active duty if, for example, the Russians lobbed a nuke into America, and if I was still alive, I could be called back to active duty. Dad wanted me to serve for four years active duty, and I wanted two years we settled on my commitment of three years active duty. I called Gunny Fox about the good news, and he set up a physical appointment for me and an appointment to take the aptitude test. I passed the physical; I did not need to wear eyeglasses to go into the Marines. I was surprised with the result of the aptitude test, and I did not need to become a grunt, which was a regular foot soldier. I had a choice of tanks, which my father said that I would be a big target, because at the time, the Russians and the Chinese had armor piercing bazookas. The effect of an armored piercing round hitting a tank would be that it would explode and fry everyone inside the tank. I thought about the prospect of dying that way, and crossed tanks off my list. I also qualified for artillery. My dad said that was a safe bet, being behind the battlefront, shooting artillery shells with a Howitzer, which was a modern day cannon. Then, the last choice was Helicopter Support, were I would be hooking up external loads to helicopters and working in landing zone operations in the field. What was cool about that was that I was most likely going to be flying around in helicopters a lot. My father said that in a combat situation I would most likely be dropped into hostile landing zones, and could be surrounded by the enemy. I took note of his warnings, but I knew that most jobs could result in the risk of being killed in a combat situation. Therefore, I went with Helicopter Support as my profession or Military Occupational Specialty 1471.

The date for my deployment was January 17, 1974, to Marine Corps boot camp at Parris Island, South Carolina. I received my deployment orders a week after Thanksgiving 1973. Once it was official that I was going into Marine Corps, my parents thought it was pointless for me to continue going to school, because I was leaving for the Marines the following month.

Judy was not happy with the idea of me leaving for the Marines, and knew that we were facing a long distance relationship in the future. I reassured her that I would be back after boot camp in three months, and we would be together for 10 days, before I would leave again. It took her little time to get her head around the situation, but once she did, she had been supportive of my decision. I didn't have the means of transportation, so I resumed hitchhiking for those last few weeks.

On my last full day at school, I said goodbye to some of the teachers that meant anything to me, and blew off the others. Most of the teachers were not supportive of my decision, the majority of them were antiwar liberals, and I was wrong for supporting the government war machine. Some of them even made speeches or comments, as part of their classroom program, to discourage other teenagers from joining the service. The end result of their reaction was more about their political point of view, and little about my educational well-being. A few were supportive of me joining the Marine Corps, one of them was my B.O.C.E.S instructor, Mr. Piazza he was also a war veteran, and he wished me success. As you might imagine, because of the antiwar/government sentiment among the young people during the 1960s and 1970s, the news of me joining the service, for the most part was not well received by my fellow classmates. In fact, after the news hit that I was joining the Marines, I was officially deemed a social outcast by the student body. A few wished me well, most hoped that I would die badly in combat. The fact that the student body ostracized me for joining the Marine Corps did not bother me, because I was never part of the mainstream social program to begin with. I was a loner. I simply could not miss something like social acceptability if I never had it to begin with. Therefore, my short answer to the Antiwar\Government activist was, "Go Fuck Yourself."

Christmas was the usual fanfare we had every year, but for me I still had this cloud of depression hanging over me. I just could not seem to shake the depression, no matter what anyone would try. The clock was ticking slowly for those last few weeks before I would leave to start my new life. I kept busy around the house helping my mom. I put my stuff in the attic, and threw out a lot of junk that I had accumulated over the years. I spent a lot of time with Judy. I even went to work with my dad a few days, and made a couple of bucks.

The night before I would start traveling to boot camp, my father took me to the American Legion to have a few drinks with him and some of his fellow veteran friends. Dad said that I could order anything from the bar. Strangely enough, I had ordered sevens and sevens, the same drink that landed me in the problems I currently had. The sip of that drink sent me back to the feeling I had on that night that I had been busted. My father introduced me to all of his friends, and every one of them had congratulated me for making the right decision to join the Marines, and only spoke of encouragement. As I sat and drank with my dad and his friends, I had a sense of social acceptance, and belonging. Although these men were much older then me, most of them had experienced war in its ugliest form, there was a sense that I was accepted as a person. After a couple of hours of drinking at the Legion, I was feeling pretty good and a little tipsy. So dad took me to the liquor store, bought a bottle of Seagram 7 and a bottle of 7-Up, and then drove home. The family going away party resumed at home. Mom and the kids waited for me to get home, and we had a family hoedown. They set up party streamers, and had chips and dip laid out on the kitchen table. This was only a family party send off, with no holds barred. Dad was also drinking seven and sevens; he was usually a beer man. Mom had broken out her BlackBerry Brandy and started to get sauced, which she hardly ever did. I was too caught up in the moment to know whether or not Ike was taking a few secret belts when no one was looking, but he was acting as crazy as I was. I had broken out some of my rock 'n roll LPs, and put them on the hi-fi, and cranked up the music-something that I was never allowed to do was blast rock 'n roll music on the family hi-fi when my parents were home. We laughed and joked around; everybody was having a great time, even me. We all danced in the living room and we partied like there was no tomorrow. The neighbors must have thought we won the lottery that night, and it was that loud on the quiet street. My parents took pictures, and captured those last moments of me as a boy. I got pretty drunk that night, and I paid for it the next morning.

I was hung over the next morning and slept in a little. I took a shower, and packed a gym bag with a change of clothes. I went downstairs and mom had made a special breakfast for dad and me. It was a weekday, so the rest of the kids were in school, and dad took the day off to drive me to the bus station. We sat, enjoyed our bacon and eggs, and had a few laughs about the party the night before. Then my parents went through parental advice about not trusting anyone except the drill instructor, and do not tell strangers about anything personal while traveling. I really had not traveled any real distances in my life growing up. I was like a country bumpkin traveling alone to Paris Island, South Carolina, an 800-mile trip. They were concerned that if I got lost I could be charged with being AWOL my first day in the service, not a good way to start out. Therefore, we ran through my itinerary a few times. In addition, Gunny Fox gave me traveling vouchers and tickets for the bus, the motel, food, the car service, and airfare. Which I found to be a bazaar concept, that people would take a piece of paper, not money, for goods and services. I kissed my mother goodbye and promised that I would write when I could. She began to cry when she hugged me, and that started me crying. Mom stood at the doorway, still crying as dad and I drove off.

We had to drive to Newburgh, New York, so I could catch a bus to Albany. As we drove those 30 miles, we talked about doing the right thing, and following my conscience. When we got to the bus depot, dad handed me $20, just in case I needed it. He told me to call him when I landed in Charleston, South Carolina, to insure that I made it. Dad said goodbye, shook my hand, grabbed my right shoulder from the driver seat and hugged me. He said, "Be careful and look out for yourself." As I broke away from his embrace, I could see that he was tearing up a little. I reassured him that I would, grabbed my bag out of the backseat, and waved as he drove off. As I sat waiting for my bus to come, I thought of how many times I saw my father actually cry, three times in my entire life, to this point. He was a much stronger person emotionally.

The 200-mile bus ride to Albany was uneventful on that gray snowy winter day. I arrived about 4 PM in the bus depot, and grabbed the car service to downtown Albany to the motel. I ate at the motel dining room. As I did, I realized that I still had not spent a dime of my own money. All the jokers were still taking the paper vouchers that Gunny gave me. I thought for a moment, that if I could copy about 1000 of the vouchers, I could live in Albany for a while. Then I dismissed the idea I did not want to live in Albany. I went to the corner store, bought some smokes and a six-pack of Bud I walked back to the motel and checked into my room. It was on the 21st floor, and it overlooked the Albany City Skyline.

It was a clean old motel with furniture from the 1940s, the TV was broken but the radio worked. I cracked open a cold one sat on the windowsill and lit a cigarette. I sat in the dark in that motel room in silence for hours looking at the Albany City Skyline. Believe me, it wasn't the impressive view that kept me looking out the window. I was looking through it as if it was a reflection of my life. In my mind that night, I went through everything that led me to that darkened motel room. What had happened was in the past, and I could never change it. The future for me was frightening and uncertain I had seen a few old boot camp movies, and I heard my uncles and my father talk about their experiences in basic training. I knew it was going to be tough. The big question was if I was tough enough to endure it, and become a Marine. Because, if I failed this test; I would had truly failed everyone. A fate I could not live with.

Conclusion

The reason I wrote this story was to depict a true memoir of my life, and to reflect the true lives of the people around me. Most importantly, this was an honest and true story about my family and me. Where I end the story of my life in this book, there was a great turning point in my family's lives. There were many horrifying tragedies that would plague my family for years after this point. It would shake their faith in God. It would also, after so many years, make their lives stronger.

This photograph was taken during my family's going away party they threw for me, the night before my trip to the Marine Corps boot camp in Paris Island, South Carolina.

This is also another photograph of me during Christmas 1973.
A kid with a lot on my mind about what the future held for
me.

CPSIA information can be obtained at www.ICGtesting.com
Printed in the USA
LVOW08s0554180715

446698LV00002B/84/P